Women & Men in Management

Second Edition

Dedicated
to Laura Graves
for her love and support
and to the memory of my grandmother
Edna Powell
for all the quarters and much more

Women & Men in Management

Second Edition

Gary N. Powell

SAGE Publications
International Educational and Professional Publisher
Newbury Park   London   New Delhi

For information address:

 SAGE Publications, Inc.
2455 Teller Road
Newbury Park, California 91320

SAGE Publications Ltd.
6 Bonhill Street
London EC2A 4PU
United Kingdom

SAGE Publications India Pvt. Ltd.
M-32 Market
Greater Kailash I
New Delhi 110 048 India

Printed in the United States of America

Library of Congress Cataloging-in-Publication Data

Powell, Gary N.
    Women & men in management / Gary N. Powell — 2nd ed.
        p.   cm.
    Includes bibliographical references and index.
    ISBN 0-8039-5223-6 —ISBN 0-8039-5224-4 (pb)
    1. Women executives.   2. Executives.   3. Sex role in the work environment.   I. Title.   II. Title: Women and men in management.
HD6054.3.P69   1993
658.4'095—dc20   93-9487

93 94 95 96 10 9 8 7 6 5 4 3 2 1

Sage Production Editor: Astrid Virding

Contents

Foreword

Gary Powell's decision to revise this book is an important one because it is one more indicator that the issues of women and men in management have not yet been resolved and, to a large extent, are still not understood.

We are being asked by a number of authors, politicians, and those in the media to accept the idea that sexism and women's issues are passe, that other business and diversity issues are more compelling in the 1990s because women have already carved out a place for themselves.

Is sexism a thing of the past? It seems that, as I read newspapers, magazines, and journals, there are signs of progress side-by-side with warnings that women are still trapped in yesterday's stereotype-driven standards. I was struck recently by two articles on the same page of *USA Today*[1]. One article extolled the fact that for the first time in history fully half of the newly-named Rhodes Scholars are women. The other article noted that a woman is beaten every 18 seconds.

The same sort of schizophrenia exists in the realm of management. On the one hand, President Clinton appointed Donna Shalala and other women to cabinet-level posts. On the other hand, women still comprise only about 5% of the executive ranks in major U.S. companies. And as Gary Powell points out in Chapter 6, fewer than half of the male executives surveyed in 1985 by *Harvard Business Review* "would feel comfortable working for a woman." John Fernandez, who has written several books based on extensive research concerning diversity in corporations, recently concluded that sexism is still socially acceptable.

Gary Powell's book examines this premise and the converse. He adds current evidence to that presented in his original 1988 version to show

how women are doing in management and the reasons behind their gains and limits. In doing so, he helps us combat assumptions that, even when well-intentioned, keep women—and many men—at a disadvantage.

A shocking finding from a nationwide research project I directed was that the biggest barrier to advancement for white women and women and men of color continues to be prejudice. Prejudice involves equating differences with deficiencies when evaluating recruits, subordinates, candidates for promotion, and so on. Assumptions form the basis for much of the prejudice that continues to hold women back. Assumptions prevail unless other information takes their place, the kind of information provided by Gary Powell.

If women have made progress since 1988 it isn't because of the passage of time. Exposure and accountability have encouraged scores of individuals to change traditional practices. Education prompts and shapes these changes. This book is an important contribution to our education.

—Ann M. Morrison
Author of *The New Leaders* and lead author of *Breaking the Glass Ceiling*
President of the New Leaders Institute in San Diego, CA

Note

1. *USA Today*, 7 December 1992, p. 12A.

Acknowledgments

Although I did all the writing (except for collaborating on one chapter) and word processing, there are many people who have contributed to the preparation of this second edition of *Women & Men in Management*. I wish to express my deep gratitude to:

1. Colleagues who read portions of the manuscript and offered helpful comments: Ellen Fagenson, Lisa Mainiero, and Stella Nkomo.
2. Diane Adams for her excellent job of copyediting.
3. Lynn Bowes-Sperry for her preparation of the index for the book.
4. Ann West and Harry Briggs at Sage Publications for helping me to initiate this project and nurturing it along.
5. Lisa Mainiero for being a terrific collaborator on Chapter 7.
6. Tony Butterfield for being my mentor and valued colleague.
7. The School of Business Administration of the University of Connecticut, for giving me the opportunity to teach the course on Women and Men in Management that won the American Assembly of Collegiate Schools of Business (AACSB) Committee on Equal Opportunity for Women Innovation Award and led to the writing of this book.
8. My many colleagues in the Women in Management Division of the Academy of Management, for providing both a forum for the sharing of research findings and a stimulus for creative thinking on this topic.
9. Louie Cohn-Haft for his counsel and friendship.
10. My parents, Norm and Zina Powell, for all their support on this project as well as everything else of significance I have ever done.
11. Tiger the Cat for unlimited love, affection, and play.
12. Most of all, Laura Graves, my wife and favorite colleague, for standing by (not behind) me and encouraging me all the way.

Introduction

Women & Men in Management, Second Edition, chronicles and examines the transition that is taking place in female/male work relationships in American organizations. Significant changes have occurred in the status of and interactions between women and men at work in recent years. In fact, some believe that all the changes that needed to take place have already happened and that a person's sex no longer has any effect on what happens to him or her at work. According to many people now entering the work force or anticipating entry, the days when women had trouble getting into jobs compared to men are long past. However, gender issues have not entirely disappeared from the workplace.

For example, consider the statistics regarding the proportions of men and women in management. The proportion of women who hold management, executive, or administrative positions in organizations has been rising consistently since 1970 and is currently 42%. However, the proportion of women who hold *top* management positions continues to be very small, no more than 5% according to most surveys. What has changed is that more women are in management. What hasn't changed is that women are concentrated in the lower levels of management and hold positions with less authority overall than men. Is it just a matter of time before the proportions of women in upper, middle, and lower management positions become approximately the same? As we shall see, maybe and maybe not.

Early Reactions to This Book

When I first told colleagues that I was planning to write a book on women and men in management, I heard a variety of reactions:

1. A male colleague smugly said, "Well, that seems to include everyone unless they are excluded by child labor laws." I could not quarrel with the accuracy of his observation, but clearly he was poking fun at the writing project.
2. Some nodded sagely and said, "Sounds great!" although it was obvious by the puzzled expressions on their faces that they had no idea what the book would be about.
3. A female colleague who is a prominent researcher in the field of women in management concluded that I must be trying to shift the focus of the field from women's issues to interactions between the sexes. However, she felt unsure about why "women" comes first in the title. She thought that this may reflect my uncertainty about whether I wish to reach a large audience with the book. As an afterthought, she wondered whether I am making a point about men usually coming first in such a title.
4. Another male colleague simply asked, "Why 'women and men' in that order, rather than 'men and women' like everyone is used to saying?" Before I could reply, someone within earshot answered, "If you need to ask a question like that, you need to read the book!"

Let's consider the issues that these reactions raise, in order.

The *first reaction* reflects the fact that my colleague did not take the project seriously. This attitude is not surprising. Until recently, men and women were assumed to be very different from one another in psychological as well as physiological attributes. The differences didn't need to be discussed, and any book or article that pertained to one sex was assumed to be irrelevant to the other. Many people still have beliefs about what women and men are "really like," how they should interact in the workplace, and the contributions that members of each sex can best make. The following statements serve as examples: Men should clean up their language when women are present. Women should be expected to act as representatives of their sex and be able to speak for "what women think" on an issue. Female subordinates should be managed differently than male subordinates. He is careful about details—she is picky. He loses his temper because he is so involved in his job—she is bitchy. Flirting, sexual innuendos, and teasing are acceptable in the workplace as long they don't have an adverse effect on productivity. Men are better at some jobs than women and vice versa, but men make the better managers.

The purposes of *Women & Men in Management* are (a) to bring to light such beliefs, (b) to critically examine their relevance to the world of work today, and (c) to recommend ways for individuals and organizations to successfully respond to them. In so doing, it will increase our understanding of the interactions between women and men in work settings. These interactions are having ever greater impact as the proportion of women in the workplace, especially in management positions, steadily increases. Although many employees are bringing new attitudes about male/female roles to their jobs, considerable resistance to the shifting of economic roles between the sexes remains. Hence problems that arise in male/female work relationships, the sources of these problems—individual, organizational, and societal—and possible solutions to them deserve our close attention.

The *second reaction*, as well as the first to some extent, reflects the fact that the term *women and men in management* is unfamiliar to many people. Until the early 1970s, the prevailing trend in the management literature was to write as if all managers were men. More recently, books in this field were devoted primarily to issues related to women in management and secondarily to issues related to male/female interactions and men in management. Reflecting the fact that women were entering the management profession in greater numbers than ever before, they advocated that women could be effective managers and highlighted the special problems that women faced in entering the management profession. The message of these books has been heard. The proportion of women in managerial positions continues to rise, and writers on the topic of management now talk about managers in terms that include both sexes.

However, this is not to say that women have been totally assimilated into the management profession and are indistinguishable from men. A successful middle manager in a Hartford, Connecticut insurance company has the mock nameplate "Boss Lady" on her desk and says that she is still called that by most of her peers (affectionately or derisively so, she does not say!). The psychologist Sandra Bem asked an audience whether they had ever known anyone personally and had not thought to notice whether the person was male or female. Few could answer the question yes. A person's sex remains an important characteristic to most of us in forming an impression of the person, and people often react to others at least in part according to their sex.

Now that women are in managerial ranks to stay, it is appropriate to focus attention on how women and men interact in the workplace rather than on whether women belong in management positions and how to get them there. Moreover, it also makes sense to recognize that men have problems related to male/female interactions too. For example, they have to cope with the fact that some men get ahead in organizations while most do not. As women have to adjust to holding positions with high status, men have to adjust to working with women who hold such positions, sometimes as their managers, often as peers, and ever more frequently as their subordinates. In discussing the issues that arise between women and men in organizations today, it is helpful to consider both female and male perspectives. In simple terms, if men have been part of the problem, they can also be part of the solution. To provide the complete background necessary for understanding these issues, we need to examine the work and prework experiences of both men and women.

The *third and fourth reactions* to the book's title reflect the fact that "women and men" is an unusual order for these two terms in writing and in speech. I have chosen "women and men" in the title simply to call attention to the typical and unconscious order ("men and women") usually used. You may have already noticed that I have been using the two orders interchangeably. If "women and men" makes you feel uncomfortable, try a little exercise: Repeat "women and men in management" aloud 25 times. Then repeat "men and women in management" aloud 25 times. Next, alternate phrases for 25 rounds: "women and men in management," "men and women in management," "women and men in management," and so on. Which phrase sounds more natural now? If it's still "men and women in management," go through the whole exercise again (and again if necessary, and again . . .). After a while, you will find that it really doesn't matter which phrase you use. That's the *real* point to be made.

However, I am not uncertain about the audience I am trying to reach with this book. Its potential audience includes *all* men and women (or women and men) who presently work in organizations, expect to work in them, or are interested in how work is conducted within them. Moreover, the colleagues who wondered why the terms appear in the order they do will probably gain from reading this book, as will many others.

Organization of the Book

The book begins its analysis of the transition in female/male work relationships by looking back in time. Chapter 1 provides a historical perspective on the economic roles of women and men. Most individuals have been exposed to "traditional" stereotypes about the traits that females and males possess and are supposed to display. To fully understand these gender stereotypes, as they shall be called, we need to understand the traditions on which they are based. The chapter traces the historical influences that have shaped these traditions and affected the distribution of work roles between women and men over the course of American history. By comparing the public norms with the economic realities at various points in time, we can better understand the present allocation of work roles.

Chapter 2 examines individual differences that affect the behavior of women and men at work and the origins of these differences. It compares gender stereotypes with the facts that have emerged from research studies about actual sex differences. It introduces the concept of androgyny as an ideal proposed by some people for how both males and females should behave. It investigates the influence of socialization experiences provided by parents, schools, and the mass media on the development of young girls and boys. It also investigates the consequences of these experiences on the health of adult women and men.

Chapter 3 explores how individuals and organizations make decisions about whether to establish an employment relationship with each other. For individuals, these decisions entail if, where, and when to work; for organizations, they entail which job applicants to hire. The chapter describes how such decisions are influenced by the sex segregation of occupations, which itself is the result of past employment decisions by individuals and organizations. Individuals' decisions are also influenced by their own personal characteristics and life situations, which may differ for males and females. Organizations' decisions to hire female or male applicants may be affected by the conscious or unconscious biases of their recruiters and by the steps they take to prevent these biases from determining hiring decisions.

Chapter 4 examines the effects of gender stereotypes on the work relationships between male and female peers. It explores whether actual differences exist between female and male peers that could serve as the basis for stereotypes. It then details the personal and situational factors that tend to promote or prevent gender stereotyping of employees by their workplace peers. It particularly focuses on the effect of the sex ratio of a group on interactions between its male and female members, and on the effect of individuals' experience in working with members of the opposite sex.

Chapter 5 considers issues pertaining to the expression of sexuality in the workplace, which may consist of sexual harassment (unwelcome sexual attention directed toward others) as well as organizational romances (welcome sexual attention directed toward others). However, both types of attention, even the welcome type, may have negative consequences for the individuals involved and their coworkers. Actions that both organizations and individuals may take to deal with sexual harassment when it occurs and to minimize the disruptive influence of organizational romances on other employees are recommended.

Chapter 6 extends the analysis of the effects of gender stereotypes to the work relationships between managers and their subordinates. It compares gender stereotypes with stereotypes of managers and then with the actual characteristics of women and men managers. Sex differences in managerial traits, behavior, effectiveness, values, commitment, stress, and responses elicited from subordinates are examined. The few sex differences that exist do not support the traditional belief that men make better managers. The belief that better managers are masculine also is unfounded, particularly in today's work environment.

Chapter 7, co-authored with Lisa Mainiero, examines the career and life patterns typically followed by men and women. Sex differences in these patterns have been diminishing but still remain. Differences in theories of career development that emphasize men's versus women's careers are documented. The chapter proposes a new conceptual framework for understanding the complexities of women's as well as men's careers that explicitly acknowledges the intersection of work and family lives. It discusses how organizations may help their employees achieve career and life goals without sacrificing the achievement of organizational goals. It also discusses how employees may contribute through their own actions to their experiencing "success" in their careers and lives.

Chapter 8 investigates issues related to the promotion of equal opportunity and appreciation of cultural diversity in organizations. It details the relevant laws and guidelines that have been enacted to restrict sex discrimination by organizations. It analyzes the effect of organizational culture on whether middle-level and lower-level managers embrace or even take seriously their organizations' professed goals regarding equal opportunity and cultural diversity. Recommendations for how organizations may best promote a proactive approach to equal opportunity and a multicultural approach to employee diversity are suggested.

Chapter 9 completes the book's analysis by looking ahead in time. It presents two alternative scenarios for the future. In one scenario, the experiences of women and men have become more similar at work and their interactions less influenced by sex-related issues. In the other scenario, traditional distinctions between the experiences of women and men at work remain or have grown larger, and an individual's biological sex is the primary influence on what his or her work life is like. The forces that seem most likely to determine which scenario, if either, will prevail in the future are identified and discussed.

In summary, *Women and Men in Management* covers a wide range of topics. It addresses pre-organizational and organizational entry issues for women and men as well as issues that arise in the workplace. It examines issues pertaining to individuals' work and personal lives and to society as a whole. It considers what it is like for men and women to work with others as peers, to manage others, and to be managed. It observes female/male relations in past eras, examines their present nature, and speculates about what they will be like in the future.

In so doing, this book offers two types of useful information to people who currently work or anticipate working in organizations. First, it gives them insight into themselves in relation to the managerial role—how they conduct or might conduct themselves as managers, and how they respond or might respond to managerial actions by others. Second, it provides insight into how other people in organizations relate to and conduct themselves in their own work roles, whether managerial or nonmanagerial. You do not need to be a manager or intend to become one to benefit from reading this book. All that you need is an interest in the world of work and how the sexes interact within it.

Changes From the First Edition

Research on the topic of women and men in management, or women in management, was first published in the mid-1970s. Thus, the first edition of this book, published in 1988, summarized and drew conclusions from about 15 years of research. Now, five years later, one-third more years have passed in which there has been an explosion of research on this topic, calling for the updating and rewriting of virtually every section of the book. Of the approximately 550 references listed in the "Notes" sections at the end of chapters, over 330 (60%) are new to this edition.

Several major changes also have been incorporated into this edition. First, the earlier Chapter 4 has been divided into two chapters—Chapter 4, "Working with People," and Chapter 5, "Dealing with Sexuality in the Workplace"—with expanded coverage of topics appearing in both chapters. Second, Chapter 7, "Getting Ahead—In Career and Life," now co-authored with Lisa Mainiero, more explicitly addresses the trade-offs between work and family concerns that most working people face. It presents a conceptual framework for examining women's and men's careers that we recently developed. Third, Chapter 8, "Promoting Equal Opportunity and Valuing Cultural Diversity," which was formerly devoted solely to issues related to promoting equal opportunity, has been expanded to give equal coverage to issues related to valuing cultural diversity in organizations. Finally, the implications sections of several chapters have been expanded.

1

Looking Back

A Silent Revolution

As a boy I lived for some time in the family of a pioneer uncle from Iowa. His log cabin was a perfect fairyland for a child because of the fascinating industries carried on in it. . . . Nearly all that was eaten and worn in the family had been manufactured by the hands of its womenfolk. In those days nothing was heard as to the "economic dependence" of the wife, of her being "supported." My aunt, busy in and about the house, was as strong a prop of the family's prosperity as my uncle afield with his team. Uncle knew it, and, what is more, *she knew* he knew it.

Gradually, however, a silent revolution has taken place in the lot of the home-staying woman. The machine in the factory has been slipping invisible tentacles into the home and picking out, unobserved by us, this, that, and the other industrial process. . . . So, one by one, the operations shift from home to factory until the only parts of the housewife's work which remain unaffected are cooking, washing, cleaning, and the care of children. . . .

With the industrial decay of the home, it is more and more often the case that the husband "supports" the wife. In the well-to-do homes—and it is chiefly here that the status of women is determined—the wife has lost her economic footing. Apart from motherhood, her role is chiefly ornamental. He is the one who counts, whose strength must be conserved, who cannot afford to be sick. . . . She is tempted to pay for support with subservience, to mold her manner and her personality to his liking, to make up to him by her grace and charm for her exemption from work. This "being agreeable" means often that she must subordinate her individuality, hide her divergent wishes and opinions, or adopt his.

Edward A. Ross[1]

Traditional sex roles, as the term is commonly used, emphasize the differences rather than the similarities between women and men. These differences are typically assumed to be innate. Traditional sex roles also suggest that women should behave in a "feminine" manner, in accordance with their presumed feminine attributes, and that men should behave in a "masculine" manner, in accordance with their presumed masculine attributes. To deviate from these prescriptions, according to traditional thinking, is to engage in abnormal behavior. These sex roles have had a profound impact on relations between women and men in our society in all spheres of life—in the family, the educational system, and the workplace, and in both management and nonmanagement ranks within the workplace.

This perspective on sex roles, although true as far as it goes, raises more questions than it answers. Does the adjective *traditional* mean that sex roles have been handed down unchanged, from generation to generation, since the beginning of civilization, or have sex roles differed over time or among cultures? If sex roles have not been constant, isn't the label of *traditional* misleading? To which traditions are we then referring? Why are we choosing these traditions over others to be called "traditional"? How were these traditions developed? How well have they reflected the actual distribution of economic roles between the sexes?

In this chapter, I will address such questions. First, the development of the traditions on which "traditional" sex roles are based will be examined, and the impact of diverse historical forces such as the rise of industrialization, the occurrence of major world wars, and the development and growth of the women's movement will be traced. Second, the compatibility of these traditions with the utilization of men and women in the labor force and management ranks over time will be explored. Finally, the implications of the difference between expressed traditions and economic realities on the work relationships that exist between men and women today will be assessed.

A Matter of Evolution?

Before beginning our historical analysis, we need to examine the view that sex roles are *not* shaped by particular historical events, but instead are simply the result of evolutionary tendencies. Evolutionary theory suggests that organisms and societies that are best able to adapt to their environment have the best chance of survival. People have used this theory to justify the notion that inborn psychological differences between the sexes complement obvious physical differences. For example, the average man is larger in stature and physically dominant over the average woman. Consequently, it has been argued as "natural" that the man assume the dominant position of manager in work organizations and that the woman assume the submissive position of subordinate. The chain of reasoning is as follows: (a) Differences exist in the division of labor between women and men, with most management positions held by men. (b) The differences evolved as our species developed. (c) The differences must have some function in ensuring our survival as a species. (d) Therefore, the differences are natural and must not be altered.[2]

This kind of argument could be used to justify almost every difference between the behavior and status of men and women that exists today. However, it has its limitations. Sex differences that may have been necessary in the past may be unnecessary at this time, and they could be undesirable in the future. As a solution to a survival problem, sex differences could remain in a society after the problem has disappeared. Moreover, some patterns of behavior may neither help nor hinder the society's survival.

Evolutionary theory has been used also as the basis for claims that sex differences that exist today were originally established in hunting-and-gathering societies. The activities of hunters of food have frequently been portrayed as more important than the activities of food gatherers. "Man the hunter" theorists have assumed that all hunting and gathering societies were similarly organized. According to them, males did most of the hunting and, along the way, developed their aggressiveness and ability to work in groups, while females depended on the males for meat and, as a result, developed their passivity. Hence, we have such conclusions as "Hunting is the master behavior pattern of the human species" and "Our intellect, interests, emotions and basic social life—all are evolutionary products of the success of the hunting adaptation."[3] However, such arguments ignore the often greater importance of gathering activities to the survival of cultures. They also diminish the intellectual and other capabilities that were required to gather food. Some "man the hunter" theorists went further to conclude that, in accordance with their hunting activities, men have always been natural killers. From this argument, it is a small leap forward to the argument that as men learned how to be successful at dominating other species during the hunt, they also learned how to be successful at dominating (managing) other people in today's work organizations.[4]

The famed anthropologist Margaret Mead pointed out the fallacy of assuming that sex differences in a particular society are natural and the result of evolution. Based on her observations of several Pacific cultures, she concluded:

> In every known society, mankind has elaborated the biological division of labor into forms often very remotely related to the original biological differences that provided the original clues. Upon the contrast in bodily form and function, men have built analogies between sun and moon, night and day, goodness and evil, strength and tenderness, steadfastness and fickleness, endurance and vulnerability. Sometimes one quality has been assigned to one sex, sometimes to the other. Now it is boys who are thought of as infinitely vulnerable and in need of special cherishing care, now it is girls. In some societies it is girls for whom parents must collect a dowry or make husband-catching magic, in others the parental worry is over the difficulty of marrying off the boys. Some peoples think of women as too weak to work out of doors, others regard women as the appropriate bearers of heavy burdens, "because their heads are stronger than men's." The periodicities of female reproductive functions have appealed to some peoples as making women the natural sources of magical or religious power, to others as directly antithetical to those powers; some religions, including our European traditional religions, have assigned women an inferior role in the religious hierarchy, others have built their whole symbolic relationship with the supernatural world upon male imitations of the natural functions of women. In some cultures women are regarded as sieves through which the best-guarded secrets will sift; in others it is the men who are the gossips. Whether we deal with small matters or with large, with the frivolities of ornament and cosmetics or the sanctities of man's place in the universe, we find this great variety of ways, often flatly contradictory one to the other, in which the roles of the two sexes have been patterned.[5]

A comprehensive study of cross-cultural occupational differences, which compiled data on the division of labor by sex in 224 mostly subsistence-level cultures, reached a similar conclusion. Only three activities—preparing and planting the soil, crafting leather goods, and making ornaments—were equally likely to be given to men or women. Other occupations were labeled masculine or feminine according to which sex was more likely to perform them. As some proponents of evolutionary theory would expect, masculine roles included hunting and trapping, while cooking and gathering herbs were feminine roles. Nonetheless, only a few occupations—metal working, weapon making, pursuit of sea mammals, and hunting—were nearly always relegated to males, and no occupation was nearly always relegated to females. Although a particular society could be quite rigid in sex roles, there was considerable variability in sex roles across societies.[6]

In conclusion, the evidence accumulated by anthropologists suggests that no one pattern of sex roles prevails across all societies. If sex roles are dictated by the lessons of evolution, different lessons have been learned by different societies. Therefore, it is unlikely that our "traditional" conceptions of sex roles are the result of principles of evolution at work. To understand the relationship between the sexes in our own society, we need to look elsewhere.

American Society Prior to 1900

Although societies around the world have differed in their conceptions of sex roles, Western societies have shared some similar notions. Throughout the recorded history of Western civilizations, a patriarchal social system in which the male has authority over the female has almost always prevailed, or at least has been the public norm.

Early American society was no exception. Puritan New Englanders, who were prominent in the founding of the American colonies, believed in a hierarchy within the family, with the man as head and the women and children as subordinates. Man's role in the home was seen as similar to God's role in the universe, that is, in charge. However, Puritans weren't the only group to endorse the concept of patriarchy. Members of other religious groups who were early American settlers shared the same attitudes regarding male supremacy. These attitudes were in force as the colonists wrested control over their affairs from Great Britain in the Revolutionary War and formed their own government.

The decision to rebel against Great Britain was made by men. The Preamble of the Constitution referred only to men. In the conferences that led to formation of the new nation, it was never considered that anyone other than men should have the same rights and privileges that men had bestowed on themselves. The right to vote was not given to women until 1920, long after it was theoretically given to men who were former slaves, and only then after a half-century of resistance. As far as the conduct of public affairs was concerned, women played little direct role in the early shaping of the American republic.[7]

Although disenfranchised, women played a considerable role in the economic system of early American society. Prior to the 1800s, the society was predominantly agrarian, with most work taking place in or around the home. Women and men were engaged in different activities—for example, men were responsible for tasks that called for lifting heavy burdens and women for matters related to clothing and food preparation—but the activities of both sexes were equally essential to the family economy. All household members, children included, worked at productive tasks.

Women became managers of shops, businesses, plantations, or farms only through the early deaths of their husbands. According to English Common Law, which governed the colonies until the Revolutionary War, a woman could not appear in court, enter into a contract, or inherit from heirs without the approval of a male relative or guardian. Nonetheless, economic needs took precedence over legalities. Women were too skilled a resource not to be fully utilized in preindustrial America.[8]

The slow rise of a market economy and the later industrial revolution altered the relationship between the sexes markedly. Better production and distribution methods began to allow the sale in the marketplace of farm produce and crafted goods that were not needed by the family. Because of the types of activities that men and women had performed, the products that men made were more likely to enter the marketplace than those produced by women. For example, milk, wheat, and wool, produced by men or both women and men, could be sold to townspeople. Butter, bread, and cloth, produced by women, could then be readily manufactured within most of those families. As a result, men, more often than women, received and thereby controlled the money coming into the family. Their control was legitimized by the religious and social doctrines that had been paid lip service but had been effectively dormant for some time.

During the same period, the American legal system was refined and tightened, and previously unwritten laws were codified. The cultural doctrines supporting male supremacy had been unofficial since English Common Law had become no longer applicable. They were now formalized in a manner compatible with the new market economy in which men dominated economic life. Wives became legally obligated to serve the wishes of their husbands, and husbands were legally elevated to the position of almost total dominance and responsibility.

The labor of wives was still valuable after the advent of the market economy, but it could not be sold as easily. Its value depended on the use the family could make of it. When piecework manufacturing methods were later developed, women who worked in their homes could also earn wages outside the home. However, by this time, the laws formalizing women's subordinate position to men were already in place. Had the laws been codified earlier, the de facto equality between the sexes then in existence might have been recognized. Had they been codified later, men and women might have been accorded equal status. The legal system was well established by the time the industrial revolution was under way.

Despite its apparent rigidity after the advent of the market economy, the economic system in America ordinarily would have been expected to continue changing to allow for the most efficient division of labor. However, the industrial revolution temporarily suspended the need for further changes by allowing economic superiority to be achieved through the superior organization of production. With surplus production, it became possible for more affluent husbands to keep their wives at home rather than allow them outside work. Thus the stay-at-home wife became a status symbol for men in American society. This division of labor outwardly copied the earlier fashion of life among European nobility, allowed the conspicuous demonstration of affluence, and reaffirmed the legally defined superior/subordinate relationship between the husband and the wife. Growing general affluence allowed the practice to spread gradually until it became institutionalized as an ideal, the standard against which other allocations of roles between the sexes were judged. However, this ideal was largely based on the experiences of white middle-class families, which differed greatly from the experiences of minority and lower-class families. Men of color tended to hold agricultural, mining, or service jobs that were considered too low-paying, insecure, dangerous, or degrading by most white men. The impact of historical forces was similar in other Western cultures.[9]

Unmarried women, who were relied on as workers in the early days of the industrial revolution, were subject to a different set of economic forces but the same social norms. To avoid the miserable working conditions and abuse of female and child labor that had taken place in British factories, Francis Cabot Lowell introduced the "Waltham system" of large-scale manufacturing to the New England textile industry in the 1810s. Factory communities built by Lowell and his associates in mill towns throughout New England were designed with adult females in mind as the workers. Primarily single and from farming families, these women were required to reside in boardinghouses under the direction of a matron employed by the company. The matron enforced regulations regarding proper behavior, including a 10 o'clock curfew, and mandatory church attendance. These arrangements were intended to assure Yankee farmers that their daughters would not be working in places of sin and corruption, and the community that the invasion of a large number of young women would not drastically alter its social fabric.

The women mainly tended the roving and spinning frames and minded the looms in the mills. Men were employed primarily as overseers, machinists, and in other heavy occupations, or in those requiring a definite skill such as printing. Men's wages were typically set at the prevailing New England wage rate for the appropriate skill or trade. Women's wages were set at a level high enough to induce them to leave the farms and stay away from other forms of employment such as domestic service, but low enough to offer an advantage for employing females rather than males and to compete with the wages of unskilled workers in British textile factories.

Female factory workers, whose ranks gradually came to include widows and wives from poorer families as well as single women, did not conform to the female role that was being developed in affluent white middle-class families. They had no choice about whether to work. Instead, their wages often made them the primary earners in their families, which became all the more important when New England's farming economy began a long period of decline in the 1830s. As a life-style of genteel leisure became the ideal for all women, those in the growing female work force were looked down on for having to work. A "cult of true womanhood," led by middle-class reformers such as Catherine Beecher, encouraged women to guard their natural place— the home—with their natural virtues of "piety, purity, submissiveness, and domesticity."[10] Thus, the spread of industrialization was affecting women throughout society. For some, it meant long hours in the factory. For others, it meant isolation in the home.[11]

The industrial revolution also greatly affected the lives of men. Toward the end of the 19th century, men were required to work in factories in increasing numbers because of the rise of heavy industry, for which women were regarded as too frail. The shift from an agricultural to an industrial society changed the ways men made use of their abilities and assessed their self-worth. In much earlier days, men proved their worth by demonstrating their physical prowess at killing animals for food. More recently, men had been admired as craftsmen for their skills at making things. Now, the role of strong provider and skilled artisan was being replaced by the role of keeper of the machines. Even though the industrial revolution provided mass-produced goods and a less strenuous way of life for most, it also robbed many men of their opportunity for creativity and accomplishment, and of their sense of purpose.[12]

By 1922, when he wrote the passage from *The Social Trend* that begins this chapter, Edward Ross could describe the dramatic contrast between the economically equal household of the log cabin in Iowa and the economically unequal households of his contemporary society. Ross's aunt and uncle knew that they were both important contributors to the family economy. They didn't perform the same roles, but they performed equally necessary ones. There was no distinction in the wages that they earned. With the rise of the market economy and then the industrial revolution, both women and men realized that the man was providing the major economic support for the family. Attitudes changed to conform to this new economic relationship. Wives changed their attitudes to make themselves more subordinate to their husbands' desires. Husbands' attitudes changed in the direction of feeling more superior to their wives than they did before, even though they weren't as fulfilled by their factory work. Whereas social doctrine had been declaring for some time that men were already superior to women, it had been expressing the official and unofficial norms of American society rather than the economic reality. Now, at least for the more affluent, reality had caught up with the norms.

Recognition of this new reality provides us some answers to the questions that were raised at the onset. Sex roles have *not* been handed down unchanged, from generation to generation, since the beginning of civilization. Cultures have differed widely in their expectations for behavior from the sexes. However, Western societies have tended to endorse a male-dominated social system. Early American society did not adhere to this norm, because of the demands of the primarily agricultural, home-based economy. The industrial revolution placed different demands on families. One member of the family, most often the man, was required to earn wages away from home while the woman continued to work at home on an unpaid basis.

Thus, we have identified the source of what have come to be known as "traditional" sex roles in our society. These sex roles, developed within white middle-class families that could afford to have the woman not earn wages outside the home, provided an ideal that was supposed to apply to all families. However, the label of *traditional* is misleading. It implies a constancy in the actual economic roles of women and men that simply has not been present in American society, although public norms about economic roles have varied less. Why did this particular set of traditions become cast as ideal, rather than traditions based on the greater sexual equality in economic roles that had prevailed before? Probably because they most agreed with the doctrine of a patriarchal social system, which had been brought to America by its original settlers. Certainly not because they were adhered to by all social classes, and not because they reflected the distribution of economic roles that was to emerge in the years to come.

American Society Since 1900

By the beginning of the 20th century, the labor force was clearly differentiated according to sex. Census statistics showed that 19% of all women and 80% of all men were in the labor force in 1900 (see Table 1.1). In other words, four out of every five women *were not* engaged in paid employment, whereas four out of every five men *were* engaged in paid employment. Only 4% of nonfarm executives, administrators, and managers were women. Men were firmly established as the dominant sex in the workplace, both in absolute numbers and in positions of authority.

In the decades between 1900 and 1940, labor force participation rates for men and women remained essentially the same, despite the occurrence of several major events. World War I, waged from 1914 to 1918, created new job opportunities for women at higher wages than they were used to earning as large numbers of men went off to war. However, no sustained change in the employment of women resulted. In fact, the labor force participation rate of women in 1920 (21%) was slightly lower

Table 1.1 Labor Force Participation Rates

Year	Percentage in the Labor Force	
	Women	Men
1870	13	75
1880	15	79
1890	17	79
1900	19	80
1910	23	81
1920	21	78
1930	22	76
1940	25	79
1950	34	86
1960	38	83
1970	43	80
1980	52	77
1990	58	76
2000 (projected)	63	76
2005 (projected)	66	73

SOURCE: 1870-1940: U.S. Department of Commerce, Bureau of the Census, *Historical Statistics of the United States: Colonial Times to 1970* (Washington, DC: Government Printing Office, 1975), pp. 127-128, series D13; 1950-1980: U.S. Department of Labor, Bureau of Labor Statistics, *Handbook of Labor Statistics* (Washington, DC: Government Printing Office, 1989), pp. 25-30, table 5; 1990: U.S. Department of Labor, Bureau of Labor Statistics, *Employment and Earnings, 39* (No. 1, January 1992), p. 163, table 2; 2000 (projected): H. N. Fullerton, Jr., "New Labor Force Projections, Spanning 1988 to 2000," *Monthly Labor Review, 112* (No. 11, November 1989), p. 8, table 4; 2005 (projected): U.S. General Accounting Office, *The Changing Workforce: Demographic Issues Facing the Federal Government* (Washington, DC: U.S. General Accounting Office, 1992), p. 23.
NOTE: 1870-1930: data for persons 10 years old and over; 1940: data for persons 14 years old and over; 1950-2005 (projected): data for persons 16 years old and over.

than it had been in 1910 (23%). Labor unions, government, and American society in general were not ready for more than a temporary change in the economic role of women. Men received priority in hiring when they returned from the war, and many women, to their resentment, were forced out of the labor force.

The passage of the Nineteenth Amendment to the Constitution in 1920, which gave women the right to vote, could have influenced economic roles in America. Backers of the amendment hoped that by ending sex discrimination in the right to vote it would stimulate the dismantling of sex discrimination in other areas of life. However, women's suffrage brought about little change in women's economic status. By 1940, the labor force participation rate of women was only 4% higher, at 25%, than it had been in 1920.

The Depression of the 1930s threw millions of Americans out of work. The unemployment rate was above 14% in each year of the decade, peaking at 25% during 1933. These conditions contributed to an identity crisis for unemployed men. In the book *Puzzled America*, published in 1935, Sherwood Anderson concluded, "The breaking down of the moral fiber of the American man through being out of a job, losing that sense of being some part of the moving world of activity, so essential to an American man's sense of his manhood— the loss of this essential something in the jobless can never be measured in dollars."[13] The Depression caused great strains in family relations, as unemployed men suffered a loss of status in their families. Those who relied on holding an authoritative role in the family and society felt humbled and disgraced. In addition, the Depression triggered resentment toward working women. With all the attention being lavished on the problems of men, the general attitude intensified that a woman who held a job was taking it away from a male breadwinner. Labor force participation rates were basically unchanged during the Depression, though, since unemployed workers who were looking for a job were still counted in the labor force.[14]

World War II, which closely followed the Depression, marked a turning point in the distribution of economic roles between women and men in the 20th century, although it did not necessarily cause the massive changes that were to follow. Similar to World War I, World War II created what was expected to be a temporarily high demand for female labor. Women were attracted to war-related industries by an advertising campaign appealing to their patriotism as well as self-interest, and they were given access to the more skilled, higher-paying jobs that were usually held by men. However, after the war was won in 1945, the labor force did not quickly "return to normal" as it had after World War I. Instead, it has never been the same.

Changes in the relative economic roles played by the sexes after World War II took several forms. The labor force participation rate of women, already at a century-high figure of 34% in 1950, rose steadily in the years to come (see Table 1.1). By 1980, over half of American women were in the labor force. The largest increase in labor force participation was among white, middle-class, well-educated women who formerly would have dropped out of the labor force for childrearing. Between 1950 and 1980, the overall participation rate for white women rose from 29% to 51%, whereas the overall participation rate for nonwhite women rose from 38% to 52%.[15] In contrast, the labor force participation rate of

Table 1.2 Participation in White-Collar Occupations

Year	White-Collar Total	Nonfarm Exec., Admin., & Managers	Professional & Technical	Clerical Workers	Sales Workers
Percentage of Total Labor Force					
1900	18	6	4	3	5
1910	21	6	5	5	5
1920	25	7	5	8	5
1930	29	7	7	9	6
1940	31	7	7	10	7
1950	36	9	8	12	7
1960	43	11	11	15	6
1970	48	11	14	17	6
1980	52	11	16	19	6
1990	58	13	—	—	—
1992	58	13	—	—	—
Percentage of Female Workers in Occupation					
1900	19	4	35	24	17
1910	24	6	41	35	22
1920	32	7	44	48	26
1930	33	8	45	52	24
1940	35	11	41	54	27
1950	40	14	40	62	34
1960	42	16	36	68	40
1970	47	16	39	75	43
1980	53	26	44	80	45
1990	56	39	—	—	—
1992	56	42	—	—	—

SOURCE: 1900-1950: U.S. Department of Commerce, Bureau of the Census, *Historical Statistics of the United States: Colonial Times to 1970* (Washington, DC: Government Printing Office, 1975), pp. 139-140, series D182-232; 1960-1980: U.S. Department of Labor, Bureau of Labor Statistics, *Handbook of Labor Statistics* (Washington, DC: Government Printing Office, 1983), pp. 44-48, table 16; 1990: U.S. Department of Labor, Bureau of Labor Statistics, *Employment and Earnings*, 37 (No. 2, February 1990), p. 29, table A22; 1992: U.S. Department of Labor, Bureau of Labor Statistics, *Employment and Earnings*, 39 (No. 5, May 1992), p. 29, table A22.
NOTE: — indicates that 1990 and later data were not compatible with earlier data.

men held fairly constant throughout the century. It still exceeded that of women, but the gap was narrowing.

The increased employment of women coincided with a rise in the proportion of "white-collar" jobs, or those that did not require manual labor, in the economy. In 1940, about one third of all jobs were white-collar, and about one third of these jobs were held by women (see Table 1.2). By 1980, over half of all jobs were white-collar, and over half of

Table 1.3 Marital Status of the Labor Force: Women

Year	Percentage Distribution of Female Labor Force			Female Labor Force as Percentage of Female Population		
	Single	Married, Spouse Present	Widowed/ Separated/ Divorced	Single	Married, Spouse Present	Widowed/ Separated/ Divorced
1890	68	14	18	41	5	30
1900	66	16	18	44	6	33
1910	60	25	15	51	11	34
1920	77	23	—	46	9	—
1930	54	29	17	51	12	34
1940	49	36	15	46	16	30
1950	32	48	20	51	24	38
1960	24	54	22	44	31	40
1970	22	59	19	53	41	39
1980	25	55	20	62	50	44
1988	25	55	20	65	57	46

SOURCE: 1890-1940: U.S. Department of Commerce, Bureau of the Census, *Historical Statistics of the United States: Colonial Times to 1970* (Washington, DC: Government Printing Office, 1975), p. 133, series D49-62; 1950-1988: U.S. Department of Labor, Bureau of Labor Statistics, *Handbook of Labor Statistics* (Washington, DC: Government Printing Office, 1989), pp. 235-239, table 55.
NOTE: 1890-1940: "Married, Spouse Present" data includes separated women; 1920: "Single" data includes widowed or divorced women.

these jobs were held by women. Women held an increasing proportion of clerical and sales jobs. Professional and technical jobs (i.e. engineers, lawyers, teachers, health technicians, and so on), about 40% of which had consistently been held by women, were growing in proportion in the economy. Most importantly for the balance of power held by women and men in the economy, the proportion of women executives, administrators, and managers in nonfarm occupations (called simply "managers" from this point on) was increasing. In 1900, this proportion was only 4%, or 1 in every 25. By 1940, it was 11%, or about 1 in every 10. In 1970, it was 16%, or 1 in every 6. In 1980, it was 26%, or 1 in every 4. By 1992, it had increased to 42%, or 2 in every 5 and ten times the proportion for 1900. Women were rapidly gaining in numbers and influence in managerial ranks, with the greatest changes taking place most recently.

The marital status of the labor force was also changing, especially for women. In 1900, single women comprised two-thirds of the female labor force (see Table 1.3). By 1960, over half of the female labor force was married. This shift did not result from a decline in working single women. The employment rate for single women increased by 19%

Table 1.4 Marital Status of the Labor Force: Men

	Percentage Distribution of Male Labor Force			Male Labor Force as Percentage of Male Population		
Year	Single	Married, Spouse Present	Widowed/ Separated/ Divorced	Single	Married, Spouse Present	Widowed/ Separated/ Divorced
1950	20	74	6	63	92	63
1960	18	76	6	56	89	59
1970	18	76	6	61	87	54
1980	26	66	8	71	81	67
1988	27	62	11	72	79	67

SOURCE: U.S. Department of Labor, Bureau of Labor Statistics, *Handbook of Labor Statistics* (Washington, DC: Government Printing Office, 1989), pp. 235-239, table 55.

between 1940 and 1988, but it more than tripled for married women during the same period. The proportion of married women who worked, which had been 6% in 1900, was still only 16% in 1940. This proportion dramatically increased after World War II, however, so that over half of all married women were employed by 1988.

The marital status of male workers changed to a lesser extent (see Table 1.4). Between 1950 and 1988, there was a 13% decline in the proportion of married men who worked and a 9% increase in this proportion for single men. However, married men still comprised over 60% of the male labor force.

The working mother moved from the periphery of the American labor force into its mainstream during the 20th century.[16] Postwar changes in the female labor force demonstrated increasing disregard for the public norm that the woman's proper place was in the home. At the beginning of the century, single women were the women most accepted into the workplace. Employment of single women required the least adjustment to the public norm; the notion that the *mother's* proper place was in the home could still be held as a standard while single women worked. The next group to enter the labor force in large numbers were older married women. Between 1940 and 1960, the proportion of 45- to 64-year-old women who worked went from 20% to 42%. These women were past their peak child-raising years. Their increasing presence in the workplace could be begrudgingly accepted by defenders of the public norm as long as *young* mothers still stayed home. The final group of women to increase its labor force participation consisted of younger married women with preschool- or school-aged children. By 1990, 75% of mothers with children between 6 and 17 years old, over 60% of those with children between 2 and 5 years old, and over 50% of those with children under 2 years old were in the labor force. The increased employment of mothers of young children ended adherence to the public norm concerning women's place by any age group.[17]

The women who entered the labor force after World War II came increasingly from the middle class. The war legitimized employment for all women regardless of their class, as female employment became a patriotic gesture rather than questionable behavior. The growth in white-collar occupations also created jobs that were not incompatible with middle-class status. Aspirations for a higher standard of living, consumerism, the desire to send children to college, and inflation made it necessary for middle-class women to work to achieve and maintain a middle-class standard of living.

However, traditional attitudes concerning women's proper place in society persisted. During the 1950s, the mass media promoted an image of family togetherness that defined the mother's role as central to all domestic activity. Betty Friedan called this attitude "the feminine mystique." It is succinctly described in the following passage:

The suburban housewife—she was the dream image of the young American women and the envy, it was said, of women all over the world. The American housewife—freed by science and labor-saving appliances from the drudgery, the dangers of childbirth and the illnesses of her grandmother. She was healthy, beautiful, educated, concerned only about her husband, her children, her home. She had found true feminine fulfillment. As a housewife and mother, she was respected as a full and equal partner to man in his world. She was free to choose automobiles, clothes, appliances, supermarkets; she had everything that women ever dreamed of.

In the 15 years after World War II, this mystique of feminine fulfillment became the cherished and self-perpetuating core of contemporary American culture. Millions of women lived their lives in the image of those pretty pictures of the American suburban housewife, kissing their husbands good-bye in front of the picture window, depositing their stationwagonsfull of children at school, and smiling as they ran the new electric waxer over the spotless kitchen floor. They baked their own bread, sewed their own and their children's clothes, kept their new washing machines and dryers running all day. They changed the sheets on the beds twice a week instead of once, took the rug-hooking class in adult education, and pitied their poor frustrated mothers, who had dreamed of having a career. Their only ambition was to be perfect wives and mothers; their highest ambition to have five children and a beautiful house; their only fight to get and keep their husbands. They had no thought for the unfeminine problems of the world outside the home; they wanted the men to make the major decisions. They gloried in their role as women, and wrote proudly on the census blank: "Occupation: housewife."[18]

Women were supposed to revel in this role and happily surrender control of and participation in economic and public life to men. According to opinion polls, both women and men accepted such an allocation of sex roles. Yet, the statistics that have been presented show that something else was actually happening in the workplace. As one observer put it, "A visitor from another planet who read the magazines and newspapers of the 1950s would never have guessed that the women portrayed as being engaged exclusively in homemaking activities were also joining the job market in unprecedented numbers."[19]

During this period, women workers were not perceived as crusading to achieve economic equality with men. Instead, their increased economic activity could be interpreted as consistent with their primary role as helpmates to their spouses. Most women who worked were citing "economic need" as the reason for their employment, even when the family income was solidly in the middle-class range. If women had not been portrayed, or portrayed themselves, as working temporarily to help meet immediate needs, they may not have been allowed to enter the workplace as easily.

Nonetheless, the contradiction between traditional attitudes and actual behavior could not last without something giving, especially when the contradiction became greater each year. What eventually "gave" was the unvarying public acceptance of traditional sex roles. In the late 1960s and early 1970s, a women's movement emerged that had a major impact on the attitudes of women, and indirectly men, about the roles each played. It was spurred both by the experiences of younger women in the civil rights movement of the 1960s and by the increasing resentment of middle-class business and professional women towards the barriers that held back their further progress. Their discontent found an early voice in Friedan's *The Feminine Mystique*, but recognition of the limits on their achievements placed by society's attitudes was not enough. This recognition now led to a full-fledged push for legislative and economic action that would bring closer the goal of equality, or at least equal opportunity, for American men and women.

The National Organization of Women (NOW), the first avowedly feminist organization since women gained the right to vote, held its inaugural meeting in October 1966. Its statement of purpose expressed concerns about discrimination in employment, education, and the legal system. It also called for a true partnership between the sexes, to be brought about by an equitable sharing of the responsibilities for home and children and the economic burden of their support. Women's groups such as NOW were successful in promoting change in a multitude of areas. Through lawsuits or the threat of them, groups pressured large corporations into initiating affirmative action programs to increase their hiring and promotion of women. Women pressured the federal government into investigating sex discrimination in federally funded contracts and federally sponsored programs and then devising programs to end it. Women's studies courses were added to the curriculum at many colleges and universities. Pressure from the women's movement reduced the emphasis on sex role stereotypes in children's books, stimulated the opening of day-care centers, and contributed to the elimination of sexist language in professional journals and of separate advertising for "women's jobs" and "men's jobs" in the classified sections of newspapers. The women's movement had impact in many ways, large and small, and a whole generation of women became aware of the possibilities that could be open to them if their lives were not lived according to traditional norms.[20]

The women's movement elicited mixed reactions in men. The men most threatened by it were those most committed to traditional roles in the family, the economy, and public affairs. They were alarmed as much because it challenged their power as because it violated their principles. Other men were concerned about the impact on their job security and future advancement as more women entered the workplace. These men were inclined to see affirmative action programs as promoting "reverse discrimination," considered as bad as the original discrimination and not a proper substitute for it.

A small number of men had the opposite reaction and promoted "men's liberation." Using consciousness-raising techniques borrowed from the women's movement, their goal was the liberation of men from the constraints imposed by the masculine sex-role stereotype. "Men's studies" courses focusing on the male experience were offered on nearly 200

college campuses by 1984. Some saw men's studies as providing a necessary complement to women's studies. Many people with an interest in
women's studies, however, believed that men's studies courses weren't
legitimate and were marginally useful at best. The director of the National
Women's Studies Association argued that *every* college course could be
called a men's studies course.[21]

Most men, however, viewed the women's movement with ambiva-
lence and anxiety. They took it seriously, but they didn't know what to
make of it or how to respond to it. In a nationwide survey of men over
16, one third said that the new relationship between women and men
had left them confused over what was expected of them. Younger men
(between ages 16 and 34) and older men (age 50 and over) were the most
confused. Given the breakdown of traditional roles, it was no longer
clear what being a man meant in American society.[22]

Many women, on the other hand, were frustrated at the lack of complete achievement of the economic, legal, and social goals originally set
forth by the women's movement. One woman in her 40s characterized
feminism as the "Great Experiment That Failed," with women of her
generation as the casualties:

> In 1973 I left what could have been a perfectly good marriage, taking
> with me a child in diapers, a 10-year-old Plymouth, and Volume 1,
> Number 1 of *Ms.* Magazine. I was convinced I could make it on my
> own. In the last 15 years my ex has married or lived with a succession
> of women. As he gets older, his women stay in their 20s. Meanwhile,
> I've stayed unattached. He drives a BMW. I ride buses.[23]

Younger women, however, tended to see such complaints as tales from
"the old days when, once upon a time, women had trouble getting into
the schools or jobs they now hold."[24]

At any rate, more than a quarter century after the formation of NOW,
the feminist agenda is far from fulfilled. Federal and state legislation
now prohibit discrimination against women in employment, education,
credit, and housing. However, women have not attained equal economic
status with men while they retain the major day-to-day share of household responsibilities.[25]

As the 1990s began, tensions between women and men over public
issues and events repeatedly emerged. For example, players on the New
England Patriots professional football team were fined by the National
Football League for locker-room harassment of a female journalist, Lisa

Olson. The response of the team's owner, Victor Kiam, to the charge of harassment was reportedly to call Olson a "classic bitch." Hounded by fans of the team when she returned to the Patriots' stadium to cover later games, Olson eventually left the country to pursue her profession in Australia.[26]

In addition, the Secretary of the Navy resigned and other naval officers were disciplined or dismissed after rampant sexual harassment at the annual convention of the Tailhook Association, a group of retired and active naval aviators, came to public light. Female naval aviators were sexually assaulted by reportedly several hundred men as they were forced to walk a gauntlet of drunken officers lining the corridor outside hospitality suites at the convention hotel. The navy helicopter pilot who was the first to complain to Navy officials about her harassment, Lt. Paula Coughlin, subsequently was the subject of a smear campaign by some of her fellow officers.[27]

Feelings ran particularly high throughout the nation when Clarence Thomas, a nominee for the U.S. Supreme Court, was accused in 1991 of sexual harassment committed a decade earlier by Anita Hill, a law professor and former subordinate of Thomas's in the U.S. Department of Education and Equal Employment Opportunity Commission. Hill's charges were dramatically aired, and vehemently denied by Thomas, in televised hearings held by the U.S. Senate Judiciary Committee. To some, the hearings signified the extent of conflict between the sexes in American society—women's strong feelings about sexual harassment and old-boy networks, and men's equally strong resentment of what they saw as unjust harassment complaints and loss of their traditional prerogatives. Battle lines were drawn over the merits of Hill's charges between men's organizations such as the National Organization for Men, feminist organizations such as NOW, and politically conservative and anti-feminist organizations such as the Eagle Forum.[28] Although Thomas's nomination was confirmed by the U.S. Senate, the intense feelings that were brought up for women and men by this and other public spectacles did not appear to be fading as the 1990s proceeded.

Implications

For manager-subordinate relationships to work best, each party needs to understand the other's needs, attitudes, skills, and goals. Without such understanding, communication is distorted, arriving at consensus solutions is difficult, and establishing the sense of teamwork and shared vision that characterizes excellent organizations is nearly impossible. One of the purposes of this book is to help men and women in both managerial and nonmanagerial roles achieve such an understanding. As we have seen, it has seldom been present in American society, because public norms and economic realities have rarely converged.

According to the historical evidence, there has been no consistent distribution of economic roles between the sexes in the United States. In early American society, cultural norms regarding male supremacy were embraced in public speech but ignored in private actions. The introduction of the market economy and the industrial revolution resulted in the least difference between these norms and economic realities. The allocation of roles between the sexes in the more affluent families of that time came to be regarded as "traditional" sex roles by our time. These roles were generally adhered to in economic life until World War II, but have been increasingly ignored since. Traditional sex roles have less to do with present-day economic realities than at any time in American history.

The changes experienced by women in the labor force over time have been striking, while the changes experienced by men have been less apparent. Men have been employed at approximately the same rate for over 120 years. However, they have been increasingly required to adapt to the presence of women as their peers, superiors, and subordinates. In turn, women entering male-dominated organizations have gone from being the only member of their sex holding a particular job, to being a member of a small group of women amid a larger group of men in the job, to sometimes being a member of the majority group and often being in charge. Adjustment has been necessary for members of both sexes at every level—personal, interpersonal, and organizational.

Yet, some important differences between the economic roles played by women and men remain. Men still hold 58% of all management positions in organizations. Even when organizations consist of predominantly female employees, the leaders are typically male. Women have had virtually no success in gaining access to the highest management positions in American corporations. Only one of the *Business Week* Top 1000 corporations has a woman chief executive, and she shares the job with her husband.[29]

The gap between male and female wages also persists. Among full-time workers, women have consistently earned lower wages than men, currently averaging less than 75 cents for every dollar earned by a man.[30]

Even with the same job in the same occupation, women's average earnings are typically lower than those of men. The highest paid occupations are those with predominantly male workers. Pay is an important indicator of the value attached to work, and the work of women continues to be valued less than the work of men in almost all major sectors of the economy.

Thus we find ourselves in a period of flux. Even though work and its rewards are not distributed equally between the sexes, enough change has occurred to make traditional sex roles no longer an appropriate guideline for workplace behavior. However, new standards of behavior have not been substituted for the old standards that have been rejected in practice. Whether consciously or unconsciously, people often take their own sex and the other's sex into account in their work transactions in some way.

What *does* it mean to be a woman or a man in today's workplace? How *should* women and men take their own sex and the other's sex into account in their workplace interactions, if at all? Widely accepted answers to these questions, promoting either a unisex standard of behavior or separate standards for men and women, have not emerged.

Due to the increase in the proportion of working women, organizations now have more interactions between people who may see themselves as more dissimilar than ever before. One of the few advantages of adhering to traditional sex roles was that men and women knew how to act with each other and what to expect. That advantage is lost for now. The only way to regain it (other than by returning to the previously prescribed roles, which is unlikely and not recommended) is for women and men to seek to understand each other better in their present work roles.

Notes

1. E. A. Ross, *The Social Trend* (New York: Century, 1922), pp. 78-80, 90-93.

2. This section of the chapter is primarily based on L. Larwood and M. M. Wood, Chapter 3, "A Question of Tradition," in *Women in Management* (Lexington, MA: Lexington Books, 1977).

3. W. S. Laughlin, "Hunting: An Integrated Biobehavior System and Its Evolutionary Importance," in *Man the Hunter*, ed. R. B. Lee and I. de Vore (Chicago: Aldine, 1968), p. 304; S. L. Washburn and C. S. Lancaster, "The Evolution of Hunting," in *Man the Hunter*, ed. Lee and de Vore, p. 293, quoted in B. L. Forisha, *Sex Roles and Personal Awareness* (Morristown, NJ: General Learning Press, 1978), p. 44.

4. C. W. Gailey, "Evolutionary Perspectives on Gender Hierarchy," in *Analyzing Gender: A Handbook of Social Science Research*, ed. B. B. Hess and M. M. Ferree (Newbury Park, CA: Sage, 1987); L. Tiger and R. Fox, *The Imperial Animal* (New York: Delta, 1971).

5. M. Mead, *Male and Female* (New York: Morrow, 1949), pp. 7-8, reprinted by permission.

6. G. P. Murdock, "Comparative Data on the Division of Labor by Sex," *Social Forces*, 15, (No. 4, 1937): 551-553.

7. C. Ferguson, Chapter 1, "The Male Ethos," in *The Male Attitude* (Boston: Little, Brown, 1966).

8. W. H. Chafe, "Looking Backward in Order to Look Forward: Women, Work, and Social Values in America," in *Women and the American Economy: A Look to the 1980s*, ed. J. M. Kreps (Englewood Cliffs, NJ: Prentice Hall, 1976).

9. E. N. Glenn and C. M. Tolbert II, "Technology and Emerging Patterns of Stratification for Women of Color: Race and Gender Segregation in Computer Occupations," in *Women, Work, and Technology*, ed. B. D. Wright (Ann Arbor: University of Michigan Press, 1987); L. A. Tilly and J. W. Scott, *Women, Work, and Family* (New York: Holt, Rinehart & Winston, 1978).

10. B. Welter, "The Cult of True Womanhood: 1820-1860," *American Quarterly*, 18 (1966), p. 152, quoted in K. V. Hansen, " 'Helped Put in a Quilt': Men's Work and Male Intimacy in Nineteenth Century New England," in *The Social Construction of Gender*, ed. J. Lorber and S. A. Farrell (Newbury Park, CA: Sage, 1991), p. 93.

11. P. Foner, ed., "Introduction," in *The Factory Girls*. (Urbana: University of Illinois Press, 1977); K. V. Hansen, " 'Helped Put in a Quilt.' "

12. J. A. Doyle, Chapter 1, "Today's Uncertain Male," in *The Male Experience* (Dubuque, IA: Brown, 1983).

13. S. Anderson, *Puzzled America* (Mamaroneck, NY: Appel, 1935), p. 46, quoted in J. L. Dubbert, *A Man's Place: Masculinity in Transition* (Englewood Cliffs, NJ: Prentice Hall, 1979), p. 210.

14. M. F. Fox and S. Hesse-Biber, Chapter 2, "Women in the Work Force: Past and Present," in *Women at Work* (Palo Alto, CA: Mayfield, 1984); Dubbert, *A Man's Place*, Chapter 7, "War to Depression: Preserving Masculine Control."

15. N. Barrett, "Women and the Economy," in *The American Woman 1987-88*, ed. S. E. Rix (New York: Norton, 1987); C. Goldin, *Understanding the Gender Gap: An Economic History of American Women* (New York: Oxford University Press, 1990), p. 17, table 2.1.

16. L. Y. Weiner, *From Working Girl to Working Mother: The Female Labor Force in the United States, 1820-1980* (Chapel Hill: University of North Carolina Press, 1985).

17. U.S. Department of Commerce, Bureau of the Census, *Historical Statistics of the United States: Colonial Times to 1970* (Washington, DC: Government Printing Office, 1975), pp. 131-132, series D29-41; U.S. Department of Labor, Bureau of Labor Statistics, *Working Women: A Chartbook* (Washington, DC: Government Printing Office, 1991), p. 50, table A-18.

18. B. Friedan, *The Feminine Mystique*, tenth anniversary ed. (New York: Norton, 1974), p. 18, reprinted by permission.

19. Chafe, "Looking Backward in Order to Look Forward," p. 20.

20. Chafe, "Looking Backward in Order to Look Forward"; C. Harrison, "A Richer Life: A Reflection on the Women's Movement," in *The American Woman 1988-89*, ed. S. E. Rix (New York: Norton, 1988).

21. Doyle, Chapter 14, "Of Clashing Values and a Questionable Future: Where to from Here?" in *The Male Experience*; M. Shiffman, "The Men's Movement: An Exploratory Empirical Investigation," in *Changing Men: New Directions in Research on Men and Masculinity*, ed. M. S. Kimmel (Newbury Park, CA: Sage, 1987); H. Brod, "A Case for Men's Studies," in *Changing Men*, ed. Kimmel; D. Petzke, " 'Men's Studies' Catches on at Colleges, Setting Off Controversy and Infighting," *Wall Street Journal, 207* (No. 29, 11 February 1986): 35.

22. B. T. Roesnner, "Men Adrift in a World of Change," *Hartford Courant, 149* (No. 273, 30 September 1986): B1.

23. K. Ebeling, "The Failure of Feminism," *Newsweek, 116* (No. 21, 19 November 1990): 9.

24. E. Goodman, "Feminists' Mid-Life Shock," *Hartford Courant, 148* (No. 8, 8 March 1985): B9.

25. Harrison, "A Richer Life."

26. B. T. Roessner, "Episode Makes Sport a Whole New Ballgame," *Hartford Courant, 153* (No. 276, 3 October 1990): B1.

27. E. Salholz, "Deepening Shame," *Newsweek, 120* (No. 6, 10 August 1992): 30-36.

28. G. Blonston and C. Scanlan, "Hill, Thomas Hold Their Ground: A Conflict Between the Sexes," *Hartford Courant, 154* (No. 285, 12 October 1991): A1, A9; S. L. Nazario, "Views of 'Women' Are as Varied as the Women," *Wall Street Journal, 218* (No. 78, 18 October 1991): B4.

29. A. T. Segal with W. Zellner, "Corporate Women," *Business Week*, No. 3269 (8 June 1992): 74-78.

30. U.S. Department of Labor, Bureau of Labor Statistics, *Employment and Earnings, 39* (No. 1, January 1992), computed from pp. 223-227, table 56.

2

Being Good Girls and Boys

Barbie Branches Out but Prince Harry Misses Out

Mattel's Barbie Is No Longer Just a Pretty Face

After 25 years of parties and dates with Ken, Mattel Inc.'s Barbie has decided to get a job. The new working-woman version of the doll made its debut this month at the American International Toy Fair in New York.

By day, the career-minded Barbie wears a pink business suit, carries a briefcase, and works at a computer terminal in her private office. At night, the sociable Barbie changes into a pink sequined evening dress in her pink and blue bedroom. "This is the first time we have positioned Barbie as a working woman," says Kathy Thorpe, a spokeswoman for Mattel, which sold $260 million worth of Barbie products last year. "Little girls see their mothers working, and their play reflects what's happening in the world."

Parents can buy the new contemporary Barbie, one of 11 models Mattel makes, for about $12, but they will have to shell out $23 more for the home and office play set. The working Barbie also comes with her own gold credit card. Unfortunately, Mattel will not let parents use it to pay for the doll.

Business Week[1]

Barbie to See Duty in Military

The heated battle over sending women into combat has gained a new recruit: Barbie has signed up for military duty.

The fashion doll, a favorite for millions of young American girls since 1959, is expanding her career options. This summer, she'll debut as an Air Force pilot, and she is scheduled to pull into Navy PXes next year as a chief petty officer. She has already been stationed in Army exchanges for several months, outfitted as a captain in a deep blue evening dress with gold braid.

All three military services are cooperating with Mattel Toys of Hawthorne, Calif., in designing the military Barbies, most of which will be sold to military families at on-base stores.

"We wanted to help provide a role model for girls," said Pam Carter, a policy officer in the Army's public affairs office who worked on the Army doll. "We're not out to recruit 9-year-old girls for the United States Army, but it does tell them they can aspire to be a soldier."

Hartford Courant[2]

Guy and Doll

Princess Diana told friends that she denied Prince Harry the doll he wanted at a London toy fair last week because of the media's presence and her fear that her No. 2 son would be dogged all his life by a photograph of him holding the doll. Harry, 7, insisted on the toy, but Diana held firm, feeling that the incident would not be reported or received empathetically. Harry came away with a toy car.

Hartford Courant[3]

What sex differences, if any, exist beyond the obvious ones? What do people believe sex differences to be? What alternatives to traditional beliefs have been proposed? How are beliefs about sex differences conveyed? What effects do they have on children and adults?

These questions, introduced from a historical perspective in the previous chapter, continue to be the subject of much attention and controversy. Some people believe that the only noteworthy differences that exist between women and men are physiological and hormonal, and that otherwise women and men are basically the same. According to this view, learned sex roles are mostly destructive to individuals and society because they are contrary to human nature. Others believe that women and men are fundamentally different in their orientation to life, including their work-related attitudes, motivation, behaviors, and skills. Such differences may be due to heredity (i.e., they are "in the genes") or environment (i.e., they result from learned sex roles rather than innate characteristics), but, in either case, they are seen as beneficial to individuals and society.

I will address these questions by reviewing the results of relevant research. Before proceeding, however, it is useful to make a distinction between two terms that are frequently used in such discussions: sex and gender. *Sex* (or "biological sex") is the term suggested by biological characteristics such as the chromosomal composition and reproductive apparatus of individuals. *Gender* is a term used in a social context. It may be defined as a scheme for categorization of individuals that uses biological differences as the basis for assigning social differences. Thus, the study of sex differences examines how males and females actually differ. In contrast, the study of gender differences focuses on how people think that males and females differ. An example of a gender difference would be a belief that females have stronger verbal skills than males. This difference does not appear to be an actual sex difference, as we shall see, but many people think that it is.[4]

Some gender differences represent beliefs that have been stable over time and held by a large proportion of the population. In particular, men have been believed to be high in "masculine" traits such as independence, aggressiveness, and dominance, and women have been believed to be high in "feminine" traits such as gentleness, sensitivity to the feelings of others, and tactfulness. Although others have called the beliefs "sex role stereotypes" or "sex stereotypes," I will refer to them as *gender stereotypes* in accordance with the sex/gender distinction.[5]

As we consider the effects of sex differences on work-related behavior, we also need to consider the effects of gender differences. Sex differences influence how people are disposed to behave in work settings. Gender differences influence how people react to others' behavior in such settings. Examining both types of differences will help us to understand male/female interactions in the workplace.

In addition, most studies of sex or gender differences have not reported the racial or ethnic group of the individuals who were the focus of the study. By ignoring issues of race and ethnicity, such studies reflect an underlying assumption that sex and gender differences are similar across all racial and ethnic groups. That is, white women and women of color are assumed to have similar personal characteristics and experiences, as are white men and men of color.[6] We need to guard against making such an assumption ourselves.

The focus of this chapter is on early influences on the behavior of females and males and their later effects. First, some of the common myths about sex differences will be examined in light of the research evidence. Next, the nature of gender stereotypes, or the traits that females and males traditionally have been believed to possess, will be considered. The concept of androgyny, a relatively recent development in thinking about sex roles, will be presented. The ways in which sex role expectations are conveyed to children, as well as the later effects of sex roles on adult health, will be examined. Finally, the chapter will consider the implications of sex differences, gender stereotypes, and sex role development on the practice of management. In other words, does a working Barbie or a military Barbie make a difference? If so, how much and what kind of a difference, and for whom?

Sex Differences: What Is the Evidence?

Watching Out for Biases

People have strong beliefs about whether there are fundamental differences between the capabilities of females and males. In fact, speculation about such differences is a national preoccupation. Americans seldom wonder whether children who differ in eye color or height also differ in intellectual abilities and personality. However, they care about whether such differences exist between girls and boys.[7]

Views about the nature of sex differences certainly have evolved over time. For example, 19th-century craniometrists argued that brain size was a good indicator of basic intelligence, and that the tendency of women to have smaller brains than men led them also to be less intelligent than men. However, this argument overlooked the fact that brain size is related to body size, and that the larger average size of males' brains is almost entirely accounted for by their larger average body size. On reviewing the existing literature on the psychology of sex differences in 1910, Helen Thompson Woolley concluded, "There is perhaps no field aspiring to be scientific where flagrant personal bias, logic martyred in the cause of supporting a prejudice, unfounded assertions, and even sentimental rot and drivel have run riot to such an extent as here."[8]

Some would say that Woolley's conclusion still applies. Researchers may bring either of two types of bias to the study of sex differences, alpha bias and beta bias. *Alpha bias* consists of the tendency to exaggerate sex differences. *Beta bias* consists of the tendency to minimize or ignore sex differences. Either type of bias can lead to a distortion of how the researcher sees reality.[9]

Such biases need not be the result of personal prejudices. The mere presence of a two-category system leads people to view the two categories as opposites, thereby demonstrating alpha bias. Since there is a biological basis that holds in most cases for categorizing people as male or female, people tend to classify males and females as different in other ways. For example, parents with two children tend to describe each in contrast to the other (e.g., "Bob is a leader, while Kathy is a follower"). However, parents with three or more children tend to focus on the unique aspects of each child (e.g., "Mary is sociable and likes to read, Tom likes art and music, Harry is mainly interested in his collection of sneakers, and Sue likes to work with her hands and loves sports"). Also, anthropologists who have done fieldwork in only two cultures tend to emphasize the differences between these cultures, whereas anthropologists with wider field experience are more aware of the diversity of human experience. No one has the opportunity to gain "wider field experience" with a third or fourth sex. However, every researcher of sex differences belongs to one of the two groups being examined. Researchers may be more likely to report sex differences that reflect favorably on their own sex.[10]

In conclusion, as we consider the findings of psychological research about sex differences, it is very important for us to be aware of the possibility of researchers' biases affecting what they do and do not report. However, this possibility should not keep us from trying to separate facts from myths about sex differences.

Sex Differences in Intellectual Skills

After arguments on the effects of physical factors such as brain size were dismissed by Woolley and others, research on sex differences in intellectual skills moved toward the use of standardized intelligence tests. At first, intelligence was viewed by test designers such as Alfred Binet as a universal concept, and tests were designed to yield a single score called an "intelligence quotient," or IQ, for every individual. Studies using Binet's test found no sex difference in general intelligence. However, researchers such as L. L. Thurstone took the concept of intelligence one step further and identified several distinct types of intellectual skills. The conceptualization of intelligence as consisting of multiple skills led to research on sex differences in specific areas such as verbal skill, spatial skill (that is, the skill to visualize figures or objects in space and how they are related to each other), and mathematical skill.[11]

In 1974, Eleanor Maccoby and Carol Nagy Jacklin published an exhaustive review of over 1,400 published studies on the psychology of sex differences.[12] Their work was the most complete of its kind ever published. They concluded that the research evidence confirmed female superiority in verbal skill appearing at about age 11 and male superiority in both mathematical and visual-spatial skill appearing at about ages 12-13. However, later researchers questioned the vote-counting technique used to summarize the results of others' studies. Maccoby and Jacklin simply tallied the number of studies that found significant differences favoring females, significant differences favoring males, or no significant sex differences in a number of general topic areas and then reached conclusions based on the "vote."

Several thousand studies since 1974 have attempted to verify, modify, or extend Maccoby and Jacklin's findings. In addition, a new statistical method called *meta-analysis* that was seen as superior to vote-counting came into vogue in the 1980s. Meta-analysis uses sophisticated quantitative methods to combine statistical evidence from different studies.[13] It yields results that are typically more complex than those yielded by vote counting. Separate meta-analyses that have been conducted on sex differences in many areas will be reported throughout this book.

A meta-analysis of sex differences in verbal skill, including all studies reviewed by Maccoby and Jacklin as well as more recent studies, concluded that such differences no longer exist. Sex differences were very small in different measures of verbal skill such as vocabulary, analogies, and general verbal ability. There was no trend in the magnitude of sex differences at different ages, countering Maccoby and Jacklin's assertion that such differences emerge around age 11. However, recently published studies reported smaller sex differences than earlier studies. The decline in reported sex differences in verbal skill in recent years could have been due to differences in how children are raised, as shall be discussed later in this chapter. However, it could also have been the result of changes in publication practices. Maccoby and Jacklin's massive work may have sensitized researchers to the importance of publishing studies in which sex differences *are not* found as well as those in which they *are* found.[14]

A meta-analysis of sex differences in spatial skills distinguished between three types of skills: spatial perception (the ability to correctly see objects as horizontal or vertical), mental rotation (the ability to rotate mentally a three-dimensional object pictured in two dimensions), and spatial visualization (the ability to visualize a simpler figure in a more complex figure). Males were superior in spatial perception and mental rotation. However, there was essentially no sex difference in spatial visualization. In addition, contrary to Maccoby and Jacklin's findings, whenever sex differences were present, they were present throughout the life span.[15]

Finally, a meta-analysis of sex differences in mathematical performance compiled findings regarding computation, understanding of mathematical concepts, and problem solving (that is, the application of math concepts to new situations). Girls were superior in computation until high school, when sex differences disappeared. There was no sex difference in the understanding of math concepts at any age. Male superiority in problem solving emerged in high school and was sustained in later years. When all types of performance were combined, there was a slight female superiority until high school and a moderate male superiority from high school through adulthood. These sex differences were present primarily for white Americans, but not for African Americans, Hispanic Americans, or Asian Americans. However, as for verbal skill, overall sex differences were smaller in more recent studies.[16]

However, performance on tests of intellectual skills is influenced by more than basic ability. For example, in a study of attitudes toward math, Jacquelynne Eccles and Janis Jacobs found that students' math performance was affected by their estimates of their mathematical abilities, their perceptions of the value of math courses, and their levels of math anxiety. These beliefs and anxiety levels, in turn, were strongly related to their mothers' beliefs concerning the difficulty of mathematics for them.[17]

Eccles and Jacobs had the unexpected opportunity to assess the effects of media reports concerning sex differences in math ability on mothers' expectations for their own children's math performance. While they were conducting their study in 1980, a study published in *Science* that received considerable media attention argued in favor of superior male mathematical ability as the cause of general sex differences in both mathematical achievement and attitudes toward math.[18] Three months later,

Eccles and Jacobs asked parents whether they had heard of the study and compared the attitudes of mothers who were aware of it (called "misinformed"—you can see their bias) with those who had not heard of it ("uninformed"). Uninformed mothers believed that the math ability of their daughters and sons was equivalent, whereas misinformed mothers of girls felt that math was more difficult for their daughters than did misinformed mothers of boys. Thus, the media reports influenced the same attitudes of parents that influence their children's attitudes toward math and subsequent math performance. In other words, parents' expectations of their children's attitudes and performance, fueled by the media campaign, may have led to a self-fulfilling prophecy.[19]

In summary, the more recent reviews of sex differences in intellectual skills based on meta-analytic techniques have yielded results that somewhat agree and somewhat disagree with those obtained by Maccoby and Jacklin in the 1970s, but are definitely more complex. Maccoby and Jacklin's conclusions regarding early female superiority in verbal skill were unsupported, as only very small sex differences were found at any age. Their conclusions regarding males' overall superior math skill emerging in adolescence were mostly supported; however, the sexes differ in their relative superiority in different types of math skill at different ages. Their conclusions concerning spatial skill were partially supported, with males demonstrating superiority in some but not all aspects of spatial skills. Also, sex differences that were present in spatial skill did not vary with age.

Although no simple conclusions can be reached, perhaps the most striking trend in these results is that sex differences in intellectual skills seem to be declining over time. This trend appeared in the meta-analyses of sex differences in verbal ability and math performance, and it has shown up in other studies as well.[20] Also, studies of the link between attitudes toward math and math performance suggest that beliefs about sex differences affect the use that individuals make of their own abilities.

Sex Differences in Social Behavior

Sex differences have been examined in many types of social behavior. Maccoby and Jacklin concluded that males are more aggressive than females beginning at about age 2, as soon as play with others begins. However, they concluded that the common beliefs that girls are more suggestible and more social than boys are myths. More recent reviews, including meta-analyses, have found differences reflecting gender stereo-types in a considerable range of social behaviors. Eleanor Maccoby later argued that (a) sex differences are minimal when males and females are observed or tested individually; and (b) sex differences emerge primar-ily in social situations, beginning in childhood, when boys and girls seg-regate themselves into same-sex groups in which distinctive interaction styles emerge.[21]

Two meta-analyses have expanded our knowledge of sex differences in aggression. One found that males were indeed more aggressive than females, but that the sex difference was greater in children than in adults. However, as for some intellectual skills, sex differences in aggression were smaller in more recent studies than in earlier studies. The other meta-analysis also found that males were more aggressive than females, but that the sex difference was more pronounced for aggression that produces pain or physical injury than for aggression that causes psy-chological or social harm.[22]

A meta-analysis of sex differences in influenceability in social settings found that men tend to be more influential and women more easily influenced, especially when there is group pressure to conform. How-ever, this difference may be due to the typical status difference in male/female interactions. When a difference in formal status exists, the male is more likely to hold the higher-level position in the organization. Also, when someone from a male-dominated occupation (e.g., physician) inter-acts with someone from a female-dominated occupation (e.g., nurse), the former usually has the greater power and status. Thus this sex dif-ference, when seen in work settings, may simply indicate that more powerful people are more influential than less powerful people.[23]

Status differences between women and men may also play an impor-tant role in nonverbal communication skills and behavior. Nonverbal communication skills include the ability to assess the meaning of non-verbal cues from others, to judge nonverbal expressions correctly, and to recall having met or seen people. Females have higher skills than males in all three areas, perhaps because they tend to have lower status. For example, the finding that women are better able to interpret non-verbal cues could reflect their being in weaker positions and having to constantly monitor others' reactions to them.[24]

Helping behavior is interesting to examine, because both females and males offer help to others but in different ways. In choosing when to offer help, both women and men are influenced by their expectations about how they are best at helping others. Males are more likely to offer heroic or chivalrous help in areas where they feel most competent as males, such as helping a motorist with a flat tire stopped by the side of a dangerous highway. In contrast, females are more likely to offer nurturant or caring help in areas where they feel most competent as females, such as volunteering to spend time with a disturbed child. These differences are also seen in occupational roles: Women are particularly well represented in occupations that involve some type of personal service, such as nurse and teacher, whereas men are especially well represented in occupations that call for placing one's life in jeopardy to help others, such as firefighter and law enforcement officer.[25] These three streams of research (on social influence, nonverbal communication, and helping behavior) suggest that when sex differences exist, they may be accounted for at least partially by situational factors.

This has been a selective review of the major findings about sex differences obtained from psychological research, since it is beyond the scope of this book to summarize the results of all of the studies on this topic. Overall, it suggests that some sex differences exist in intellectual skills and social behavior, but that they may be diminishing over time and may be attributable to factors other than personal characteristics. Now that we have reviewed the evidence about sex differences, let us turn to the question of what people traditionally have believed to be sex differences. Sex differences themselves play only a small role in influencing male/female interactions in the workplace; gender differences may have greater importance.

Gender Differences: What Are the Beliefs?

The terms *masculinity* and *femininity* were introduced in the previous chapter to describe beliefs about what males and females are really like. These terms usually are used in a historical sense. That is, they typically refer to "traditional" beliefs that have been handed down about the personal attributes of men and women. These beliefs are not necessarily held by all members of society at any given time. For the most part, they have been unguided by the research evidence about sex differences. Nevertheless, most members of society have been exposed to such beliefs and have been expected to live up to them at some time in their lives. Before we examine the influence of these beliefs, it is necessary to document exactly what they are.

Before we proceed, try the following exercise. In your mind, put together a mental image of the "typical woman"; then try to imagine an image of the typical woman that most people would agree on. Next, provide five adjectives or phrases that complete these two sentences: (1) I think the typical woman is _____. (2) Most other people think the typical woman is _____. Now repeat the whole exercise, this time thinking about the "typical man."[26]

Let's consider your responses. You probably feel that most people would answer in a more biased manner than you, invoking gender stereotypes of what the two sexes are like. But, have you noticed the bias of the exercise itself? It is likely to have led you to focus on the differences between the sexes, when, in fact, there is considerable overlap and similarity between their characteristics.

One of the earliest and best-known studies of gender stereotypes was conducted in this manner. Inge Broverman and her colleagues asked a group of college students in an early-1970s study to list characteristics, attitudes, and behaviors in which they believed women and men differ. Examining the 122 items that appeared on the initial list, a second group rated the extent to which they agreed that the items were typical of an adult man or an adult woman. Analysis of these results yielded 41 items that were believed to differentiate between men and women. The men and women who responded to the survey were in almost perfect agreement on the items. These items divided into two clusters. First, men were seen as more competent than women, rating higher on such items as "very direct," "very worldly," "very skilled in business," "can make decisions easily," and "almost always acts as a leader." However, women were seen as more warm and expressive than men, rating higher on such items as "very tactful," "very gentle," "very aware of feelings of others," "very talkative," and "easily expresses tender feelings." Both competence and warmth/expressiveness were seen as desirable characteristics. However, since 29 of the 41 differentiating items were favorable to the masculine rather than the feminine stereotype, the researchers concluded that masculinity is more valued than femininity in American society.[27]

Another group of researchers adapted the survey used by Broverman et al. to examine gender stereotypes but followed a different procedure. They asked a group of college students to rate the *typical* adult male and female on 138 items (the original 122 items plus 16 extra) and another group to rate the *ideal* adult male and female. Fifty-five items were identified as "stereotypic" based on differences between the ratings of the typical male and female. The 23 items that had ratings for both ideal males and ideal females on the masculine side of the scale were labeled as "male-valued." Examples of these items are "makes decisions easily," "feels superior," "acts as a leader," and "independent." The 18 items that were rated higher on the feminine side of the scale for both ideal males and ideal females, such as "emotional," "devotes self to others," "understanding," and "gentle," were labeled as "female-valued." The other 13 items (one was dropped as uninterpretable) had ratings on the masculine side for the ideal male and on the feminine side for the ideal female; these items were labeled as "sex-specific." When the male-valued and male-specific items were compared with the female-valued and female-specific items, the same groupings of competence versus warmth and expressiveness were seen.[28]

Research conducted since these studies has found little change in the gender stereotypes originally documented. Beliefs about sex differences appear to have remained essentially the same since the late 1960s, despite the increased attention given to gender stereotypes in the popular media and the considerable changes that have taken place in the work world since then.[29] There has even been consensus in the perceived attributes of women and men across cultures. A study of gender stereotypes in 30 different nations found evidence for common male and female stereotypes. The male stereotype was seen as stronger and more active than the female stereotype. The male stereotype was characterized by high needs for dominance, autonomy, aggression, and achievement, whereas the female stereotype was characterized by high needs for deference, nurturance, and affiliation. However, some variations have also been found in the male and female stereotypes invoked in different cultures.[30]

As noted before, just asking about the characteristics of two categories can force the categories to be seen as opposites. However, not all women are stereotyped as having exactly the same traits, nor are all men viewed the same. For example, women have been further stereotyped as falling into one of five categories: sex object, career woman, housewife, athlete, or "women's libber." Similarly, men have been categorized into four distinct types: businessman, athletic man, blue-collar working man, and macho man. It seems clear that people apply more than gender stereotypes in considering the sexes. They also apply more specific stereotypes to members of each sex.[31]

Although beliefs about sex differences have not changed much over the years, beliefs about the relationship between masculinity and femininity have changed. So have our notions of what females and males should be like. Let's turn now to the origin and development of the concept of androgyny.

Androgyny: The Best of Both Worlds?

Until the 1970s, masculinity and femininity generally were believed to be opposites. If a person was high in masculinity, he or she was regarded as low in femininity, and vice versa. Although studies had shown that some characteristics regarded as ideal for adults in general were feminine and others masculine, it still was considered appropriate for an individual to conform to his or her gender stereotype. Males were supposed to be masculine, females were supposed to be feminine, and anyone who fell in the middle or at the "wrong" end of the scale was considered to be maladjusted and in need of help.

Sandra Bem challenged these assumptions and beliefs in a series of studies. As others had done, she identified masculine items as those that were seen as more desirable for men than women and feminine items as those seen more desirable for women than men. However, instead of every item being regarded as masculine at one end of the scale and feminine at the other end, each masculine item was now regarded as "high in masculinity" at one end of the scale and "low in masculinity" at the other end, and each feminine item as "high in femininity" at one end and "low in femininity" at the other. This procedure resulted in masculinity and femininity being defined as separate and independent, rather than opposing, sets of characteristics in the Bem Sex-Role Inventory (BSRI).[32] Another instrument developed at about the same time, the Personal Attributes Questionnaire (PAQ), also presented independent measures of masculinity and femininity.[33]

The BSRI contained 20 masculine items, 20 feminine items, and 20 filler items to disguise the purpose of the instrument. Individuals were asked to rate the extent to which they thought each item was characteristic of themselves. Masculinity and femininity scores were calculated by averaging individuals' self-ratings for the respective items. Therefore, rather than measuring beliefs about others, the BSRI measured beliefs about oneself in relation to traditional concepts of masculinity and femininity. Bem called these beliefs an individual's *sex role identity*. She adopted a four-quadrant classification scheme for sex role identity as follows:[34]

Femininity Score

		High	Low
Masculinity Score	High	Androgynous	Masculine
	Low	Feminine	Undifferentiated

Thus were born the concept of psychological androgyny and a means of measuring it. The term *androgyny* comes from the Greek roots *andr* (man) and *gyne* (woman). It means both masculine and feminine. Once this term entered psychologists' vocabularies, a sense of its appropriate place in the realm of human behavior needed to be developed. This was offered by Bem and others in studies that soon followed. An androgynous sex role identity was found to be associated with higher self-esteem, a more flexible response to situations that seemed to call for either feminine or masculine behaviors, and a host of other positive factors. The individual who adheres to gender stereotypes no longer seemed the ideal of psychological health. Instead, the androgynous individual, whose self-image and behavior are less narrowly restricted along sex role lines, was seen to be more psychologically flexible and more ready to meet the complex demands of society. In short, androgyny was proposed as the new ideal.[35]

It is easy to understand why the concept of androgyny has such appeal. Androgyny is intended to represent the "best of both worlds," both highly valued masculine behaviors and highly valued feminine behaviors. It appears to present a desirable means for individuals to move beyond the rigid constraints of sex roles. If we believe in the concept and promise of androgyny, males and females no longer need to act differently by conforming to the appropriate gender stereotype. Under the new standard, they should behave similarly and adopt characteristics of both stereotypes.

Not surprisingly, Bem's work triggered a backlash. Some criticized her for poor science because her beliefs in what is "right" for individuals were made so obvious. This is not a very good argument; *all* scientific research is value-laden, but most researchers are not as explicit in stating their values. More telling criticism was made of the items that comprised the BSRI. Here, Bem appears to have been victimized by her own methodology. The average desirability of the masculine items in the BSRI for a man was similar to the average desirability of the feminine items for a woman. However, the desirability of the various items had not been assessed for an adult in general. Other researchers found that the masculine characteristics were more desirable than the feminine characteristics overall when rated for an adult of unspecified sex. Bem accepted this criticism, and developed a Short BSRI that eliminated most of the items regarded as undesirable for adults.[36]

Others have maintained that the masculinity and femininity components of androgyny do not equally contribute to psychological well-being, flexibility, and adjustment. According to this argument, masculinity rather than androgyny yields positive outcomes for individuals in American society. For example, a meta-analysis of the relationship between sex role identity and self-esteem concluded that masculinity has a far greater influence on self-esteem than femininity. Further research is needed to settle the dispute over the relative utility of being androgynous, thereby displaying a combination of masculine and feminine characteristics, or simply being masculine.[37]

Still others have argued that masculinity and femininity could be further divided into independent concepts and that it made no sense to talk about masculinity and femininity in themselves. For example, masculinity could consist of separate characteristics pertaining to dominance or aggressiveness and to autonomy or independence. Bem counterargued that strong beliefs about sex differences suggest that the terms masculinity and femininity refer to meaningful concepts for people, even if the concepts themselves can be broken down further. She acknowledged that her early results had generated inappropriate goals and subsequently proposed the elimination of society's dependence on gender as the primary means of classifying people. Rather than everyone becoming androgynous individuals, she advocated the development of an environment where everyone is free to be themselves rather than being expected to live up to any standard of psychological health.[38]

So, here is where the controversy over androgyny stands. Traditional beliefs about gender differences, or what females and males *are really like*, are held by many people. However, different conceptions of what females and males *should be like* have been proposed. One view argues for conformity to feminine and masculine gender stereotypes. Another view argues that people should break free from gender stereotypes and pursue an androgynous ideal. Still another view argues that there should be no standard conception of ideal behavior for females and males and that people should simply be themselves, whatever that may be. People who reject gender stereotypes as standards do not necessarily agree with the proposition that androgynous people lead better lives. Midst this turmoil, children still are being brought into the world and raised by adults who have beliefs about differences between girls and boys and how they should behave.

Sex Role Development in Children: What Are the Influences?

Although the concept of androgyny offers a vision of a society free of the influence of gender stereotypes, that society has not arrived yet. Boys still grow up under the heavy influence of the masculine stereotype and girls under the influence of the feminine stereotype. To explain the effects of these influences, we need to examine how young males and females are encouraged to live up to the expectations of the appropriate sex role and be "good boys" and "good girls."

Three types of factors have been claimed by different theorists to influence the early development of females and males: biological, environmental, and cognitive. No agreement has been reached as to which has the greater influence, but all three factors appear to have at least some effect. To understand these effects, we need to consider the basic arguments of each theory.[39]

Those who focus on the effects of *biological* factors argue that the characteristics and behaviors that children display are determined mostly by their biological sex. According to this argument, boys behave the way they do simply because they are male, and girls behave as they do because they are female, although the underlying reasons proposed for biological effects differ. For example, the creationist perspective attributes male-female differences to distinct acts of creation by God. Others argue that sex differences in levels of hormones such as testosterone and androstenedione are responsible for sex differences in behavior.

Those who focus on the effects of *environmental* factors argue that girls and boys are induced to act in accordance with sex roles by being rewarded for engaging in the "right" behaviors and punished for engaging in the "wrong" behaviors by adults and other children. Children may also choose to imitate models of the same sex. According to this theory, parents play a large role in shaping their children's behavior but other people, institutions, and the society at large can have a considerable effect as well.

Both of these theories depict the role of the individual child in its own development as essentially passive. In the biological view, the child's biological sex determines the nature of development. In the environmental view, the reinforcement patterns specified by others determine the nature of development. The *cognitive* theory of development assumes a more active infant or child—one who participates in, is influenced by, and in turn influences the forces that contribute to his or her development. Although these forces are similar to the reinforcing influences suggested by the environmental theory, they are more subject to modification according to the cognitive theory.

Some sex differences in characteristics and behavior emerge very early in life—according to some studies, as early as 3 weeks of age. However, this does not mean that the differences are necessarily biological in origin, because researchers have observed differences in parental behavior toward male and female children at an equally early age. In fact, some studies have shown that simply *labeling* a neutrally clothed child as female or male, no matter which sex the child actually belongs to, can elicit responses consistent with gender stereotypes. Children's beliefs about what activities are appropriate for girls and boys emerge at a later age. One study concluded that kindergarten children are still learning stereotypes about what the typical boy or girl chooses for activities, whereas third-graders have more firm ideas. The third-grader is more likely to agree with the proposition: "She is a girl, so she will behave as a girl." Children are not born with knowledge about gender stereotypes but learn about them as they grow older.[40]

The "heredity versus environment" question is far from settled, and it is beyond the scope of this book to settle it here. Instead, while recognizing that heredity and biological factors have at least some influence on the behavioral development of children (although their effects are not well understood), I shall focus on the interactions with external forces suggested by both the environmental and cognitive theories. Although these two theories differ considerably in their basic assumptions, they agree on the predominant influence of culturally determined gender stereotypes. We shall now examine some of the important people and institutions that contribute to the adoption of sex-typed characteristics and behaviors by girls and boys.

Parents

Parents are in a position to have a special effect on child development. They provide the opportunity for imitation of their own behavior, and they provide reinforcements for their children's behavior. Children are more likely to imitate same-sex models than opposite-sex models, although they could presumably imitate any adult to whom they were exposed. Because parents are highly available and powerful, they are the models children are most likely to copy, particularly during the pre-school years. Parents who are absent, however, are unavailable as role models.[41]

Parents' values affect how they raise their children. For example, parents who claim that opportunities for both sexes should be equal in the adult world are more likely to encourage their children to deviate from gender stereotypes than parents who advocate separate roles for women and men. Also, parents' beliefs about their children's abilities affect how those children view their own abilities, as we saw earlier in the effects of mothers' beliefs on their children's math performance. Whether innate intellectual and behavioral differences between the sexes exist or not, many parents believe that they do and act accordingly.[42]

A meta-analysis found few differences in parents' actual treatment of boys and girls. Minimal differences were found in amounts of interaction, encouragement of achievement, warmth and nurturance, encouragement of dependence or independence, and disciplinary strictness displayed toward sons and daughters of all ages. However, parents, especially fathers, showed a strong tendency to encourage sex-typed activities in their children. This tendency was seen in such diverse areas as assignment of household responsibilities and play activities. One study found that sons in dual-earner families spend only one third as much time on household chores as sons in traditional families, while daughters in dual-earner families spend 25% more. In addition, parents tend to offer their sons and daughters different types of toys and physical environments. Boys are provided with more sports equipment, tools, and vehicles; remember that Prince Harry got a car whether he wanted it or not. Girls, however, are provided with more dolls (including working and military Barbie dolls), jewelry, and children's furniture. And, not surprisingly, more pink and less blue is seen in girls' rooms than in boys' rooms.[43]

Encouragement of sex-typed activities in children contributes to other behavioral differences. For example, a study of 11 cultures found similarity in the way girls and boys respond to "lap children" (those aged 0-1 year). Lap children draw positive responses and nurturing behavior from children as young as 2 years old as well as from adults. However, girls are more often assigned to take care of lap children than boys. As a result, girls develop greater nurturing skills, and nurturance becomes a style of interaction that is both familiar and enjoyable to them. The researchers suggested that if boys were assigned greater care of lap children than girls, they would be the sex to develop greater nurturing tendencies and skills. There also could be later effects on their own children. A cross-cultural study of nonindustrial societies found that fathers' participation in child-rearing enhances the public status of women. Closer father-child relationships were associated with greater female participation in community decision making and access to positions of authority. Thus, differences in the tasks that females and males are assigned as children and adopt as parents promote sex differences in behavior.[44]

In conclusion, in their creation of household environments and in their encouragement or assignment of activities, parents contribute to the arousal of different interests and development of different abilities in their daughters and sons. In so doing, they both convey and reinforce the message that girls and boys are different. The same theme emerges as we consider school experiences.

School

Once they enter school systems, children are subjected to the influence of additional authority figures besides their parents. They have more adult models to choose from, and they have more occasion to be rewarded or punished for their own behavior. One of the first messages children receive at school is the sex-typing of positions in the school system itself. Men typically run the system, whereas women work in it; 95% of school superintendents and 72% of principals are male, but 72% of all elementary and secondary school teachers are female. Furthermore, students see differences in how female and male administrators approach their jobs. Women superintendents and principals take fewer trips away from the building, tour their buildings more often, observe classrooms and teachers more often, and in general interact more with teachers and students than men do.[45]

Most of today's adults were exposed to classroom readers that depicted girls and boys in exclusively stereotypical ways. An early study of elementary readers found that males were portrayed more often, appeared in a wider variety of roles, and were more active than females, who tended to be passive and hold domestic roles. A more recent study found less-pronounced differences in the rate of portrayal for males and females and in the variety of roles assigned to each. Adult women appeared more often than previously, but still not as often as men or in as wide a range of occupations. Girls appeared just as often as boys, and in a wider variety of roles than previously. However, girls were still depicted as needing to be rescued more than boys. They could be brave, but they still could not get themselves out of trouble as well as boys could.[46]

Although blatant sex-typing in schools has been reduced sharply in recent years, the subtler forms of socialization pressures remain. These originate from the attitudes and behaviors of the teachers themselves. Teachers act as powerful mediators of sex role standards. Teachers seldom see themselves as feeling differently toward girls and boys or treating them differently. However, classroom observations at all grade levels reveal considerable differences in both male and female teachers' interactions with students. Boys tend to receive more positive and negative attention than girls. They are questioned more, criticized more, and have more ideas accepted and rejected. Girls volunteer more often than boys but are not called on as often. Overall, boys receive more attention, encouragement, and "airtime" than girls. However, these findings are not consistent across all races. Several studies have found that teachers have lower expectations for the academic performance of African American boys than African American girls and prefer them less as students.[47]

One study demonstrated that teachers can be taught how to avoid classroom behaviors that favor boys over girls, thereby minimizing their own contribution to the presence of stereotypical sex differences in their students. This suggests a possible solution to the problem of teachers' reinforcement of traditional beliefs about gender differences. However, the problem remains: Teachers have different reactions to female and male students, even when race is taken into account. In so doing, they have a significant effect on what girls and boys think of themselves, and on what they learn about how to function in society.

The Mass Media

The mass media, particularly television, influence childhood development by providing opportunities for modeling and information-seeking outside family and school. The average American household is tuned to a television over 7 hours a day. During their school years, children spend more time watching television than in the classroom. They see an estimated 350,000 television commercials by age 17. By the mid-20s, watching television is the third most time-consuming activity of their days, after work and sleep. Thus the messages that television conveys not only represent the culture in which they appear but are also a large part of it. Television may be the great socializer in American society. It teaches what is important and how to behave. It may also teach gender stereotypes.[48]

Stereotypical behavior by females and males has persistently characterized both children's and adult's television programming. For example, a study of Saturday morning children's programs found that 68% of the major characters were male and that male characters engaged in more activity than female characters. Boys therefore had more opportunity to imitate same-sex models than girls. Also, the sexes tended to appear in different roles. Females were more often presented in relationships with others such as family or friends, while males were more often portrayed in roles independent of others or at work. In prime-time television programs, about 65% of all characters are male, a proportion that has changed little over the years. In successful family-oriented series, the husband's role is typically exaggerated and the wife's role underplayed. Men tend to be older and have higher status positions, and they more successfully combine paid employment with marriage. Women are less likely to be seen as working outside the home than men; those that do are less likely to be married than working men. Women tend to be attractive according to conventional standards—the proportion of television females with blonde hair, about 35%, is more than twice as large as the proportion of blondes in the general population. The females and males in rock videos, another form of television programming, are not exactly representative of the general population either. Despite dramatic changes in the outside world, the world of television programming has been remarkably stable in its portrayal of women and men and in its underrepresentation of female characters.[49]

In television commercials, men typically have been presented as more knowledgeable (e.g., the "Man from Glad," "Mr. Goodwrench") and women as more bewildered (the grateful housewife). Although men and women now appear equally as often in commercials, they differ in the kinds of products they endorse. Females are more likely to promote products used in the home, whereas males are more likely to promote products used outside the home. Men also drink more beer, typically after they have overcome a physical challenge such as driving cattle or simply made it to the end of the work day ("For all you do, this Bud's for you"). Commercials use male narrators about 90% of the time. When female narrators are used, it is typically for feminine products associated with body care. Also, commercials for the same type of product make different appeals to men and women. The emphasis of jeans commercials for men is on being an individual and doing one's own thing, whereas the emphasis for women is on enhancing one's appearance.[50]

Magazine advertising has conveyed similar messages. Until recently, ads rarely showed women in working roles and never showed them as executives or professionals. Several stereotypes of women's roles occurred regularly: (a) women's place as in the home; (b) women as not making important decisions; (c) women as dependent and in need of men's protection; and (d) men regarding women as sex objects, not as people. Women most often were portrayed as happy and diligent homemakers, beautiful and dependent social companions, or most concerned with being blond, thin, or having other physical characteristics they did not possess.[51]

The depiction of sex roles in newspaper comic strips has changed somewhat in recent years with the introduction of strips featuring working women, such as "For Better or For Worse" and "Sally Forth." Not much change has taken place in older comic strips such as "Dennis the Menace" and "The Born Loser" (although Blondie now owns a catering business). However, the image of the career woman in the comics is far from positive. She is a superwoman, cleaning the house, taking care of the children, fixing the car, *and* maintaining a career, and suffers from stress and sleepless nights as a result. She is often portrayed as hard, dominating, and critical of her husband, never being satisfied with anything he does. The portrait of the career woman's husband is equally negative; he tends to be ineffectual, weak, and lazy. In sum, the message of the comics has been described as "if you are a woman and want a happy home, do not have a career, and if you are a man, never marry a career woman."[52]

The ultimate effects of television and other media portrayals of sex roles have been the subject of considerable debate. Some theorists claim that television viewing cultivates conceptions of social reality. The basic premise of cultivation theory is that "the more time people spend watching television, the more likely they are to perceive the real world in ways that reflect the patterns found in television." In support of cultivation theory, studies have found that both children and adults who watch more television are more aware of gender stereotypes, see themselves in more stereotypical terms, and hold more traditional attitudes toward men's and women's roles.[53]

However, television viewing does not always reinforce gender stereotypes. One study found that perceptions of the proportion of women in nine different occupations, including doctor, nurse, lawyer, college teacher, and grade school teacher, differed from U.S. census data and also from the proportion of women seen in these occupations in prime-time television programming. Respondents erred consistently in the direction of sexual equality in the chosen professions. That is, their estimates were closer to a 50-50 split of women and men in occupations than was really the case. The researchers concluded that respondents' distortions may have resulted from their watching television *news* rather than other programming, even though more than three quarters of network news reports are filed by men. They may have learned from news programs about trends toward a more equal distribution of men and women in different types of jobs, and then confused the trends with the status quo.[54]

Overall, there is little evidence that the mass media, especially television, portray women and men in less stereotypical roles now than in the past. There is also debate over how much television contributes to the formation and reinforcement of gender stereotypes. However, given how much television is watched by Americans of all ages, it has enormous potential to influence perceptions of reality.

Sex Role Adherence in Adults: What Are the Consequences?

Until recently, according to public norms, adherence to traditional sex roles was seen as one of the best routes to happiness and harmony with nature. Since androgyny has been offered as an alternative, the consequences of fitting the appropriate sex role are no longer so clear. They may be argued as either positive or negative, depending on one's beliefs about the merits of androgynous people versus masculine men and feminine women.

One way to investigate the results of adherence to sex roles is to examine sex differences in various measures of mental and physical health. We need to proceed with caution in using this approach. When we consider data on differences between females and males, we do not know whether we are examining the effects of biological differences, environmental differences, or cognitive differences. Pressures to conform to sex roles are only one aspect of the environment that could influence behavior and health. However, such statistics are likely to provide some indication, if not definitive proof, of the possible consequences of adhering to sex roles.

The data on mortality, health, and health-related actions can be interpreted in this light. The feminine sex role places a much greater emphasis on self-awareness and the expression of feelings, including admission of difficulties, than the masculine sex role. It also encourages dependency on others. Therefore, women could be more inclined than men to report symptoms of mental illness and to make use of or be committed to mental health facilities, even if they were no worse off in mental health. Women are also more likely to admit that they are experiencing ill health in general and to take appropriate coping actions that reduce the likelihood of their illnesses becoming major.

The masculine sex role can be particularly hazardous to health. An estimated three-fourths of the sex difference in life expectancy has been attributed to sex-role related behaviors. Aggressiveness and competitiveness cause men to put themselves in dangerous situations, thereby leading them to suffer more accidents. Emotional inexpressiveness causes psychosomatic and other health problems. Lack of self-awareness keeps men from being sensitive to signals that all is not well for them. The male role encourages the taking of risks that endanger health and discourages men from taking adequate medical care of themselves. In response to women's redefinitions of their own role, a "modern male role" has emerged that encourages men to use their interpersonal and emotional capabilities to promote smooth collaboration with others toward achievement (such as by being managers) and within heterosexual relationships. However, staying emotionally "cool" remains a major value associated with the male role.[55]

The statistics are striking. In 1900, the expectation of longevity at birth was 48 years for women and 46 years for men. In 1990, it was 79 years for women and 72 years for men. The sex difference in mortality favoring women has been present for individuals of all races throughout the century. When quality of life is taken into account, the female advantage in "well-life" expectancy is about three years. Nonetheless, males die at a higher rate than females for all age groups, ranging from less than 4 years old to greater than 85 years old. Life expectancy has increased substantially for women and men, but the difference favoring women has also increased.[56]

Health statistics vary considerably. Even when illnesses due to reproductive functions are excluded, women suffer more from acute conditions and nonfatal chronic conditions than men. Women report more depression and are treated more for mental illness. They report a greater amount of physical ailments such as headaches, dizziness, and stomach upsets. Women use more prescription medicines and over-the-counter drugs than men. They restrict their activities due to health problems about 25% more days per year than men, and they spend about 40% more days per year in bed.[57]

In contrast, men suffer more from major physical ailments. They suffer 50-60% more injuries from ages 17 to 44. They are more susceptible to visual and hearing problems and paralysis than women at all ages. Men have a higher rate of problem drinking and exhibit more stress-related disorders such as cirrhosis of the liver and suicide. They are more likely to exhibit the Type A behavior pattern—characterized by extreme amounts of competitiveness, striving for achievement, aggressiveness, haste, impatience, and feelings of being under pressures of time and responsibility—that contributes to coronary heart disease. Men also suffer more from life-threatening diseases such as atherosclerosis and emphysema. They experience more overall long-term disability due to chronic health problems than women.

A study of men who have been successful at work found that when they experience dissatisfaction or problems at work, most don't talk about them at home. Instead, they choose to compartmentalize the problems of work and internalize their stress, keeping the home as a refuge. These men are happy to report their triumphs, but they are reluctant to report difficulties that might suggest incompetence, weakness, or immaturity. This behavior is consistent with the traditional male role. A traditional man feels that just as it is his wife's role to deal with home and children, it is his role to deal with work. To ask for her support in dealing with work problems suggests that he isn't up to handling his work by himself. Also, he may see his wife as getting upset too easily. Telling her about his work problems might only make her anxious, thereby giving him one more problem.[58]

Women's and men's health are influenced by both work and family roles. Paid employment has a positive effect on their health, particularly if their feelings are positive about it. Work rewards such as challenge, recognition from one's supervisor, and helping others at work contribute to better health, and work concerns such as overload, poor supervision, and discrimination lead to worse health. Also, higher wages, more hours of paid work, and less hours of housework and caring for children are associated with better health. These latter factors favor men's health, because men tend to earn higher wages, spend more time at work, and spend less time doing housework or child care. One study concluded that, if women's and men's social roles were more equal, women would experience better health than men, consistent with their greater longevity.[59]

Moreover, husbands and wives affect each other's health. Several studies have shown that wives' employment can have a negative impact on their husbands' mental health. Husbands of wives working full-time tend to feel less adequate as breadwinners than husbands of housewives do, and this leads to their feeling less satisfied with their jobs and life in general. Although not examined, this effect is probably greatest for husbands with more traditional attitudes toward male and female roles. However, husbands' employment can have a negative impact on their wives' health. One study found that the wives of husbands in more stressful occupations had shorter life expectancies. We would expect this effect also to work in reverse, with husbands of wives in more stressful occupations having shorter life expectancies.[60]

In summary, women experience more frequent illness and short-term disability, but their problems typically do not endanger their lives. In contrast, men suffer from more life-threatening diseases that cause more permanent disability and earlier death. Women are "sicker" in the short run, but men are sicker in the long run. Spouses also affect the health of each other.

The different data on health and mortality that have been considered reveal limitations of both the masculine and feminine roles. Adherence to the feminine role means surrendering control over many aspects of one's life to others. This lack of control contributes to feelings of depression that, in their extreme form, may lead to treatment in mental health facilities. In contrast, adherence to the masculine role means suppressing one's feelings and always striving (or pretending) to be in control of one's own life. The effects of this unbridled push for dominance by men are seen in higher mortality rates, Type A behavior, coronary heart disease rates, and other symptoms of ill health. These effects are often found in management ranks, suggesting that the managerial role, too, has its risks.

This analysis suggests that for women and men to lead healthy and long lives (besides having a spouse who is conducive to health), it is indeed desirable for them to experience the "best of both worlds." They benefit from having the ability to be aware of and express their feelings and to form empathetic relationships with others (associated with the feminine sex role), combined with the ability to be in control and free of excessive dependence on others (associated with the masculine sex role). While we work toward a society that is free of a dependence on gender as the primary means for categorizing people, androgyny seems to offer a healthier standard of living than traditional sex roles.

Implications

I began this chapter by posing several questions about sex differences, gender differences, and their general effects. Before we move on, it is appropriate to explore the initial implications of the answers provided to these questions.

Sex differences in intellectual skills and social behavior could affect the kinds of occupations that males and females choose. For example, some traditionally male occupations such as accounting and engineering particularly call for mathematical or visual-spatial skill. Males have demonstrated superiority in both math performance from high school on, although less so in recent years, and in some types of spatial skills. This could explain in part why these occupations are male-dominated. However, parents' expectations fueled by media reports have been shown to influence their children's performance on tests of intellectual skills, suggesting that occupational choices are also influenced by social forces. Also, some traditionally female occupations such as grade school teaching particularly call for verbal skill, and no female superiority in verbal skill has been demonstrated. I shall discuss the range of influences on how people choose occupations, including management, at greater length in Chapter 3.

Males' higher aggression and concern for dominance, although they diminish with age and have been less evident in recent years, could have an impact on managerial behavior and performance. Aggression could be exhibited, for example, in a tendency to verbally attack subordinates, peers, or superiors in organizations. Eventually the overly aggressive individual would be likely to experience negative repercussions, ranging from formal or informal reprimands to poor performance evaluations (unless he or she is a top executive or owner). However, aggression also could be channeled into more positive forms of behavior, such as an eagerness to "attack" challenging assignments. Thus aggression

in the workplace may be a double-edged sword, having both construc-
tive and destructive implications for behavior. High aggressiveness in
itself does not make a person more, or less, likely to be a good manager.[61]

Women have been found to be more susceptible to attempts at influence and more adept at nonverbal communication than men. The first
difference suggests that women might be more passive members of
work groups and organizations. If this were true, it would certainly
hinder their work performance. However, women's greater nonverbal
abilities would have a positive effect on their communications with
coworkers at all organizational levels.

Beliefs about sex differences include a much wider range of characteristics than actual sex differences. These beliefs also have a much greater
effect than sex differences, as seen in a range of evaluative activities and
organizational situations. Recruiters and other organizational representatives evaluate the suitability of applicants for employment. Managers evaluate the performance of their subordinates, who in turn
evaluate the kind of leadership demonstrated by their managers. Work
group members evaluate the contributions of other members. Promotion decisions are based on evaluations of the past performance and
future potential of candidates for promotion. In each of these situations,
others' evaluations of an individual materially affect the effectiveness
and progress of that individual in the organization. These evaluations
are based on beliefs about what the individual is like, which are influenced by whether the individual is male or female. Thus, stereotypical
beliefs that women are more nurturant or that men are better leaders
have an influence on evaluations far beyond what the actual facts may
dictate. Ways of dealing with gender stereotyping in the workplace will
be discussed in Chapter 4.

Androgyny has been presented not so much as a belief about what
individuals are like but as a prescription advocated by some for what
individuals should be like. In particular, it has been offered as a model
for the effective manager. We shall discuss the merits of this prescription
at length in Chapter 6. The long-term benefits of androgyny for individuals in general remain to be seen.

Important influences on childhood development such as parents,
school, and the media have their own organizational analogues. Individuals may react to authority figures in organizations based on how their
parents treated them earlier in life and their reactions to the treatment.
Early school experiences also are likely to condition responses to authority.

Television has provided numerous models for leadership, ranging from Captain James Kirk of *Star Trek* and Lou Grant to Wonder Woman and Murphy Brown, and we can expect it to continue to provide models that influence both children and adults. News reports in television and the other media also influence perceptions of basic abilities of individuals as well as social roles and norms.

However, these influences need not be taken for granted. Changes are needed in the ways in which parents, teachers, the media, and society at large view gender issues. Parents and teachers need to be aware of the powerful effect of expectations on what children learn. National groups such as the Parent-Teacher Association (PTA) can play a vital role in bringing this information to parents. University schools of education and other institutions that provide teacher training can also ensure that teachers enter the profession with an awareness of how their expectations and the ways in which they interact with students affect student performance. The media can do a better job of presenting factual information about individual abilities and social forces to children as well as adults. Nonstereotypic and complex findings may not make as interesting copy as stereotypic and simple findings. Nonetheless, the media have a responsibility to accurately inform the public about gender issues, no matter how complicated the message may be.[62]

The division of labor in society regarding child care may play a particularly strong role in bringing about sex differences. If interacting with lap children brings forth nurturing skills in caregivers of both sexes, we need to reconsider who gives the care to children. Presently, females do most of it and males do little of it, leading women to develop more nurturing tendencies than males. There seems to be no compelling reason, biological or otherwise, why this should be the case.[63]

The implications of health data for adults on the practice of management are disturbing. Managers occupy a high-stress role that contributes to many symptoms of ill health including coronary heart disease and dependence on alcohol and other drugs. In Chapter 6, we will more fully discuss how the managerial role contributes to stress, what makes some managerial jobs more stressful than others, and whether female and male managers differ in their experiences with or responses to stress.

We are left wondering what the short-term and long-term effects of working and military Barbie dolls will be, if any. As the opening passages to this chapter make clear, the dolls are being marketed to girls rather than boys. Unless sex differences in the toys chosen by children and their parents disappear, girls will be more exposed to the dolls than boys. Thus any direct effect the dolls have on attitudes or expectations about society will be seen primarily in girls. As a result, girls could expect to see a more sex-integrated workplace and military, whereas boys could have less reason to expect the same. However, girls could indirectly affect boys' expectations through their contacts with them in the classroom, schoolyard, and home.

What might cause a comparable direct effect on boys' attitudes and expectations? Princess Diana, as well as other parents, reading this book? Dolls aimed directly at boys? If so, what characters should such dolls represent? Female warriors? Male nurses? Video games in which females rescue males or people in danger muster their own resources and rescue themselves (rather than males rescuing females)? Electronic sports games (football, basketball, baseball, and so on) with co-ed teams? *Real* professional and college sports with co-ed teams? What could cause changes for both girls and boys? A female president of the United States? More female CEOs and senior executives? It will be interesting to find out, if we get the chance.

Gender stereotypes are mostly out of touch with facts about sex differences, are strongly held by many people, and are under attack by others. Given these conflicts, it will be interesting to see how the standards of behavior for "being good girls and boys" continue to evolve. Meanwhile, we shall next consider how the early experiences of girls and boys are translated into decisions, made either by them or for them, about the pursuit of occupations.

Notes

1. Reprinted from the March 4, 1985, issue of *Business Week* by special permission, © 1985 by McGraw-Hill, Inc.

2. "Barbie Doll to See Duty in Military," *Hartford Courant*, 153 (No. 62, 3 March 1990): A2.

3. "Guy 'N Doll," *Hartford Courant*, 154 (No. 111, 20 April 1992): A2.

4. C. W. Sherif, "Needed Concepts in the Study of Gender Identity," *Psychology of Women Quarterly*, 6 (1982): 375-398; R. K. Unger, "Toward a Redefinition of Sex and Gender," *American Psychologist*, 34 (1979): 1085-1094.

5. I. K. Broverman, S. R. Vogel, D. M. Broverman, F. E. Clarkson, and P. S. Rosenkrantz, "Sex Role Stereotypes: A Current Appraisal," *Journal of Social Issues*, 28 (No. 2, 1972): 59-78.

6. R. Ely, "Gender Difference: What Difference Does It Make?" *Proceedings of the Annual Meeting of the Academy of Management*, ed. J. L. Wall and L. R. Jauch (Miami Beach, 1991); P. T. Reid and L. Comas-Diaz, "Gender and Ethnicity: Perspectives on

Dual Status," *Sex Roles*, 22 (1990): 397-408; P. T. Reid, "Racism and Sexism: Comparisons and Conflicts," in *Eliminating Racism: Profiles in Controversy*, ed. P. A. Katz and D. A. Taylor (New York: Plenum, 1988).

7. C. N. Jacklin, "Female and Male: Issues of Gender," *American Psychologist*, 44 (1989): 127-133.

8. J. S. Hyde, "Meta-Analysis and the Psychology of Gender Differences," *Signs*, 16 (1990): 55-73; H. T. Woolley, "A Review of the Recent Literature on the Psychology of Sex," *Psychological Bulletin*, 7(No. 18, 1910): 335.

9. R. T. Hare-Mustin and J. Maracek, "The Meaning of Difference: Gender Theory, Postmodernism, and Psychology," *American Psychologist*, 43 (1988): 455-464.

10. D. Belle, "Ironies in the Contemporary Study of Gender," *Journal of Personality*, 53 (1985): 400-405; W. S. Barnes, "Sibling Influences within Family and School Contexts," Unpublished doctoral dissertation, Harvard Graduate School of Education, 1984; G. Bateson, "Insight in a Bicultural Context," *Philippine Studies*, 16 (1968): 605-621; A. H. Eagly and L. L. Carli, "Sex of Researchers and Sex-Typed Communications as Determinants of Sex Differences in Influenceability: A Meta-Analysis of Social Influence Studies," *Psychological Bulletin*, 90 (1981): 1-20.

11. Hyde, "Meta-Analysis and the Psychology of Gender Differences."

12. E. E. Maccoby and C. N. Jacklin, *The Psychology of Sex Differences* (Stanford, CA: Stanford University Press, 1974).

13. Hyde; A. H. Eagly and W. Wood, "Explaining Sex Differences in Social Behavior: A Meta-Analytic Perspective," *Personality and Social Psychology Bulletin*, 17 (1991): 306-315; J. S. Hyde, "Introduction: Meta-Analysis and the Psychology of Gender," in *The Psychology of Gender: Advances through Meta-Analysis*, ed. J. S. Hyde and M. C. Linn (Baltimore, MD: Johns Hopkins University Press, 1986).

14. J. S. Hyde and M. C. Linn, "Gender Differences in Verbal Ability: A Meta-Analysis," *Psychological Bulletin*, 104 (1988): 53-69.

15. M. C. Linn and A. C. Petersen, "Emergence and Characterization of Sex Differences in Spatial Ability: A Meta-Analysis," *Child Development*, 56 (1985): 1479-1498; M. C. Linn and A. C. Petersen, "A Meta-Analysis of Gender Differences in Spatial Ability: Implications for Mathematics and Science Achievement," in *The Psychology of Gender*, ed. Hyde and Linn.

16. J. S. Hyde, E. Fennema, and S. J. Lamon, "Gender Differences in Mathematics Performance: A Meta-Analysis," *Psychological Bulletin*, 107 (1990): 139-155.

17. J. S. Eccles and J. E. Jacobs, "Social Forces Shape Math Attitudes and Performance," *Signs*, 11 (1986): 367-380.

18. C. P. Benbow and J. C. Stanley, "Sex Differences in Mathematical Ability: Fact or Artifact?" *Science*, 210 (1980): 1262-1264.

19. R. A. Jones, *Self-Fulfilling Prophecies: Social, Psychological, and Physiological Effects of Expectancies* (New York: John Wiley, 1977).

20. A. Feingold, "Cognitive Gender Differences Are Disappearing," *American Psychologist*, 43 (1988): 95-103.

21. Maccoby and Jacklin, *The Psychology of Sex Differences*; E. E. Maccoby, "Gender and Relationships: A Developmental Account," *American Psychologist*, 45 (1990): 513-520.

22. J. S. Hyde, "How Large Are Gender Differences in Aggression? A Developmental Meta-Analysis," *Developmental Psychology*, 20 (1984): 722-736; A. H. Eagly and V. J. Steffan, "Gender and Aggressive Behavior: A Meta-Analytic Review of the Social

Psychological Literature," *Psychological Bulletin, 100* (1986): 309-330; J. S. Hyde, "Gender Differences in Aggression," in *The Psychology of Gender*, ed. Hyde and Linn.

23. A. H. Eagly and W. Wood, "Gender and Influenceability: Stereotype versus Behavior," in *Women, Gender, and Social Psychology*, ed. V. E. O'Leary, R. K. Unger, and B. S. Wallston, (Hillsdale, NJ: Lawrence Erlbaum, 1985); Eagly and Carli, "Sex of Researchers and Sex-Typed Communications"; A. H. Eagly, *Sex Differences in Social Behavior: A Social-Role Interpretation* (Hillsdale, NJ: Lawrence Erlbaum, 1987).

24. J. A. Hall, "On Explaining Gender Differences: The Case of Nonverbal Communication," in *Sex and Gender: Review of Personality and Social Psychology*, vol. 7, ed. P. Shaver and C. Hendrick (Newbury Park, CA: Sage, 1987).

25. A. H. Eagly and M. Crowley, "Gender and Helping Behavior: A Meta-Analytic Review of the Social Psychological Literature," *Psychological Bulletin, 100* (1986): 283-308; Hyde, "Meta-Analysis and the Psychology of Gender Differences."

26. L. Larwood and M. M. Wood, Chapter 2, "Women and Management: Culturally Biased Perspectives," in *Women in Management* (Lexington, MA: Lexington Books, 1977), used by permission.

27. Broverman et al., "Sex Role Stereotypes."

28. J. T. Spence, R. Helmreich, and J. Stapp, "Ratings of Self and Peers on Sex Role Attributes and Their Relation to Self-Esteem and Conceptions of Masculinity and Femininity, *Journal of Personality and Social Psychology, 32* (1975): 29-39.

29. D. N. Ruble and T. L. Ruble, "Sex Stereotypes," in *In the Eye of the Beholder: Contemporary Issues in Stereotyping*, ed. A. G. Miller (New York: Praeger, 1982); D. J. Bergen and J. E. Williams, "Sex Stereotypes in the United States Revisited: 1972-1988," *Sex Roles, 24* (1991): 413-423.

30. J. E. Williams and D. L. Best, *Measuring Sex Stereotypes: A Multination Study*, revised edition (Newbury Park, CA: Sage, 1990), pp. 244-245.

31. C. M. Noseworthy and A. J. Lott, "The Cognitive Organization of Gender-Stereotypic Categories," *Personality and Social Psychology Bulletin, 10* (1984): 474-481; K. Deaux, W. Winton, M. Crowley, and L. L. Lewis, "Level of Categorization and Content of Gender Stereotypes," *Social Cognition, 3* (1985): 145-167; B. Six and T. Eckes, "A Closer Look at the Complex Structure of Gender Stereotypes," *Sex Roles, 24* (1991): 57-71; R. D. Ashmore, F. K. Del Boca, and A. J. Wohlers, "Gender Stereotypes," in *The Social Psychology of Female-Male Relations: A Critical Analysis of Central Concepts*, ed. R. D. Ashmore and F. K. Del Boca (Orlando: Academic Press, 1986).

32. S. L. Bem, "The Measurement of Psychological Androgyny," *Journal of Consulting and Clinical Psychology, 42* (1974): 155-162.

33. J. T. Spence and R. L. Helmreich, *Masculinity and Femininity: Their Psychological Dimensions, Correlates, and Antecedents* (Austin: University of Texas Press, 1978).

34. S. L. Bem, "On the Utility of Alternative Procedures for Assessing Psychological Androgyny," *Journal of Consulting and Clinical Psychology, 45* (1977): 196-205.

35. E. Lenney, "Androgyny: Some Audacious Assertions Toward Its Coming of Age," *Sex Roles, 5* (1979): 703-719.

36. E. J. Pedhazur and T. J. Tetenbaum, "Bem Sex Role Inventory: A Theoretical and Methodological Critique," *Journal of Personality and Social Psychology, 37* (1979): 996-1016; S. L. Bem, *Bem Sex-Role Inventory: Professional Manual* (Palo Alto, CA: Consulting Psychologists Press, 1981). Although Bem intended the Short BSRI to replace the original version of the BSRI in future research, the original version

continues to be widely used. It and the PAQ have been the two instruments most commonly used to measure individuals' sex role identity.

37. C. Markstrom-Adams, "Androgyny and Its Relation to Adolescent Psychosocial Well-Being: A Review of the Literature," *Sex Roles, 21* (1989): 325-340; M. C. Taylor and J. A. Hall, "Psychological Androgyny: Theories, Methods, and Conclusions," *Psychological Bulletin, 92* (1982): 347-366; W. H. Jones, M. E. O'C. Chernovetz, and R. O. Hansson, "The Enigma of Androgyny: Differential Implications for Males and Females?" *Journal of Consulting and Clinical Psychology, 46* (1978): 298-313; B. E. Whitley, "Sex Role Orientation and Self-Esteem: A Critical Meta-Analytic Review," *Journal of Personality and Social Psychology, 44* (1983): 765-778; L. Dimitrovsky, J. Singer, and Y. Yinon, "Masculine and Feminine Traits: Their Relation to Suitedness for and Success in Training for Traditionally Masculine and Feminine Army Functions," *Journal of Personality and Social Psychology, 57* (1989): 839-847.

38. S. L. Bem, "Gender Schema Theory: A Cognitive Account of Sex Typing," *Psychological Review, 88* (1981): 354-364.

39. Jacklin, "Female and Male"; M. Lewis and M. Weinraub, "Origins of Early Sex-Role Development," *Sex Roles, 5* (1979): 135-153.

40. M. Stern and K. H. Karraker, "Sex Stereotyping of Infants: A Review of Gender Labeling Studies," *Sex Roles, 20* (1989): 501-522; T. J. Berndt and K. A. Heller, "Gender Stereotypes and Social Inferences: A Developmental Study," *Journal of Personality and Social Psychology, 50* (1986): 889-898.

41. Maccoby and Jacklin, Chapter 8, "Sex Typing and the Role of Modeling," and Chapter 9, "Differential Socialization of Boys and Girls," in *The Psychology of Sex Differences*.

42. J. K. Antill, "Parents' Beliefs and Values about Sex Roles, Sex Differences, and Sexuality: Their Sources and Implications," in *Sex and Gender*, vol. 7, ed. Shaver and Hendrick; Eccles & Jacobs, "Social Forces Shape Math Attitudes and Performance."

43. H. Lytton and D. M. Romney, "Parents' Differential Socialization of Boys and Girls: A Meta-Analysis," *Psychological Bulletin, 109* (1991): 267-296; M. H. Benin and D. A. Edwards, "Adolescents' Chores: The Difference between Dual- and Single-Earner Families," *Journal of Marriage and the Family, 52* (1990): 361-373; A. Pomerleau, D. Boldue, G. Malcuit, and L. Cossette, "Pink or Blue: Environmental Gender Stereotypes in the First Two Years of Life," *Sex Roles, 22* (1990): 359-367.

44. B. B. Whiting and C. P. Edwards, *Children of Different Worlds: The Formation of Social Behavior* (Cambridge, MA: Harvard University Press, 1988), pp. 270-271; S. Coltrane, "Father-Child Relationships and the Status of Women: A Cross-Cultural Study," *American Journal of Sociology, 93* (1988): 1060-1095.

45. American Association of University Women (AAUW), *How Schools Shortchange Girls* (Washington, DC: AAUW Educational Foundation, 1992), p. 7; C. Shakeshaft, Chapter 6, "Differences Between the Ways Women and Men Manage Schools," in *Women in Educational Administration*, updated edition (Newbury Park, CA: Sage, 1989).

46. P. Purcell and L. Stewart, "Dick and Jane in 1989," *Sex Roles, 22* (1990): 177-185.

47. AAUW, "The Classroom as Curriculum," in *How Schools Shortchange Girls*; M. Guttentag and H. Bray, "Teachers as Mediators of Sex-Role Standards," in *Beyond Sex Roles*, ed. A. G. Sargent (St. Paul, MN: West, 1977); M. Sadker and D. Sadker, "Sexism in the Schoolroom of the '80s," *Psychology Today, 19* (No. 3, March 1985): 54-57; B. R. Sandler, "The Classroom Climate for Women," in *The American Woman 1987-88*, ed. S. E. Rix (New York: Norton, 1987); S. I. Ross and J. M. Jackson, "Teachers' Expectations

for Black Males' and Black Females' Academic Achievement," *Personality and Social Psychology Bulletin, 17* (1991): 78-82.

48. D. M. Davis, "Portrayals of Women in Prime-Time Network Television: Some Demographic Characteristics," *Sex Roles, 23* (1990): 325-332; L. Z. McArthur and S. V. Eisen, "Television and Sex-Role Stereotyping," *Journal of Applied Social Psychology, 6* (1976): 329-351.

49. McArthur and Eisen, "Television and Sex-Role Stereotyping"; Davis, "Portrayals of Women in Prime-Time Network Television"; N. Signorielli, "Television and Conceptions About Sex Roles: Maintaining Conventionality and the Status Quo," *Sex Roles, 21* (1989): 341-360; M. L. Moore, "The Family as Portrayed on Prime-Time Television, 1947-1990: Structure and Characteristics," *Sex Roles, 26* (1992): 41-61.

50. D. J. Bretl and J. Cantor, "The Portrayal of Men and Women in U.S. Television Commercials: A Recent Content Analysis and Trends over 15 Years," *Sex Roles, 18* (1988): 595-609; L. T. Lovdal, "Sex Role Messages in Television Commercials: An Update," *Sex Roles, 21* (1989): 715-724; L. Strate, "Beer Commercials: A Manual on Masculinity," in *Men, Masculinity, and the Media*, ed. S. Craig (Newbury Park, CA: Sage, 1992); S. M. Ogletree, S. W. Williams, P. Raffeld, B. Mason, and K. Fricke, "Female Attractiveness and Eating Disorders: Do Children's Television Commercials Play a Role?" *Sex Roles, 22* (1990): 791-797.

51. D. E. Sexton and P. Haberman, "Women in Magazine Advertisements," *Journal of Advertising Research, 14* (No. 4, August 1974): 41-46.

52. L. Mooney and S. Brabant, "Two Martinis and a Rested Woman: 'Liberation' in the Sunday Comics," *Sex Roles, 17* (1987): 419; S. Brabant and L. Mooney, "Sex Role Stereotyping in the Sunday Comics: Ten Years Later," *Sex Roles, 14* (1986): 141-148.

53. M. Morgan, "Television and Adolescents' Sex Role Stereotypes: A Longitudinal Study," *Journal of Personality and Social Psychology, 43* (1982): 948; P. E. McGhee and T. Frueh, "Television Viewing and the Learning of Sex-Role Stereotypes," *Sex Roles, 6* (1980): 179-188; L. Ross, D. R. Anderson, and P. A. Wisocki, "Television Viewing and Adult Sex-Role Attitudes," *Sex Roles, 8* (1982): 589-592.

54. C. Mc Cauley, K. Thangavelu, and P. Rozin, "Sex Role Stereotyping of Occupations in Relation to Television Representations and Census Facts," *Basic and Applied Social Psychology, 9* (1988): 197-212; D. Croteau and W. Hoynes, "Men and the News Media: The Male Presence and Its Effect," in *Men, Masculinity, and the Media*, ed. S. Craig.

55. I. Waldron, "Why Do Women Live Longer Than Men?" *Journal of Human Stress, 2*, No. 1 (Part I, March 1976): 2-13, and No. 2 (Part II, June 1976): 19-30; J. Harrison, "Warning: The Male Sex Role May Be Dangerous to Your Health," *Journal of Social Issues, 34* (No. 1, 1978): 65-86; S. M. Jourard, "Some Lethal Aspects of the Male Role," in *The Transparent Self* (New York: Van Nostrand, 1971); J. H. Pleck, *The Myth of Masculinity* (Cambridge: MIT Press, 1981).

56. U.S. Department of Commerce, Bureau of the Census, *Statistical Abstract of the United States*, 111th edition (Washington, DC: Government Printing Office, 1991), p. 73, table 105; U.S. Department of Commerce, Bureau of the Census, *Historical Statistics of the United States: Colonial Times to 1970*, series B107-115 (Washington, DC: Government Printing Office, 1975), p. 55; R. M. Kaplan, J. P. Anderson, and D. L. Wingard, "Gender Differences in Health-Related Quality of Life," *Health Psychology, 10* (1991): 86-93.

57. L. M. Verbrugge, "Gender and Health: An Update of Hypotheses and Evidence," *Journal of Health and Social Behavior, 26* (1985): 156-182.

58. R. S. Weiss, Chapter 5, "Bringing Work Stress Home," in *Staying the Course: The Emotional and Social Lives of Men Who Do Well at Work* (New York: Free Press, 1990).

59. L. M. Verbrugge, "The Twain Meet: Empirical Explanations of Sex Differences in Health and Mortality," *Journal of Health and Social Behavior, 30* (1989): 282-304; R. L. Repetti, K. A. Matthews, and I. Waldron, "Employment and Women's Health: Effects of Paid Employment on Women's Mental and Physical Health," *American Psychologist, 44* (1989): 1394-1401; R. C. Barnett, H. Davidson, and N. L. Marshall, "Physical Symptoms and the Interplay of Work and Family Roles," *Health Psychology, 10* (1991): 94-101; J. Rodin and J. R. Ickovics, "Women's Health: Review and Research Agenda as We Approach the 21st Century," *American Psychologist, 45* (1990): 1018-1034; C. E. Bird and A. M. Fremont, "Gender, Time Use, and Health," *Journal of Health and Social Behavior, 32* (1991): 114-129; I. Waldron, "Effects of Labor Force Participation on Sex Differences in Mortality and Morbidity," in *Women, Work, and Health*, ed. M. Frankenhaeuser, U. Lundberg, and M. Chesney (New York: Plenum Press, 1991).

60. G. L. Staines, K. J. Pottick, and D. A. Fudge, "Wives' Employment and Husbands' Attitudes Toward Work and Life," *Journal of Applied Psychology, 71* (1986): 118-128; B. C. Fletcher, "Marital Relationships as a Cause of Death: An Analysis of Occupational Mortality and the Hidden Consequences of Marriage—Some U. K. Data," *Human Relations, 36* (1983): 123-134.

61. C. N. Jacklin and E. E. Maccoby, "Sex Differences and Their Implications for Management," in *Bringing Women into Management*, ed. F. E. Gordon and M. H. Strober (New York: McGraw-Hill, 1975); P. J. Caproni, "Aggression in the Workplace: Gendered and Hierarchical Views" (Paper delivered at the Annual Meeting of the Academy of Management, San Francisco, 1990).

62. C. N. Jacklin, "Female and Male."

63. C. N. Whiting and Edwards, *Children of Different Worlds*; C. N. Jacklin, "Female and Male."

3

Entering the World of Work

I'm Gonna Be an Engineer

When I went to school I learned to write and how to read
Some history, geography, and home economy,
And typing is a skill that every girl is sure to need,
To while away the extra time until the time to breed
And then they have the nerve to ask, "What would I like to be?"
I says, "I'm gonna be an engineer!"
"No, you only need to learn to be a lady
The duty isn't yours, for to try and run the world
An engineer could never have a baby
Remember, dear, that you're a girl."

Peggy Seeger
["I'm Gonna Be an Engineer," by Peggy Seeger.
© 1976 by Stormking Music Inc. All rights reserved.]

Individuals make their own decisions about whether to work, and what kind of work they will do. No one is forced into one type of work or blocked from another. We live in a free country where individuals have the liberty to choose the role, if any, they wish to play in the economy. Right?

Right only in a restricted sense. Americans *are* free to direct their own lives. The government doesn't assign jobs to people; they choose jobs for themselves. However, people are influenced in their decisions about work by several factors aside from their own interests and capabilities. First, they are influenced by society's norms about who should or should not work. American society generally frowns on welfare if people are capable of working. However, according to traditional norms, women have been discouraged from entering the workplace. Second, people are influenced by others' expectations of their interests and capabilities. Third, they are influenced by the choices that the marketplace presents as they consider various occupations. Fourth, they are influenced by the decisions made by organizations about their applications for employment.

We have already examined general beliefs regarding sex differences and their influence on how children are brought up. Now we will get more specific and look at the choices that individuals make, both about whether or not to work and about the occupations they pursue if they decide to work. Choices are influenced by the perceived characteristics of occupations, which may seem to welcome certain types of workers and not others. Choices also are influenced by the personal characteristics, background, and life situations of the individuals themselves, and by the decision-making processes used by recruiters and other organizational representatives that lead to the hiring of certain applicants and not others. Let's begin by examining the occupational choices available to individuals as they contemplate entering the world of work.

The Choices Available: Sex Segregation in the Workplace

If the workplace were completely integrated with regard to sex, the percentages of the male and female labor force in each of the occupations in which people work would be equal. For example, if 5% of all males were engineers, 5% of all females would be engineers, and the same would hold true for all occupations. As one sex increased in proportion in the labor force relative to the other, the percentages of members of that sex in different occupations would remain equal to the equivalent percentages for the other sex.

Sex segregation exists when females and males are *not* similarly distributed across occupations. The extent of sex segregation in the workplace at any time may be measured by a "segregation index," as shown in Table 3.1. An index value of zero indicates complete sex integration, whereas an index value of 100 indicates complete sex segregation.[1]

Table 3.1 Example of Sex Segregation Index

Occupation	Percentage of Male Labor Force	Percentage of Female Labor Force	Absolute Difference
1	40%	20%	40 − 20 = 20%
2	25	10	25 − 10 = 15
3	15	40	40 − 15 = 25
4	20	30	30 − 20 = 10
	100%	100%	70%

NOTE: Sex segregation index = Sum of absolute differences/2 = 35%.

In the example in Table 3.1, the segregation index value of 35% means that 35% of the male labor force would have to change occupations for the distribution of males across occupations to match that of females, or vice versa. For example, if 10% of the males shifted from Occupation 1 to Occupation 4, 10% shifted from Occupation 1 to Occupation 3, and 15% shifted from Occupation 2 to Occupation 3, the distributions for males and females would be equal and a total of 35% of the males would have changed occupations.

Sex segregation was a remarkably stable feature of the American workplace during this century until the 1970s. The sex segregation index varied between 66% and 69% between 1900 and 1970, but then dropped to 59% in 1980 and 57% in the late 1980s. Decreases in the index since 1970 have been primarily due to the increased number of females in male-dominated occupations, particularly at the managerial and professional levels. Nonetheless, the segregation index is still very high. Over half of the male or female labor force would have to change jobs for sex segregation to be eliminated completely.[2]

The extent of sex segregation in the workplace can be seen in greater detail by examining the employment of women and men in specific occupational categories, as summarized in Table 3.2. Although not as detailed as the data on which segregation indices are calculated, which have encompassed from 250 to 400 occupations at different times of assessment, the table is detailed enough to give us an idea of how men and women differ in the jobs they hold.

Occupations are classified as male-intensive, female-intensive, or neutral according to a conservative spread of 20 percentage points around the female (or male) proportion of the work force. According to Table 3.2, women hold 45.9% of all jobs in the labor force. Therefore,

Table 3.2 Employment of Women and Men in Occupations

Occupation	Percentage of Male Labor Force	Percentage of Female Labor Force	Percentage of Female Workers in Occupation	Occupation Type
Executive, administrative, & managerial	**13.8**	**11.6**	**41.7**	
Officials & administrators, public administration	.6	.5	44.1	
Other executive, administrative, & managerial	10.2	7.3	37.7	
Management-related occupations	3.0	3.8	51.6	
Professional specialty	**12.3**	**16.1**	**52.6**	
Engineers	2.6	.3	8.7	M
Mathematical & computer scientists	1.0	.5	30.1	
Natural scientists	.5	.2	27.9	
Health diagnosing occupations	1.2	.3	19.1	M
Health assessment & treating occupations	.5	3.9	87.4	F
Teachers, college & university	.8	.6	37.7	
Teachers, except college & university	1.7	6.0	75.2	F
Lawyers & judges	.9	.3	21.4	M
Other professional specialties	3.1	4.0	52.2	
Technicians & related support	**3.5**	**3.8**	**47.7**	
Health technologists & technicians	.5	2.3	80.8	F
Engineering & science technicians	1.4	.4	21.1	M
Other technicians	1.6	1.1	35.9	
Sales occupations	**11.6**	**12.4**	**47.5**	
Supervisors & proprietors	4.0	2.5	35.0	
Sales representatives, finance & business services	2.1	1.6	39.1	
Sales representatives, commodities, except retail	2.0	.7	22.4	M
Sales workers, retail & personal services	3.4	7.5	64.8	
Sales-related occupations	.1	.1	59.3	
Administrative support, including clerical	**6.0**	**27.8**	**79.7**	F
Supervisors	.6	.7	53.3	
Computer equipment operators	.4	.8	62.2	
Secretaries, stenographers, & typists	.1	8.1	98.5	F

(Continued)

Table 3.2 Continued

Occupation	Percentage of Male Labor Force	Percentage of Female Labor Force	Percentage of Female Workers in Occupation	Occupation Type
Financial records processing	.3	4.0	91.0	F
Mail & message distributing	.9	.6	34.3	
Other administrative support, including clerical	3.7	13.6	75.6	F
Service occupations	**10.2**	**17.6**	**59.4**	
Private household	.1	1.4	95.7	F
Protective service	2.6	.7	19.1	M
Food service	3.6	5.9	58.1	
Health service	.3	3.5	88.9	F
Cleaning & building service	2.8	2.2	40.2	
Personal service	.8	3.9	81.4	F
Precision production, craft, & repair	**18.6**	**2.2**	**9.0**	**M**
Mechanics & repairers	6.6	.2	2.6	M
Construction trades	7.3	.2	1.9	M
Other precision production, craft, & repair	4.7	1.8	24.4	M
Operators, fabricators, & laborers	**19.7**	**7.5**	**24.5**	**M**
Machine operators, assemblers, & inspectors	7.1	5.3	39.0	
Transportation & material moving	6.9	.7	8.1	M
Handlers, equipment cleaners, helpers, and laborers	5.7	1.5	17.9	M
Farming, forestry, & fishing	**4.3**	**1.0**	**15.7**	**M**
Farm operators & managers	1.6	.4	15.4	M
Other farming, forestry, & fishing	2.7	.6	15.9	M
TOTALS	**100.0**	**100.0**	**45.9**	

SOURCE: U.S. Department of Labor, Bureau of Labor Statistics, *Employment and Earnings, 39* (No. 5, May 1992), computed from p. 29, table A-22.
NOTE: Occupation Type equals M for a male-intensive occupation and F for a female-intensive occupation. No symbol indicates a neutral occupation. The table includes both full-time and part-time employees.

male-intensive occupations are defined as those in which 25.9% or less of the work force is female. Female-intensive occupations are defined as those in which 65.9% or more of the work force is female. The remaining occupations, in which 26.0% to 65.8% of the workers are female, are defined as neutral.

Almost half of all women (46.7%) are working in female-intensive occupations, while almost half of all men (46.2%) work in male-intensive occupations. More than one quarter of the female labor force is in the "administrative support, including clerical" occupations, whereas only 6% of the male labor force is employed in these areas. Women also dominate half of the various service occupations. In contrast, almost 40% of the male labor force is employed in the "precision production, craft, and repair" and "operators, fabricators, and laborers" occupations, while less than 10% of the female labor force work in the same occupations. Farming, forestry, and fishing are also dominated by men.

Professional, technical, and sales occupations are male-intensive, female-intensive, or neutral according to the particular occupation being considered. Less than 10% of all engineers are women, which may give us a clue as to why the older narrator of "I'm Gonna Be an Engineer" felt discouraged when she was a girl from even considering the profession. Health-diagnosing (e.g., medicine) and the legal professions are also male-intensive. Health assessment and treating (e.g., nursing) and teaching except at the college and university level are female-intensive. Technical occupations in the health area are female-intensive, whereas those in engineering and science are male-intensive. The sale of commodities is a male-intensive occupation, whereas other types of sales occupations are neutral.

Table 3.2 suggests that the greatest disparities in female and male employment are occurring outside of the executive, administrative, and managerial occupations. These occupations, which were male-intensive by the same 20-point-spread criterion until the mid-1970s, are now neutral in their overall composition. However, the percentages of female workers in the occupational categories shown do not tell the entire story. Women managers are employed to a far greater extent at the lower managerial levels than they are in *top* management positions; half of the entry-level management corps is female. However, as reported in Chapter 1, only one of the CEOs of the *Business Week* Top 1000 corporations is female. In addition, the proportion of female senior executives (that is, those with jobs within three managerial levels of the CEO's job) is less than 5%, as is the proportion of senior executives who are people of color. Thus, although the lower managerial ranks have become neutral, the top managerial levels remain male-intensive.[3]

Not only do women tend to work in different occupations than men; they also differ in earnings. The median wage for full-time female workers is 74% of what full-time male workers earn. This ratio stayed at about 60% from 1920, when about one fifth of women were in the labor force, to 1980, when over half of women were in the labor force. The decrease in the earnings gap since 1980 has resulted from the increased employment of women in male-intensive occupations. Nonetheless, the gap in earnings remains considerable, primarily due to the low wages earned in female-intensive occupations.[4]

The earnings gap is also due, however, to a sex difference in wages within almost every occupation. To cite a few examples, the ratio of female-to-male earnings among full-time workers is 86% for engineers, 54% for physicians, 90% for registered nurses, 80% for college and university teachers, 83% for grade school teachers, 88% for social workers, 75% for lawyers, 76% for computer operators, 82% for bartenders, 83% for janitors and cleaners, 68% for machine operators, assemblers, and inspectors, 78% for bus drivers, and 89% for farm workers. Looking at the managerial ranks, female managers earn 66% as much as male managers. These earning gaps exist in part because men tend to hold the higher-paying jobs within each occupation. They also exist because men typically earn more than women for the same job.[5]

However, earnings aren't the only indication of the disparity between male-intensive and female-intensive occupations. Women also experience less career mobility than men. By receiving less on-the-job training, women have fewer resources than men to advance their status and wages. Workers in female-intensive occupations typically have few opportunities to move from entry level to advanced levels of pay and prestige, achieving their maximum status in a relatively short period of time. As a result, women tend to gain less occupational standing over the course of their careers than men. Because women are concentrated in lower-paying occupations and industries that are less likely to provide pension coverage, they are also at a disadvantage at retirement.[6]

We have portrayed a workplace that to a large extent is sex-segregated, generating employment patterns that convey a powerful message to young people as well as adults who are planning to enter or reenter the job market. The message is that although all occupations are theoretically open to all qualified individuals, (a) the lower-paying, less-valued occupations are more appropriate for females; (b) the higher-paying, more-valued occupations are more appropriate for males;

and (c) men's work is often rewarded more than women's work for the same job.

However, the sex segregation of occupations does not dictate decisions about employment. Otherwise, change in the proportions of women and men in particular occupations would have never occurred. To understand more about the process by which employment begins for individuals, we need to examine other influences.

Decisions by Individuals

Individuals' decisions regarding initial employment are made in three stages. In the first stage, both occupational aspirations, or preferences for the occupation in which they would like to work, and expectations for the occupation in which they will actually work, are formed. (The term *occupation* is used broadly here to include nonpaying lines of work, such as staying at home to care for one's family, as well as paid employment.) The second stage consists of the decision to work or not at a particular point in time, a decision that is influenced by occupational aspirations and expectations previously formed and by the individual's current life situation. In the third stage, the individual decides to explore some job opportunities and not others, and decides to choose one job over another if the need for such a choice arises. These latter decisions are influenced more by the characteristics of the jobs under consideration and organizational recruiting practices.

Occupational Aspirations and Expectations

Occupational aspirations represent dreams that girls and boys have of "what they would like to be when they grow up." For example, Peggy Seeger's aspiring engineer had such a dream. Occupational expectations, however, represent the work individuals actually believe they will do. Expectations take into account perceptions of constraints such as limited opportunities or personal qualifications on the achievement of these dreams. The discrepancy between aspirations and expectations indicates the extent to which individuals believe that such constraints may prevent realization of their aspirations.

Studies of the occupational aspirations of preschool and elementary school children indicate that sex differences appear at an early age.

Children tend to see activities, including work, in sex-appropriate terms, viewing some as appropriate only for females and others as appropriate only for males. Girls' early aspirations often focus on the female-intensive occupations of teacher and nurse, whereas those of boys are typically spread over a wider range of occupations, although mostly male-intensive ones.

Margaret Mooney Marini and Mary Brinton found similar sex differences in the occupational aspirations of adolescents. Using data collected from a nationally representative sample, they calculated a segregation index for the occupational aspirations of youths aged 14 to 22. In this case, the segregation index indicated the proportion of one sex that would have to change occupational aspirations to make the distributions of aspirations for the two sexes equal. The segregation index value was 68% for youths aged 14 to 15 and 62% for youths aged 20 to 22. The segregation index for the existing work force was 59% at about the time the survey data were collected. Although the occupational aspirations were slightly less sex-typed for the older youths, the aspirations of the youths as a whole were just as sex-segregated as the occupations held by people who were then employed.[7]

Marini and Brinton further classified the occupational aspirations of the 14- to 22-year-olds according to whether they were for male-intensive, female-intensive, or neutral occupations. Their definitions, slightly different than the ones we used before, were that male-intensive occupations had less than 30% women, female-intensive occupations had 60% or more women, and neutral occupations had 30% to 59% women. Based on these categories, 86% of the males aspired to male-intensive occupations, and only 4% aspired to female-intensive occupations. In contrast, 53% of the females aspired to female-intensive occupations, and 35% aspired to male occupations. Thus males were more likely than females to prefer occupations dominated by their own sex.

Most studies have concluded that occupational expectations are more sex-typed than occupational aspirations. For example, a study of 11th-grade students found no difference between the mean percentage of men employed in occupations aspired to (83%) and expected (82%) by boys. However, the mean percentage of women employed in occupations aspired to by girls (67%) was significantly lower than the mean percentage of women employed in occupations in which the girls expected to work (75%). Girls saw greater constraints on their aspirations than boys, expecting to work in occupations more female-intensive than those they preferred.[8]

Work-related values have been changing over time, especially among women. Since the 1960s, there has been a dramatic increase in the value that female college freshmen (or freshwomen) place on status-attainment goals such as "having administrative responsibility," "obtaining recognition from colleagues," and "becoming an authority in my field." There has been less of an increase in the value placed on such goals by men, resulting in a narrowing of value differences between the sexes. Young women today have less traditional aspirations, and aspirations more like those of young men, than in earlier times. However, sex differences in occupational aspirations remain.[9]

In addition, occupational aspirations may be influenced by personal and background characteristics. For example, according to several studies, precollege African American women have a higher level of aspirations than their white counterparts. Such differences are less evident for college students and adults in general. Also, a study of girls' aspirations during childhood and adolescence found that "pioneers" who aspired to male-intensive occupations were more likely to have working mothers and highly-educated parents than "nonpioneers," demonstrating the importance of family characteristics. In general, women who aspire to male-intensive occupations tend to be fundamentally different in experience and socialization from those with more traditional aspirations.[10]

Let's now shift our focus from occupational aspirations in general to managerial aspirations in particular. Several studies have found that females aspire to managerial careers to a lesser degree than males.[11] However, other factors may contribute to the sex difference in managerial aspirations.

Some colleagues and I asked undergraduate business students at three universities to answer the question, "If you *had* to choose, in which of the following levels of an organization would you most like to work?" The possible responses were top management, middle management, lower management, and rank and file. Less than 5% of the students marked the lower management or rank and file categories, so we used only the top management and middle management categories in our analysis. Students also described themselves on the Bem Sex-Role Inventory and were classified as masculine, feminine, androgynous, or undifferentiated according to their BSRI masculinity and femininity scores (see Chapter 2).[12]

Table 3.3 presents the proportions of individuals who aspired to top management in each of the sex role identity groups for each sample.

Table 3.3 Percentage of Individuals Aspiring to Top Management

Sample/Sex Role Identity Group	Males N	Males Percentage	Females N	Females Percentage	Significance of Sex Difference
University 1					
Androgynous	46	73.9	29	51.7	n. s.
Masculine	91	83.5	16	81.3	n. s.
Feminine	25	60.0	66	45.5	n. s.
Undifferentiated	61	62.3	26	57.7	n. s.
TOTAL	223	73.1	137	53.3	<.001
University 2					
Androgynous	97	76.3	58	60.3	n. s.
Masculine	212	78.8	16	87.5	n. s.
Feminine	78	56.4	130	46.9	n. s.
Undifferentiated	177	63.8	63	47.6	<.05
TOTAL	564	70.6	267	52.4	<.001
University 3					
Androgynous	39	66.7	31	54.8	n. s.
Masculine	49	83.7	14	57.1	n. s.
Feminine	14	64.3	50	40.0	n. s.
Undifferentiated	34	58.8	26	30.8	n. s.
TOTAL	136	70.6	121	43.8	<.001

SOURCE: L. A. Mainiero, G. N. Powell, and D. A. Butterfield, "Sex Role Identity: A Predictor of Managerial Aspirations" (Paper delivered at the Annual Convention of the American Psychological Association, Toronto, 1978).
NOTE: Significance level pertains to the chi-square value for the relationship between managerial aspiration level and sex in each row, degrees of freedom = 1. The symbol n. s. indicates lack of significance at the .05 significance level. The proportion of masculine individuals aspiring to top management is significantly greater than the proportion of feminine individuals aspiring to top management for each sex in each sample at the .05 significance level.

Results were similar for the three samples. The proportion of males aspiring to top management was significantly larger than that of females. However, when males and females with a particular sex-role identity were compared, sex differences in managerial aspirations disappeared in all cases except one. These results can be explained by examining the sex-role identity distributions for males and females. In each sample, the greatest proportion of males was masculine and the greatest proportion of females was feminine. Masculine individuals aspired to top management in greater proportions than feminine individuals. Therefore, males were shown to have stronger managerial aspirations. However, sex-role identity was the real cause of the sex difference in managerial aspirations.

These results suggest that sex-role identity, which seems to be more the result of socialization experiences than of basic sex differences, may have a substantial effect on the formation of occupational aspirations and expectations. Whether they are female or male, masculine individuals may aspire to and expect to succeed in more male-intensive occupations, whereas feminine individuals may aspire to and expect to succeed in more female-intensive occupations. The aspirations and expectations of androgynous and undifferentiated individuals may be less affected by the sex segregation of occupations.

In summary, when individuals make choices about the occupations in which they would like to work and expect to work, they are likely to be influenced by the distribution of male and female workers across occupations and by their own socialization experiences. The fact that expectations mirror the sex segregation of occupations more than aspirations, particularly for females, shows the constraining nature of these influences. In turn, such aspirations and expectations act to maintain the existing level of sex segregation. Changes in occupational aspirations are to be expected, as the increased labor force participation of women affects the socialization of children. However, aspirations and expectations would have to change considerably for sex differences in them to disappear.

The Decision to Work

The decision to work differs from the formation of occupational aspirations in several ways. First, it takes economic considerations more into account, whereas the choice of aspirations is primarily a psychological process. Second, the decision to work may involve the needs and wishes of a spouse and/or children, whereas the choice of aspirations involves only the needs and wishes of the individual. Third, the decision to work depends on job availability, whereas aspirations are formed with the assumption that the occupational choice will be available.[13]

Most people work for the money. They need to support themselves in some manner unless they are independently wealthy. When there are two wage-earners in a family, it would seem that the economic need to have both working is less severe than the need to have at least one work. However, as mentioned in Chapter 1, desire for the higher standard of living possible with two incomes creates the economic need. In any event, a majority of both women and men say that they work out of economic necessity.

Women and men respond similarly to questions about working for noneconomic reasons, such as satisfying their needs for accomplishing something, working with friendly coworkers, achieving some level of status and prestige, and the like. A majority of both working women and working men say that they would continue to work if they did not need to. We don't really know if they would act in accordance with these convictions if put to the test, but the statements themselves suggest that both sexes gain nonmonetary pleasures from working.

Our society usually regards males as *not* having a decision to make about whether they work. Of course they work—they are men! The socialization of children, even when both parents work, typically stresses the male's role as the primary wage-earner in the family. Whether they are single, married without children, married with children, widowed, separated, or divorced, most men work until they are ready to retire. Statistics on participation rates according to marital status (see Table 1.4) show that at least two thirds of the men in each category are in the labor force. Eighty-five percent of men aged 20-24, over 90% of those aged 25-34, 35-44, and 45-54, and 67% of those aged 55-64 are in the labor force. Except for the drop in the employment rate of the older group, which is primarily due to earlier retirements, these statistics have changed little over the past 40 years. However, there is an 11% range present in the labor force participation rates of white (77%), Hispanic (82%), and African American (71%) men.[14]

Women, in contrast, have experienced more change in their employment status during the same period. As a result, most of the research conducted on the decision to work has focused on factors that affect women's decisions. These may be divided into personal and situational factors, although the two types of factors may have a combined influence.

Personal factors that could affect women's decisions to work include demographic characteristics such as age, race, and education, as well as personality characteristics (although this influence has seldom been examined). Age plays less of a role in determining whether women work than it did in the past. About 70% of women aged 20-24, 25-34, 35-44, and 45-54, and 43% of those aged 55-64 are in the labor force. Racial or ethnic group also plays a diminished role in women's decisions to work. Due to the increased employment of white women, only 5 percentage points (as compared to the 11-point range for men) separate the labor force participation rates of white (56%), Hispanic (53%), and African American (58%) women. The kinds of jobs held by women differ according to their racial or ethnic group, with Hispanic and African

American women concentrated more in lower-paying occupations, but this factor no longer appears to affect their decisions to work.[15]

Women have been attaining ever higher levels of education since the 1950s, when they were receiving less than one third of the bachelor's and master's degrees awarded. Since 1982, women have received over half of the bachelor's and master's degrees awarded each year. They now receive one third of the MBA degrees awarded, up from only 4% in 1970. The employment status of women is highly related to their level of educational attainment. The more education a woman has received, the greater the likelihood that she is in the labor force.[16]

Furthermore, the amount of education a woman receives greatly affects the kind of job she can attain. In 1989, 57% of the women employed in managerial or professional occupations had completed 4 or more years of college, whereas only 15% of those in technical, sales, or administrative support occupations and 5% of those in service occupations had achieved the same level of education. (A similar trend existed for men.) If women's level of educational attainment continues to rise, we can expect to see further changes in the nature of their employment.[17]

Situational factors may also affect women's decisions to work, especially married women. A woman's husband—whether he is employed and living with her, what his occupation, income, and attitudes are, and whether he is expected to be geographically mobile—may influence her decision. The more positive the husband's attitude towards his wife's working outside the home, the more likely she is to work. If the husband is unemployed or not present, the wife is also more likely to work. However, the higher the husband's income and the higher the prestige and responsibility associated with his job, the less likely the wife is to work. The woman's decision to work may be constrained by limited job selection in the location of the husband's job. If a woman is expected to be ready to move should her husband be transferred or take a job in another location, she may be less inclined to invest her energies in a career that does not lend itself to relocation.[18]

Children—how many, their ages, and the availability of child care arrangements—have less of an effect on whether women work than in previous years. However, as noted in Chapter 1, mothers of children under the age of 6 are still less likely to work than mothers of children between the ages of 6 and 17 only. Organizations as a whole do little to accommodate the child-care needs of working parents, a subject we will return to in Chapter 7. When suitable child-care arrangements are not available, it is typically the wife rather than the husband who sacrifices employment to care for children.

A small proportion of individuals, when they decide to work, decide to own and operate their own businesses. Although men are more likely than women to be self-employed, women's share of nonfarm solely-owned businesses has increased to 30%. Also, more couples are starting businesses together. The increase in small businesses jointly owned by a husband and wife has been greater in recent years than the increase in those solely owned by either women or men. Women-owned businesses are concentrated in the retail and personal service industries; they are less prevalent in male-intensive fields such as finance, manufacturing, and research and development. However, businesses headed by women are not any more or less likely to fail, or to be successful in terms of growth in earnings, than those headed by men.[19]

Both female and male entrepreneurs tend to be more highly educated, energetic, independent, self-confident, competitive, and goal-oriented than the labor force in general. They are likely to have had negative experiences in working for other people that led them to venture out alone. Female entrepreneurs also tend to be first-born or only children with entrepreneurial fathers, suggesting that they received special attention and opportunities for development of self-confidence and modeling in childhood. Although we have been generally referring to the decision to work for others in this chapter, we should recognize that some people decide to work for themselves.[20]

In summary, the decision to work is seldom made without consideration given to the economic needs of the household. It is also influenced by noneconomic factors. Education has a particularly strong effect on women's decisions to work; situational factors, particularly pertaining to husband and children, are also considered by women. In contrast, men typically do not consider whether to work, but when to retire.

Decisions About Job Opportunities

Individuals' decisions to pursue particular occupations are influenced primarily by their aspirations and their perceptions of the opportunities currently available. Decisions about particular job opportunities are influenced more by the inclination to actively explore potential job openings, the characteristics of the jobs that are being considered, and the recruiting practices used by the organizations that offer these jobs. Sex differences in job search tendencies, preferences for job characteristics, or responses to recruiting practices could lead male and female applicants to take different types of jobs.

Little research has been conducted on sex differences in the job search process. However, one interesting study examined differences in males' and females' job search behavior. College seniors interviewing for jobs were presented with five types of responses that employers typically give to letters of inquiry from applicants: no response, a letter indicating no opening but your letter and resume will be kept on file, a letter indicating that your letter and resume are being circulated, a letter showing some interest in you by including a job application form and / or requesting further information, and a request for a job interview. The seniors were then asked what each response would mean about the employer's interest in them and what future actions they would take in light of the response, such as writing again, calling, or dropping the company from their job search. There were no sex differences in interpretations of company responses, job search strategies, or attitudes toward the job search process. This evidence suggests that, once they decide to look for a job, men and women do not approach the job search process differently.[21]

Whether women and men differ in their preferences for job characteristics is a question that has long been debated. Frederick Herzberg and his colleagues guided early research on the question with the distinction between extrinsic and intrinsic characteristics of jobs. Extrinsic characteristics of jobs are provided by sources other than the job itself: Pay, the opportunity for promotion, pleasant working conditions, and recognition for good work are all provided by the organization, peers, or supervisors. Intrinsic characteristics pertain more to the nature of the job. Variety, opportunity for achievement and challenge, and level of responsibility are all intrinsic characteristics that may provide satisfaction separately from the job's extrinsic characteristics. According to Herzberg, males place greater importance on intrinsic and less importance on extrinsic job characteristics than females.[22]

However, more recent studies that have incorporated women aspiring to or already in managerial roles have yielded results in which the sexes have converged or actually switched places in preferences, results that differ sharply from Herzberg's findings. For example, female MBAs in one study placed higher importance than men on intrinsic job characteristics related to professional growth (e.g., challenging work, the opportunity to use their education, and the opportunity to develop professionally), whereas male MBAs placed greater importance on salary considerations, especially long-term career salary potential.[23]

Philip Manhardt provided a possible explanation for these conflicting results by relating individuals' preferences for job characteristics to their general commitment to work. On studying new college recruits in an insurance company in the late 1960s, he discovered that female graduates placed less importance on long-range aspects of a job that are related to career success than male graduates. However, he also observed that, when the sample of females was restricted to those who rated having a career first among their major life satisfactions, sex differences in importance of job characteristics were almost completely eliminated. Manhardt concluded, "Given equal perceived importance of a career and probability of continued employment, there is no reason to expect that women would not value success in business and show as much 'desire to get ahead' as men." By this reasoning, when women's commitment to work is similar to that of men, sex differences in preferences for job characteristics are less likely to appear.[24]

Other research supports this theory and suggests yet other factors that influence preferences for job characteristics. A study of data collected from national samples of adults revealed similar patterns in men's and women's preferences. Both sexes, when choosing from a list of one intrinsic and four extrinsic characteristics, identified the intrinsic characteristic of meaningful work as most important to them and rank ordered the four extrinsic characteristics of income, opportunity for promotion, job security, and working hours as increasingly less important to them in that sequence. Similar to earlier results, a sex difference in general commitment to work was found, especially among married individuals. Members of both sexes with a higher commitment to work were more likely to prefer meaningful work and less likely to prefer high income and short working hours. In addition, individuals with higher occupational prestige, education, and income were more likely to select meaningful work as their first choice. Individuals with lower occupational prestige, education, and income were more likely to select income, opportunity for promotion, or job security as their first choice.[25]

The conflict felt between work and home roles may also influence preferences for job characteristics. Typically women experience higher levels of work-home role conflict than men. However, both women and men who report high levels of role conflict express a strong desire for corporate policies that would help them deal with the conflicting demands of work and home, such as child-care leaves, flexible work hours, and assistance with daily child-care arrangements.[26] Thus, although there may be some differences in preferences in job characteristics due to sex, differences due to other factors such as occupational prestige, education, income, commitment to work, and work-home role conflict are likely to be far greater.

Finally, women and men could differ in their responses to the recruiting practices used by organizations. Most research on recruiting practices has focused on the characteristics of recruiters and their behavior in interviews. Factors such as the recruiter's personality, knowledge of the job opportunity being discussed, ability and willingness to answer questions, and demonstrated interest in the applicant have been shown in some studies to affect applicants' evaluations of job opportunities. However, differences in the responses of male and female applicants to recruiter characteristics or their interview behaviors generally have not been found.[27]

Thus men and women do not seem to differ significantly in their job search behavior, preferences for job characteristics, or reactions to organizational recruiting practices. Although aspirations and expectations affect the jobs for which they apply, women and men respond quite similarly to job opportunities. They differ to a greater extent in their decisions to work, although the gap between the outcomes of their decisions has become smaller in recent years. They differ most in their occupational aspirations and expectations, which reflect the current level of sex segregation in the workplace.

Individuals' decisions about work obviously have a great influence on how they begin their work careers. Sex differences in these decisions are primarily attributable to differences in occupational aspirations and expectations, which in turn are influenced by socialization pressures from parents, schools, and the mass media. However, organizations' decisions also affect the entry of women and men into the workplace. We shall next examine the decisions made by organizations about individuals who approach them concerning job opportunities.

Decisions by Organizations

Recruiters, personnel officers, and managers have little information on which to base their decisions to hire one applicant for a job over others. Referrals are a major source of applicants; however, the portrayals of individuals conveyed by referrals are invariably glowing. Decisions about which applicants other than walk-ins or referrals to interview are typically based on resumes, which present some information about applicants' backgrounds and experiences but little about their personal qualities. When recruiting is conducted on college campuses, decisions about which applicants to consider further are based on interviews that last no more than 20 to 30 minutes. The recruiter is likely to have read the resumes of up to a dozen applicants in less than an hour at the beginning of the day. As initial screening devices, campus interviews are necessary for organizations to reduce the large number of applicants who could possibly be considered to a select few who receive closer scrutiny. However, these interviews lead by necessity to quickly formed impressions that present only a blurred picture of the applicant. Follow-up interviews collect more information about applicants, but not enough so that employers can be absolutely sure that they are making the right choice.[28]

When judgments about individuals are based on very little data, as is the case when organizations make hiring decisions, these judgments are likely to be influenced by stereotypes. Gender stereotypes receive the most attention in this book, but stereotypes may also be based on such factors as age, race, ethnic group, class, religion, and geographical region of origin. Decision makers with limited information about applicants tend to make more biased decisions than those with more information. For example, a meta-analysis of the effect of applicant gender and qualifications on hiring recommendations found that qualifications had by far the greater effect, although the effect of gender was still significant. The best way to prevent gender stereotypes from affecting decisions, then, is to collect as much information as possible about all applicants. However, this is a costly solution that organizations are unlikely to embrace. Thus we are left with the fact that, as long as gender stereotypes are widely accepted, they are likely to affect decisions about applicants in some way.[29]

Gender stereotypes work both ways. Female applicants may be rated as more qualified, offered higher starting salaries, given more challenging job assignments, and hired more often than male applicants with equivalent credentials, or vice versa, depending on the job being hired for. Males typically receive more favorable evaluations for male-intensive jobs and females for female-intensive jobs. For example, males may be preferred over females for the jobs of engineer (you remember the song), physician, and security guard, whereas females may be preferred over males for the jobs of secretary, nurse, and grade school teacher.

This may occur because the characteristics seen as necessary for success in such jobs are characterized as either masculine or feminine, thereby calling for the appropriate sex. However, it may simply result from a belief that the sex that occupies or applies for a job in greater numbers must be better at it. In either case, the effect of the type of job on hiring decisions is to maintain the existing pattern of sex segregation in the workplace.[30]

This effect has particular relevance to hiring for managerial positions. The job of manager at any level has been male-intensive until recently, and the job of manager at upper levels remains highly male-intensive. Thus, if the same effect of type of job were to hold, we should expect to see males receive preferential treatment. In fact, most studies of hiring for managerial jobs have found such a preference. However, having information about applicants' competence can eliminate this preference.[31]

Gender may affect hiring decisions in other ways. For example, a study of simulated hiring for managerial positions in a bank found that male applicants were preferred when the work group to be managed was predominantly male and that female applicants were preferred when the group was predominantly female. Another simulation of initial placement decisions for newly hired engineers found that women engineers received less challenging first job assignments than male engineers when they were about to enter an all-male work group, whereas the presence of a competent female engineer in the work group resulted in male and female engineers receiving first job assignments with similar levels of challenge. Also, a woman is more likely to be hired as a higher education administrator if the proportion of women in the same type of job across institutions is higher, the proportion of women administrators in the same institution is higher, and the predecessor in the position is a woman. Thus the sex of subordinates, coworkers, and people being replaced may affect organizations' hiring and placement decisions.[32]

Applicants' marital status, considered with their biological sex, could also influence organizations' decisions. For example, hiring decisions could be affected by traditional notions concerning the commitment of women to family responsibilities as opposed to those associated with a career. Married women could be regarded as less suitable than married men or single workers for a position that called for extensive travel. We do not know, however, how prevalent this effect is.

Recruiter characteristics may also have an impact on organizations' decisions about applicants. Sex apparently does not affect these decisions, as male and female recruiters seldom differ in their responses to applicants; however, personality traits and beliefs may affect their evaluations. One study found that recruiters who were high in authoritarianism, reflecting a tendency to stress roles of dominance and submission in male-female relationships, preferred male applicants over female applicants for an administrative trainee position; those who were moderate or low in authoritarianism did not differ in their evaluations of male and female applicants. A separate study found that recruiters who tended to believe in gender stereotypes were more likely to discriminate against applicants of the sex seen to be inappropriate for a job than recruiters who did not endorse the stereotypes. These findings suggest that organizations need to be careful in their selection of recruiters if they are to avoid hiring decisions based more on gender stereotypes than on applicants' actual qualifications.[33]

An applicant's appearance seems to affect recruiters' hiring decisions. A meta-analysis concluded that people's perceptions of the social competence of others reflect the notion that "what is beautiful is good." When applying for managerial jobs, however, physical attractiveness can be a handicap for women. Whereas attractive males have been favored over unattractive males for such positions, unattractive females have been favored over attractive females for them. A possible explanation for this result is that attractiveness leads others to judge an individual more in accordance with gender stereotypes, that is, an attractive woman is seen as more feminine and an attractive man as more masculine than their less attractive counterparts. Attractiveness would then enhance a male's credentials and diminish a female's credentials for a stereotypically male job such as manager, even though it is no longer male-intensive except at high levels. However, this explanation also suggests that unattractive males are preferred over attractive males for stereotypically female jobs such as nurse and receptionist, which has less been the case; physical attractiveness is generally an asset for men, independent of the type of job. In the same vein, one study found that "babyfaced" applicants were favored for jobs emphasizing nurturing skills, whereas "maturefaced" applicants were favored for jobs emphasizing leadership skills.[34]

Manner of dress may also affect recruiters' decisions about an applicant's suitability for a managerial position. A study of female applicants found that those with more masculine dress (e.g., emphasis on vertical and angular lines, straight silhouettes, large-scale details, dark or dull colors, and heavy textures) were seen as more forceful, self-reliant, dynamic, aggressive, and decisive, and received more favorable hiring recommendations than those with more feminine dress (e.g., emphasis on horizontal and curved lines, rounded silhouettes, small-scale details, light colors, and soft, delicate textures). Although women are not expected to adopt a specific business uniform as much as men are, they are expected to adopt traditional male attire to some extent. However, male applicants for professional positions who wear ill-fitting suits, unironed shirts, ties that are too short, or tacky tie clips create negative impressions. Socks that are white, beige, brightly colored, or large-patterned and shoes that are in poor condition or do not convey a professional image are also out for men.[35]

These findings regarding the effect of appearance on hiring decisions are disturbing, because they focus on a person's appearance rather than qualifications. People have little control over their attractiveness or "facial maturity" as perceived by others. Applicants have more control over their dress than their basic appearance, but dress still seems a frivolous basis for deciding whom to hire for a managerial position. However, some executives claim that if an applicant wears an outfit judged by others to be inappropriate to an employment interview, he or she probably doesn't understand the realities of the work world and would be an ineffective performer.

The biases that have been described operate most often at an unconscious level. Recruiters who endorse gender stereotypes probably do not say to themselves, "I will take my belief in gender stereotypes into account in evaluating applicants." And recruiters who are presented with an attractive female applicant and an attractive male applicant for the same managerial job hopefully do not think, "Wow! What an attractive woman! That rules her out for this position. The attractive man will be much better in it." However, some decision makers consciously use what they believe are other people's biases as the basis for decisions about applicants. If they believe, for example, that their employees or customers will feel uncomfortable with a female manager or engineer or a male secretary or receptionist, they may go along with the expected wishes of others in their hiring decisions even if they have no personal objections to hiring a member of the sex deemed inappropriate for the position. For example, a study of law firms found that many were reluctant to hire female attorneys due to the expected loss of clients who they believed preferred males in these positions.[36]

So far, we have seen a gloomy picture of how organizations make decisions about applicants. However, things may not be as bad as this picture suggests. Almost all of the research studies described have had participants, who were either organizational recruiters or college students, evaluate either fictitious resumes or hypothetical applicants seen in videotaped mock interviews. Such studies deliberately keep the amount of information about applicants small, so that the effect of the variable under investigation can be most readily identified. Hardly any studies have been conducted of decisions made about real applicants.

The few studies of actual employment interviews that have been conducted generally have not found applicant sex to affect recruiters' decisions. For example, Laura Graves and I examined the effects of several variables besides applicant sex on recruiters' evaluations of applicants in campus interviews. We found that the applicant's subjectively measured qualifications, such as communications ability, knowledge of the job being applied for, and initiative, had the greatest effect on recruiters' evaluations, whereas applicant sex had no effect. Recruiters tended to see stronger subjective qualifications in applicants with high grade point averages whom they viewed as similar to themselves and whom they liked. These results support the point made earlier that, when more information is available about applicants, applicant sex has less of an effect on decisions.[37]

Thus organizations have considerable opportunity to discriminate between male and female applicants in their hiring decisions. They may do so because of the unconscious biases of organizational recruiters, or because of conscious beliefs about the biases of others. Since so little information is available when decisions are made, the biases described probably affect decisions to some extent, although to what extent is unknown. Further research on actual decisions about applicants is necessary to determine the size of this effect. However, we know enough to conclude that organizations need to guard against possible biases in their decisions about applicants if they are to prevent sex discrimination from taking place.

Implications

We shall examine the implications of the research results presented in this chapter in two ways. First, we will consider how organizations can improve their management of recruitment activities, including how they present themselves to applicants (and the outside world) and how they decide which applicants to hire. Second, we will consider how individuals can improve their prospects for attaining a satisfying and rewarding job.

What Organizations Can Do

Occupational aspirations and expectations, which begin being formed by individuals at very early ages, are the characteristics of individuals most responsible for maintaining the sex segregation of occupations. The differences in boys' and girls' aspirations and expectations mirror the existing level of sex segregation to a large extent. Women and men differ to a lesser extent in their decisions on whether to work, and they differ very little in their decision making about whether to take particular jobs. Thus, if organizations wish to contribute to a lower level of sex segregation in the workplace, they can have a considerable impact by influencing the formation of occupational aspirations and expectations. To do so, they need to play a more conscious role in the socialization of children.

How can organizations best play this role? Many organizations already distribute materials to high school guidance counselors about opportunities in their industries. These materials portray both women and men in various occupations to a greater extent than ever before. However, high school is not the place for organizations to start. If they expect to have any appreciable impact on the development of occupational aspirations and expectations, organizations also need to direct activities toward younger children. One way to do this is to send speakers to elementary schools, Cub Scout and Brownie troops, and other places where young children congregate, to talk about the opportunities in their industries and the workplace, stressing that they will be looking for both good women and good men. The best speakers would be members of the sex least represented in the occupations being talked about, or mixed-sex teams to demonstrate that both sexes belong in the occupations. For example, if the singer of "I'm Gonna Be an Engineer" succeeds despite the admonishments of everyone around her, she would be an ideal speaker on opportunities in the engineering professions. Films that are distributed to schools and youth groups can be used to convey similar themes.

Organizations can also use the mass media, especially television, more effectively for the same purpose. The opportunities for organizations to use television to have a positive influence on the aspirations and expectations of children are largely untapped. For example, organizations do very little recruiting of applicants on television. Only one large organization currently recruits via television: the Armed Forces of the United States. Although the Marines are still looking for "a few good men," recruiting advertisements for the other military services typically portray both sexes as fitting in them. Of course, these advertisements are not too realistic—nobody dies, or even gets their hair messed up—but they do convey the message that both sexes belong. These advertisements not only attract applicants; they also give a message to young children that may influence their occupational aspirations and expectations more than military Barbie dolls ever will.

Television ads are too costly a way for most organizations to solicit applicants. After all, the Armed Forces don't pay for their heavy use of television—*we* do as taxpayers. However, organizations can prepare public-service messages for television stressing that both women and men belong in their industries. Organizations also need to monitor the influence of their current uses of television on children's aspirations and expectations. They can discourage reliance on gender stereotypes in advertisements for their products and services and in the programs they support with their advertising.

Organizations also need to devote more attention to their own recruitment-related activities. Most do a poor job of managing college recruitment. CEOs have little involvement in it, and it is seldom regarded as a key strategic function. Companies rely primarily on brochures, which are too general and unswervingly positive to have much of an effect, to communicate with prospective applicants. Recruiter performance is most often evaluated on procedural grounds, such as whether the recruiter kept appointments and filed necessary reports, rather than on actual results. Performance as a recruiter has little impact on individual rewards, especially for recruiters who are line managers.[38]

This casual concern for the recruitment function may be because organizations have had no trouble in attracting applicants in recent years. When applicants are abundant, organizations can fill vacancies without paying attention to whether they are doing a good job at it. However, the mere ability to fill vacancies is not a good measure of recruiter effectiveness. Tracking the performance, satisfaction, turnover rate, and subsequent career success of new hires is necessary to provide data on the quality of hiring decisions and the long-term effectiveness of recruiting practices.[39]

Organizations can improve their recruitment performance by paying close attention to the selection and training of recruiters and others who make hiring decisions. Screening of applicants for recruiter positions should include assessment of beliefs in gender stereotypes and personality traits such as authoritarianism to determine their ability to make unbiased decisions about applicants. Training of prospective as well as current recruiters is necessary. A survey of *Fortune* 1000 companies found that less than half offered a standardized training program for recruiters and, of those, less than half required that recruiters actually receive training before beginning their assignments. When training occurred at all, it focused on interviewing skills and what to look for in applicants more than on development of interview content and what to tell applicants about the company.[40] Organizations can do much more to train people involved in the recruitment process, whether as full-time recruiters or managers hiring for their own departments, to look beyond sex-role identity and not rely on stereotypes.

Organizations can also reduce the likelihood of sex discrimination by standardizing and formalizing their recruitment practices, and then monitoring these practices to ensure their effectiveness. As noted before, sex discrimination is most likely to occur when little information is available about applicants. Structured interviewing can ensure that similar and sufficient information is collected on all applicants by requiring interviewers to ask questions in the same topic areas. Providing interviewers with specific job requirements, rather than general platitudes about the type of applicant being sought, has been shown to reduce biases and improve the reliability of judgments. Use of rating techniques such as behaviorally anchored rating scales (BARS) can help interviewers to rate applicants' qualifications in a detailed and systematic fashion. In addition, use of multiple interviewers may reduce the biases in judgments that would result if only one interviewer rated the applicant.[41]

In summary, organizations need to take the recruitment function much more seriously to improve their effectiveness in attracting and selecting the most qualified applicants regardless of their sex, race, or any other job-irrelevant personal characteristic. Also, by seeking to influence occupational aspirations and expectations formed at an early age, they can work toward ensuring that they will have qualified applicants of both sexes in their applicant pools in the long run.

What Individuals Can Do

Successful placement requires joint decision making, by applicants as well as employers. Applicants need to know *how* to search for the information they need to make a fully informed decision, *where* to look, and *what* information to look for.[42]

First, they should clarify their own goals and preferences for a work environment. Just looking for any job, whatever it may be, is not a useful strategy because it provides little guidance on how to proceed in finding that job. Making a list of preferred job characteristics is helpful. For example, a survey of college seniors found that they rated the following job characteristics in descending order of importance as shown: challenging/interesting work, opportunity to use abilities, opportunity to learn, opportunity to show superiors effective performance, variety of activities, competent/sociable coworkers, opportunity for rapid advancement, type of work or service being performed, salary, training programs, freedom to do the job my own way, job security, company reputation, location, fringe benefits, job title, company size, and opportunity for extensive travel. Applicants can gain from rank ordering the same list of job characteristics for themselves before beginning their job search.[43]

Second, besides utilizing campus placement facilities if they are college students, applicants should make use of outside, informal sources such as friends and acquaintances to identify potential employers. Only large organizations looking to fill large numbers of jobs are likely to interview on college campuses. Yet, most of the growth in jobs in the American economy in recent years has been generated by smaller rather than larger firms. Thus looking off-campus as well as on-campus for a job is important. Most job seekers obtain employment through informal sources, rather than more formal sources such as employment agencies and newspaper advertisements.[44]

Third, applicants should be prepared to make a good impression in interviews. The research results discussed earlier are relevant—it is important to dress the part. Applicants may be successfully trained on how to present themselves effectively in job interviews. As a result, applicant-training workshops have become common, and most applicants gain from attending such workshops if they are available. If not, having practice interviews with friends who are willing to play the interviewer role may be beneficial. All the information that applicants provide in interviews is likely to be considered. Therefore, they should make sure they make their positive qualities known, just as most organizations do in presenting themselves to applicants in their literature and in person.[45]

Fourth, applicants should carefully assess the merits of each potential employer. Such information can be difficult to obtain, but it is critical to making a good job choice and is available if the right questions are asked at the right time to the right people in a sensitive manner. Applicants should not expect to get very much information out of the initial employment interview other than whether there seems to be a potential match. However, if they proceed past that point to have further discussions with an employer, they will need further information to make a decision. Female applicants may gain from reading books such as *The Best Companies for Women* by Baila Zeitz and Lorraine Dusky to get an impression of what particular companies would be like to work for.[46]

Finally, applicants should select the job that provides the best match between their preferred job characteristics and the work environment capable of satisfying them. This assumes multiple job opportunities, which may not be the case for all applicants. However, it is best to be prepared for such a decision. Applicants who follow all of these steps, whether they are female or male, will enhance their chances of being successfully employed.

Conclusions

Actions taken by individuals and organizations ultimately affect the distribution of the sexes across all types of jobs. Individuals' aspirations and expectations have tended to support the existing sex segregation of occupations. Thus it is not surprising that research has shown that more males aspire to management positions, especially top management, than females. As suggested earlier, individuals' sex role identities may provide the best explanation for sex differences in managerial aspirations. If sex-role identity is primarily the result of socialization experiences, the cause of sex differences in managerial aspirations then becomes gender stereotyping, which puts pressure on males and females of all ages to conform. Thus, sex differences in aspirations may not disappear unless sex differences in the socialization experiences that promote traditional sex-role identities disappear first.

Decisions by organizational representatives also affect the sex composition of occupations. The job of manager often has been defined as masculine, with men seen as more suited for it than women. Many studies have documented a bias toward the hiring of male applicants for managerial positions, even when the qualifications of female and male applicants have been equivalent. These results also reflect the influence of gender stereotypes that suggest that men are more appropriate for leadership roles than women.

Thus we have the conditions present for a self-fulfilling prophecy: Individuals' and organizations' decisions are affected by and often reinforce the current level of sex segregation in occupations. Given these conditions, it is a wonder that change occurs in the level of sex segregation in any occupation.

Yet, such change has been occurring. The sex segregation index value has been gradually dropping in recent years. The managerial ranks, and those of many other professions, have a greater proportion of women than ever before. The forces supporting the status quo, consisting of gender stereotypes and the existing level of sex segregation, are powerful. However, the desire for a higher standard of living, which has provided an economic reason for both adult members of a household to work, and the women's movement, which has provided an ideological reason for women to seek to exercise more economic power over their own lives, have also been powerful forces supporting change in the sex segregation of occupations.

The decisions made by individuals about whether they wish to enter the workplace and in what capacity, and the decisions made by organizations about which applicants they hire to fill job openings, are extremely complex. Both types of decisions are affected, but not fully determined, by the prevalence of gender stereotypes in our society. Otherwise, the singer of "I'm Gonna Be an Engineer," and other individuals who once aspired to and now work in occupations in which their sex is in the minority, would have never achieved their dreams.

Notes

1. O. D. Duncan and B. Duncan, "Residential Distribution and Occupational Stratification," *American Journal of Sociology, 60* (1955): 493-503.

2. F. D. Blau and M. A. Ferber, Chapter 5, "Differences in Occupations and Earnings: Overview," in *The Economics of Women, Men, and Work*, 2nd ed. (Englewood Cliffs, NJ: Prentice Hall, 1992); S. M. Bianchi and N. Rytina, "The Decline in Occupational Sex Segregation during the 1970s: Census and CPS Comparisons," *Demography, 23* (1986): 79-86; E. Gross, "Plus ca Change...? The Sexual Structure of Occupations over Time," *Social Problems, 16* (1968): 198-208.

3. A. B. Fisher, "When Will Women Get to the Top?" *Fortune*, 126 (No. 6, 21 September 1992): 44-56; Korn/Ferry International, *Executive Profile: A Decade of Change in Corporate Leadership* (New York: Korn/Ferry International, 1990), pp. 22-23, tables 58 and 61; A. T. Segal with W. Zellner, "Corporate Women," *Business Week*, No. 3269 (8 June 1992): 74-78.

4. U.S. Department of Labor, Bureau of Labor Statistics, *Employment and Earnings*, 39 (No. 1, January 1992), computed from pp. 223-227, table 56; M. M. Marini, "Sex Differences in Earnings in the United States," *American Review of Sociology*, 15 (1989): 343-380.

5. U.S. Department of Labor, Bureau of Labor Statistics, *Employment and Earnings*, 39 (No. 1, January 1992), computed from p. 223-227, table 56; A. A. Kemp and E. M. Beck, "Equal Work, Unequal Pay: Gender Discrimination within Work-Similar Occupations," *Work and Occupations*, 13 (1986): 324-347; J. Pfeffer and A. Davis-Blake, "The Effect of the Proportion of Women on Salaries: The Case of College Administrators," *Administrative Science Quarterly*, 32 (1987): 1-24.

6. B. F. Reskin and H. I. Hartmann, Chapter 1, "The Significance of Sex Segregation in the Workplace," in *Women's Work, Men's Work: Sex Segregation on the Job* (Washington, DC: National Academy Press, 1986).

7. M. M. Marini and M. C. Brinton, "Sex Typing in Occupational Socialization," in *Sex Segregation in the Workplace: Trends, Explanations, Remedies*, ed. B. F. Reskin (Washington, DC: National Academy Press, 1984).

8. M. M. Marini and E. Greenberger, "Sex Differences in Occupational Aspirations and Expectations," *Sociology of Work and Occupations*, 5 (1968): 147-178.

9. R. Fiorentine, "Increasing Similarity in the Values and Life Plans of Male and Female College Students? Evidence and Implications," *Sex Roles*, 18 (1988): 143-158; L. W. Harmon, "Longitudinal Changes in Women's Career Aspirations: Developmental or Historical?" *Journal of Vocational Behavior*, 35 (1989): 46-63; J. A. Jacobs, Chapter 4, "Trends in Young Women's Occupational Aspirations," in *Revolving Doors: Sex Segregation and Women's Careers* (Stanford, CA: Stanford University Press, 1989).

10. A. J. Murrell, I. H. Frieze, and J. L. Frost, "Aspiring to Careers in Male- and Female-Dominated Professions: A Study of Black and White College Women," *Psychology of Women Quarterly*, 15 (1991): 103-126; D. E. Sandberg, A. A. Ehrhardt, C. A. Mellins, S. E. Ince, and H. F. L. Meyer-Bahlburg, "The Influence of Individual and Family Characteristics upon Career Aspirations of Girls During Childhood and Adolescence," *Sex Roles*, 16 (1987): 649-668; L. M. Subich, G. V. Barrett, D. Doverspike, and R. A. Alexander, "The Effects of Sex-Role-Related Factors on Occupational Choice and Salary," in *Pay Equity: Empirical Inquiries*, ed. R. T. Michael, H. I. Hartmann, and B. O'Farrell (Washington, DC: National Academy Press, 1989).

11. M. D. Fottler and T. Bain, "Sex Differences in Occupational Aspirations," *Academy of Management Journal*, 23 (1980): 144-149.

12. L. A. Mainiero, G. N. Powell, and D. A. Butterfield, "Sex Role Identity: A Predictor of Managerial Aspirations" (Paper delivered at the Annual Convention of the American Psychological Association, Toronto, 1978).

13. V. F. Nieva and B. A. Gutek, Chapter 3, "Factors Affecting Women's Decision to Work," in *Women and Work: A Psychological Perspective* (New York: Praeger, 1981).

14. U.S. Department of Labor, Bureau of Labor Statistics, *Handbook of Labor Statistics* (Washington, DC: Government Printing Office, 1989), pp. 25-30, table 5.

15. U.S. Department of Labor, Bureau of Labor Statistics, *Handbook of Labor Statistics*, pp. 25-30, table 5.

16. U.S. Department of Education, *Digest of Educational Statistics 1990* (Washington, DC: Government Printing Office, 1991), p. 232, table 220, and p. 263, table 243.

17. U.S. Department of Commerce, Bureau of the Census, *Statistical Abstract of the United States 1991*, 111th ed. (Washington, DC: Government Printing Office, 1986), p. 399, table 655.

18. Nieva and Gutek, Chapter 3, "Factors Affecting Women's Decision to Work," in *Women and Work*; E. Lehrer and M. Nerlove, "Female Labor Force Behavior and Fertility in the United States," *Annual Review of Sociology, 12* (1986): 181-204.

19. U.S. Department of Labor, Women's Bureau, *Facts on Working Women: Women Business Owners*, Publication No. 89-5, 1989 (Washington, DC: Department of Labor); B. Brown, "Partners in Life and Also in Business," *Wall Street Journal, 213* (No. 44, 6 March 1989): B1; A. J. Kalleberg and K. T. Leicht, "Gender and Organizational Performance: Determinants of Small Business Survival and Success," *Academy of Management Journal, 34* (1991): 136-161.

20. R. D. Hisrich and C. G. Brush, Chapter 1, "A Historical Perspective," in *The Woman Entrepreneur* (Lexington, MA: Lexington Books, 1986); D. D. Bowen and R. D. Hisrich, "The Female Entrepreneur: A Career Development Perspective," *Academy of Management Review, 11* (1986): 393-407.

21. B. Z. Posner, J. Schmidt-Posner, and W. A. Randolph, "Can Applicants' Characteristics Explain the Sex Structuring of Organizations?" *Psychological Reports, 56* (1986): 343-350.

22. F. Herzberg, B. Mausner, R. O. Peterson, and D. F. Capwell, *Job Attitudes: Review of Research and Opinion* (Pittsburgh: Psychological Service of Pittsburgh, 1957).

23. W. J. Bigoness, "Sex Differences in Job Attribute Preferences," *Journal of Organizational Behavior, 9* (1988): 139-147; N. J. Beutell and O. C. Brenner, "Sex Differences in Work Values," *Journal of Vocational Behavior, 28* (1986): 29-41; O. C. Brenner and J. Tomkiewicz, "Job Orientation of Males and Females: Are Sex Differences Declining?" *Personnel Psychology, 32* (1979): 741-750; K. M. Bartol and P. J. Manhardt, "Sex Differences in Job Outcome Preferences: Trends among Newly Hired College Graduates," *Journal of Applied Psychology, 64* (1979): 477-482.

24. P. J. Manhardt, "Job Orientation of Male and Female College Graduates in Business," *Personnel Psychology, 25* (1972): 361-368.

25. W. B. Lacy, J. L. Bokemeier, and J. M. Shepard, "Job Attribute Preferences and Work Commitment for Men and Women in the United States," *Personnel Psychology, 36* (1983): 315-329.

26. U. J. Wiersma, "Gender Differences in Job Attribute Preferences: Work-Home Role Conflict and Job Level as Mediating Variables," *Journal of Occupational Psychology, 63* (1990): 231-243.

27. G. N. Powell, "Applicant Reactions to the Initial Employment Interview: Exploring Theoretical and Methodological Issues," *Personnel Psychology, 44* (1991): 67-83; M. M. Harris and L. S. Fink, "A Field Study of Applicant Reactions to Employment Opportunities: Does the Recruiter Make a Difference?" *Personnel Psychology, 40* (1987): 765-784; M. S. Taylor and T. J. Bergmann, "Organizational Recruitment Activities and Applicants' Reactions at Different Stages of the Recruitment Process," *Personnel Psychology, 40* (1987): 261-285.

28. This section of the chapter is based primarily on research reviewed in G. N. Powell, "The Effects of Sex and Gender on Recruitment," *Academy of Management Review*, 12 (1987): 731-743.

29. H. L. Tosi and S. W. Einbender, "The Effects of the Type and Amount of Information in Sex Discrimination Research," *Academy of Management Journal*, 28 (1985): 712-723; J. D. Olian, D. P. Schwab, and Y. Haberfeld, "The Impact of Applicant Gender Compared to Qualifications on Hiring Recommendations: A Meta-Analysis of Experimental Studies," *Organizational Behavior and Human Decision Processes*, 41 (1988): 180-195.

30. M. E. Heilman, "Sex Bias in Work Settings: The Lack of Fit Model," in *Research in Organizational Behavior*, vol. 5, ed. L. L. Cummings and B. M. Staw (Greenwich, CT: JAI, 1983); P. Glick, C. Zion, and C. Nelson, "What Mediates Sex Discrimination in Hiring Decisions?" *Journal of Personality and Social Psychology*, 55 (1988): 178-186; R. D. Arvey, H. E. Miller, R. Gould, and P. Burch, "Interviewer Validity for Selecting Sales Clerks," *Personnel Psychology*, 40 (1987): 1-12; J. Rosenstein and M. A. Hitt, "Experimental Research on Race and Sex Discrimination: The Record and the Prospects," *Journal of Occupational Behavior*, 7 (1986): 215-226; M. E. Heilman, "The Impact of Situational Factors on Personnel Decisions Concerning Women: Varying the Sex Composition of the Applicant Pool," *Organizational Behavior and Human Performance*, 26 (1980): 386-395.

31. M. E. Heilman, "Information as a Deterrent against Sex Discrimination: The Effects of Applicant Sex and Information Type on Preliminary Employment Decisions," *Organizational Behavior and Human Performance*, 33 (1984): 174-186.

32. G. L. Rose and P. Andiappan, "Sex Effects on Managerial Hiring Decisions," *Academy of Management Journal*, 21 (1978): 104-112; M. S. Taylor and D. R. Ilgen, "Sex Discrimination against Women in Initial Placement Decisions: A Laboratory Investigation," *Academy of Management Journal*, 24 (1981): 859-865; A. M. Konrad and J. Pfeffer, "Understanding the Hiring of Women and Minorities in Educational Institutions," *Sociology of Education*, 64 (1991): 141-157.

33. K. Simas and M. McCarrey, "Impact of Recruiter Authoritarianism and Applicant Sex on Evaluation and Selection Decisions in a Recruitment Interview Analogue Study," *Journal of Applied Psychology*, 64 (1979): 483-491; C. Sharp and R. Post, "Evaluation of Male and Female Applicants for Sex-Congruent and Sex-Incongruent Jobs," *Sex Roles*, 6 (1980): 391-401.

34. A. H. Eagly, R. D. Ashmore, M. G. Makhijani, and L. C. Longo, "What Is Beautiful Is Good, But . . . : A Meta-Analytic Review of Research on the Physical Attractiveness Stereotype," *Psychological Bulletin*, 110 (1991): 109-128; P. C. Morrow, "Physical Attractiveness and Selection Decision Making," *Journal of Management*, 16 (1990): 45-60; M. E. Heilman and L. R. Saruwatari, "When Beauty Is Beastly: The Effects of Appearance and Sex on Evaluations of Job Applicants for Managerial and Nonmanagerial Jobs," *Organizational Behavior and Human Performance*, 23 (1979): 360-372; L. A. Zebrowitz, D. R. Tenenbaum, and L. H. Goldstein, "The Impact of Job Applicants' Facial Maturity, Gender, and Academic Achievement on Hiring Recommendations," *Journal of Applied Social Psychology*, 21 (1991): 525-548.

35. S. M. Forsythe, "Effect of Applicant's Clothing on Interviewer's Decision to Hire," *Journal of Applied Social Psychology*, 20 (1990): 1579-1595; S. M. Forsythe, M. F. Drake, and C. E. Cox, "Influence of Applicant's Dress on Interviewer's Selection Decisions," *Journal of Applied Psychology*, 70 (1985): 374-378; C. J. Scherbaum and D.

H. Shepherd, "Dressing for Success: Effects of Color and Layering on Perceptions of Women in Business," *Sex Roles, 16* (1987): 391-399; K. A. Hughes, "Businesswomen's Broader Latitude in Dress Codes Goes Just So Far, Male Executives Also Suffer for Their Sartorial Mistakes," *Wall Street Journal, 210* (No. 45, 1 September 1987): 33.

36. C. F. Epstein, *Women in Law* (New York: Basic Books, 1981).

37. L. M. Graves and G. N. Powell, "An Investigation of Sex Discrimination in Recruiters' Evaluations of Actual Applicants," *Journal of Applied Psychology, 73* (1988): 20-29.

38. S. L. Rynes and J. W. Boudreau, "College Recruiting in Large Organizations: Practice, Evaluation, and Research Implications," *Personnel Psychology, 39* (1986): 729-757; J. W. Boudreau and S. L. Rynes, "Giving It the Old College Try," *Personnel Administrator, 32* (No. 3, 1987): 78-85.

39. L. M. Graves, "College Recruitment: Removing Personal Bias from Selection Decisions," *Personnel, 66* (No. 3, 1989): 48-52.

40. Rynes and Boudreau, "College Recruiting in Large Organizations."

41. D. L. Collinson, D. Knights, and M. Collinson, "Conclusion: The Vicious Circles of Job Segregation," in *Managing to Discriminate* (London: Routledge, 1990); R. L. Dipboye, Chapter 9, "Strategies for Improving Selection Interviews," in *Selection Interviews: Process Perspectives* (Cincinnati: South-Western, 1992).

42. This section of the chapter is based primarily on T. A. Kolenko, "College Recruiting: Models, Myths, and Management," in *Human Resource Management: Perspectives and Issues*, 2nd ed., ed. G. R. Ferris, K. M. Rowland, and M. R. Buckley (Boston: Allyn and Bacon, 1990).

43. B. Z. Posner, "Comparing Recruiter, Student, and Faculty Perceptions of Important Applicant and Job Characteristics," *Personnel Psychology, 34* (1981): 329-339; R. P. Seidel and G. N. Powell, "On the Campus: Matching Graduates with Jobs," *Personnel, 61*, no. 4 (1983): 66-72.

44. D. P. Schwab, S. L. Rynes, and R. J. Aldag, "Theories and Research on Job Search and Choice," in *Research in Personnel and Human Resources Management*, vol. 5, ed. K. M. Rowland and G. R. Ferris (Greenwich, CT: JAI, 1987).

45. Dipboye, "Strategies for Improving Selection Interviews."

46. B. Zeitz and L. Duffy, *The Best Companies for Women* (New York: Simon and Schuster, 1988).

4

Working With People

Impressions From the Office and the Battlefield

The Office

The family picture is on HIS desk.
—Ah, a solid, responsible family man.
The family picture is on HER desk.
—Umm, her family will come before her career.
HIS desk is cluttered.
—He's obviously a hard worker and a busy man.
HER desk is cluttered.
—She's obviously a disorganized scatterbrain.
HE is talking with his co-workers.
—He must be discussing the latest deal.
SHE is talking with her co-workers.
—She must be gossiping.
HE'S not at his desk.
—He must be at a meeting.
SHE'S not at her desk.
—She must be in the ladies' room.
HE'S not in the office.
—He's meeting customers.
SHE'S not in the office.
—She must be out shopping.
HE'S having lunch with the boss.
—He's on the way up.

SHE'S having lunch with the boss.
—They must be having an affair.
The boss criticized HIM.
—He'll improve his performance.
The boss criticized HER.
—She'll be very upset.
HE got an unfair deal.
—Did he get angry?
SHE got an unfair deal.
—Did she cry?
HE'S getting married.
—He'll get more settled.
SHE'S getting married.
—She'll get pregnant and leave.
HE'S having a baby.
—He'll need a raise.
SHE'S having a baby.
—She'll cost the company money in maternity benefits.
HE'S going on a business trip.
—It's good for his career.
SHE'S going on a business trip.
—What will her husband say?
HE'S leaving for a better job.
—He knows how to recognize a good opportunity.
SHE'S leaving for a better job.
—Women are not dependable.

Natasha Josefowitz[1]

The Battlefield

Senior Pentagon officials insisted Tuesday that rules barring women
from combat should continue, but some senators on the Armed Services Committee endorsed allowing them to fly warplanes in combat.
The crowded hearing was the first formal congressional inquiry devoted solely to allowing women to fly combat aircraft since the Persian Gulf war, in which five women were classified as killed in action
although they did not formally have combat roles.

"I totally support seeing some changes," said Lt. Brenda M. Holdener,
a Navy helicopter pilot at Norfolk Naval Air Station in Virginia who

supervised 30 sailors in the Red Sea during the war. "I'm very selfish—I'd like to see it changed because it would afford me more opportunities."

Maj. Christine Prewitt, an Air Force pilot from Andrews Air Force Base, Md., said men and women go through identical pilot training. "If you make that cut, you should be able to go on and fly," she said.

Robert H. Barrow, commandant of the Marine Corps from 1979 to 1983, said, "Combat is finding and closing with and killing or capturing the enemy. It's uncivilized, and women can't do it." Barrow warned that allowing women into combat roles will cripple military morale. "Women give life, sustain life, nurture life—they can't take it. If you want to make a combat unit ineffective, assign women to it. It would destroy the Marine Corps—as simple as that—something no enemy has been able to do in over 200 years."

Gen. Merrill A. McPeak, the Air Force chief of staff, said he would choose a male pilot instead of a female aviator even if the choice hurt combat effectiveness. "I admit that doesn't make much sense, but that's the way I feel about it," he said.

Gen. A. M. Gray, the current Marine commandant, said his female troops were not pressing for changes. "We don't see this request (from female Marines) to want to fly airplanes or be in the ground combat arms," he said. "We believe that our women understand that you need women, and you need men and they're different—thank goodness—and it will always be that way."

Mark Thompson[2]

In her poem, Natasha Josefowitz describes gender stereotypes of women and men in office environments. Of course, the distinctions between the sexes that she draws are exaggerated and not intended to reflect reality. Not so with those drawn by senior Pentagon officials, however. Whether such distinctions reflect reality or not, people frequently use gender stereotypes to estimate and evaluate not only their own abilities and performances but those of others as well. Responses to coworkers are heavily influenced by the stereotypes people use to interpret others' behavior.

Does gender stereotyping belong in the workplace? Are there any real differences between female and male peers, that is, individuals who hold the same types of jobs or work at the same level? If so, what are the differences, and when are they most often exhibited? If not, why do men and women in some situations feel awkward and uncomfortable in working together, and in other situations act as if each other's sex makes no difference at all?

In this chapter, I shall address issues pertaining to gender stereotyping of workplace peers. First, we shall consider whether gender stereotypes have any relation to actual sex differences exhibited at work. Although basic sex differences may be diminishing over time, female and male peers still could differ in ways that affect their work relationships. By reviewing research on task-oriented groups, we shall reach a conclusion about the extent of sex differences between women and men peers.

Second, we shall examine the effects of gender stereotypes such as those portrayed in the poem and the conditions under which they come into play. Sometimes, individuals bring a belief in gender stereotypes with them to their work relationships. Other times, it is the work environment that leads individuals to make more use of gender stereotypes than they would otherwise. Both personal and situational factors that contribute to gender stereotyping in work settings will be described.

Third, we shall explore the ways in which gender stereotyping influences the interactions between peers in skewed groups (i.e., groups in which the ratio of females to males is either very high or very low). In particular, we shall examine the effects of groups possessing "token" members of one sex on interactions between the tokens and the more dominant sex.

Finally, we shall discuss the implications of gender stereotyping and token-dominant dynamics in groups, identifying ways in which organizations and individuals can offset their negative effects.

Do Female and Male Peers Differ?

In our examination of behavior related to entry to the workplace, we found that the closer individuals get to making decisions about particular jobs, the less they differ according to sex. There are larger sex differences in early occupational aspirations and expectations, smaller sex differences in decisions to work, and minimal sex differences in decisions about job opportunities. If the same pattern of diminishing sex differences were to hold after individuals enter the workplace, we would expect negligible sex differences in peers' behavioral tendencies and responses to work situations. To investigate whether this expectation is warranted, we shall review research on a variety of topics related to behavior in task-oriented groups.[3]

One stream of research has examined the effect of the sex composition of groups on group performance. A meta-analysis of laboratory studies found that, overall, all-male groups tended to perform better than all-female groups. In addition, groups differed in the type of task that they performed best, perhaps due to differences in the preferred interaction styles of women and men found in separate meta-analyses. All-male groups were better at activities that called for high amounts of task-oriented behavior, such as "brainstorming" or generating possible solutions to a problem. All-female groups, in contrast, were better at activities that called for high amounts of social behavior, such as reaching a consensus on the best solution to a problem. Such differences are consistent with gender stereotypes. However, mixed-sex groups were slightly superior to both all-male and all-female groups. Although the activities at which these groups were best at were not identified in the meta-analysis, we might expect them to excel at activities that call for more of a balance between task-oriented and social behavior.[4]

Differences are most likely to appear, however, in newly formed groups in which members have little information about each other's competence. Sex differences in task versus social roles played in newly formed groups seem to result from group members' belief in gender stereotypes, particularly that males are more competent at tasks than females. However, when the group has some history and members have gained information about each other's competence, sex differences in interaction style tend to disappear. Members who are seen as higher in competence, regardless of whether they are women or men, tend to engage in more task behavior and less social behavior than group members who are seen as less competent.[5]

Other research has examined whether men or women emerge more often as leaders in groups that have no formally assigned leader. This question is particularly important because of the current trend in organizations toward maintaining fewer managerial levels and relying on work teams to provide their own direction. A meta-analysis of sex differences in the emergence of leaders distinguished between task leadership, social leadership, and leadership in general. Task and social leaders were considered to be individuals who made significant contributions to groups through their task-related or social behavior respectively. In support of gender stereotypes, emergent task leaders tended to be male whereas emergent social leaders tended to be female. When the type of leadership was unspecified, men emerged most often as leaders. However, the tendency for men to emerge as leaders was less prevalent in (1) groups that had been intact for longer periods of time, (2) studies conducted in real-world as opposed to laboratory settings, and (3) studies that were recently published.[6]

Individuals who are high in the tendency to dominate seem likely to emerge as group leaders. Since men tend to be more aggressive than women, it is not surprising that they also engage in more dominating behavior toward their opposite-sex peers. Various studies have found that women talk less, are interrupted more, and are disagreed with more than men.[7] Since the tendency to dominate is more compatible with the masculine than the feminine gender stereotype, what happens when high-dominance women work with low-dominance men?

Edwin Megargee assigned high-dominance and low-dominance individuals to dyads (pairs) and asked each dyad to decide on a leader before they proceeded to work on a task together. As expected, in same-sex dyads, individuals who were high in the tendency to dominate tended to be chosen as group leaders. In mixed-sex dyads where the male was high in dominance and the female low, the male tended to be chosen as leader. However, when the female was high in dominance and the male was low, the male still tended to be chosen as leader.[8]

These results were obtained, however, from newly formed dyads in which members had very little information about each other. In such circumstances, gender stereotypes of men as leaders might be expected to hold most often. To test how well gender stereotypes hold when more information is available about group members, other researchers conducted a variation of Megargee's study. They gave members of dyads information about each other's competence at the task they were about to do prior to the selection of a leader. In dyads where the high-dominance female was also more competent than the low-dominance male, the female tended to be chosen as the leader more often than when information about task competence was unavailable. Such information contributed to the selection of the more competent person, female or male, as leader, rather than the selection of the male on the basis of gender stereotypes.[9]

Women and men may not be acting in as stereotypical fashion in groups as they once were. Ross Webber examined interactions between the sexes in four-person student teams formed in graduate business courses at Columbia and Wharton. Each team worked together for 13 weeks at analyzing cases and writing group reports. Teams were studied at two different periods of time, the early 1970s and the early 1980s. In the 1970s teams, women who were the minority in a team typically did not strive for the leadership role and were excluded from power if they did. Although perceived by the men as contributing little to group performance, women on these teams preferred their minority status. However, conflict levels were at their highest in female-majority teams. Not only did men feel resentful of their minority status, but every male on a female-majority team felt that he was the leader.[10]

There was a dramatic improvement in relations between the sexes in the 1980s teams. Women were much more likely to exercise leadership, whether they were the minority or the majority, and they were increasingly seen by their male colleagues as being successful leaders. Conflict levels declined considerably on female-majority teams. In addition, men were much less threatened when working with women than before. Although these results were obtained from an elite sample, they suggest that the ability of women and men to work together in groups has significantly improved.

One of the sentiments not expressed in Josefowitz's poem is that women have been regarded by many people as possessing a special ability to sense the feelings and thoughts of others ("women's intuition"). One study investigated task-oriented dyads to determine whether the role that an individual plays as leader or subordinate affects his or her level of sensitivity. It found no distinction between women and men in sensitivity to others. Instead, individuals in the subordinate role, regardless of sex, were more sensitive to leaders than leaders were to subordinates. Because women have been in the subordinate role in our society more frequently than men, what has been called "women's intuition" might more appropriately be called "subordinates' intuition." These results suggest that the assigning of roles to group members may override any potential sex difference in their sensitivity to other members.[11]

The concept of "fear of success" received a great deal of attention in the 1960s and 1970s as a personality characteristic that was supposed to distinguish between women's and men's responses to task-oriented situations. Matina Horner proposed that women have particular anxieties concerning success, because success is incompatible with the feminine gender stereotype and thereby may lead to rejection by others. As a result, Horner argued, women possess a motive to avoid success that is not present in men, leading them to lower their aspirations for success in groups or deny responsibility for their success when it occurs.[12]

This concept was initially popular because it reinforced different aspects of people's notions regarding the capabilities of the sexes. For some, it meant not that women were incapable but that they feared the consequences if they did well and performed to their full capabilities. For others, it justified a belief that women are less equipped than men to deal with situations that call for an achievement orientation.

However, Horner's theory failed to hold up under scrutiny. In later studies, fear of success appeared in women mostly for activities that were considered appropriate only for men. In activities considered appropriate for women or men, motives for avoiding success showed no sex difference. Apparently individuals of both sexes shy away from success when it will result in social disapproval. Thus fear of success seems a legitimate response of individuals to the anticipated reactions of others in special circumstances, rather than a generalized personality trait possessed more by women that affects their efforts to be successful in groups.[13]

Rather than sex differences or fear of success, sex role identity differences could influence behavior in peer groups. Androgyny is supposed to contribute to behavioral flexibility, which is necessary when people need to solve problems together. Androgynous individuals, who are able to play both task and social roles and to lead as well as follow, may tend to share the roles they perform in groups. In contrast, masculine individuals may tend to adopt task roles and act as the leader more than feminine individuals. In groups of masculine men and feminine women, the men may be more likely to lead and the women to follow.

Studies of the relationship between sex role identity and behavior in a task-oriented group support the notion that individuals who are high in masculinity, whether men or women, take a more active task role and emerge more often as group leaders. In groups where men are masculine and women feminine, men tend to dominate the leadership role. However, androgynous women and men tend to share leadership in mixed-sex task groups, particularly when they have some social support from other group members of their sex who are also androgynous. Thus the sex role identity of group members appears to have an important effect on their behavior in groups.[14]

I have not reviewed *all* of the research on sex differences in task-oriented groups, as it would be beyond the scope of this book to do so. However, the research findings presented suggest an explanation for the existence of differences between female and male peers in certain group situations. Sex differences reflecting gender stereotypes typically have been found in laboratory studies that ask strangers to work on a task together. When group members know something about each other or have been assigned a role in the group, sex differences tend to disappear. Men and women appear to adopt stereotypical roles when they are in unfamiliar situations, but drop such roles when the situation is more familiar and they have worked together longer. In addition, sex differences supporting gender stereotypes are less evident than before. Sex-role identity differences among group members may provide a better explanation for individual differences in behavior. However, we must also look to other explanations for the prevalence of gender stereotyping in the workplace.

Gender Stereotyping at Work

As the opening passages suggest, gender stereotypes can have considerable impact on how members of both sexes are regarded in work settings. The research evidence about whether women or men are evaluated more favorably for equivalent performance is mixed. Early reviews documented pro-male bias in most studies; however, a meta-analysis of sex differences in evaluations of performance in laboratory studies found little evidence for bias in favor of either sex. In addition, the presence or absence of a sex difference in evaluations was mostly unaffected by such factors as the sex of the evaluators, the physical attractiveness of the individuals being evaluated, and how recently the study was published.[15]

However, the meta-analysis did not examine the effect of individuals' adherence to gender stereotypes on their evaluations of others. A study in which college students were told that their evaluations would be used to make salary, promotion, and tenure decisions for professors uncovered such an effect. Women professors were evaluated less favorably by students who adhered to a traditional stereotype of women. However, evaluations of men professors were unaffected by gender stereotypes.[16]

Gender stereotypes, when applied to workplace peers, typically have less to do with the people being stereotyped than with the people doing the stereotyping and the situations in which stereotypes are made. Certain characteristics, both of individuals and situations, lead people to stereotype others.

Individuals who hold traditional attitudes towards women and their role in society are more likely to see working women and men in stereotypical terms than individuals with less traditional attitudes. A variety of personal characteristics appear to influence such attitudes. For example, one study found that the more frequently people attended church, the more traditional were their attitudes toward women. Regular churchgoers may consider and be more influenced by religious teachings about women rather than their own experiences. However, older and more educated individuals had less traditional attitudes toward women. Maturity and education, which broaden a person's knowledge and expose people to a greater variety of information about women, may enable them to distinguish women's actual characteristics from those assigned by the feminine gender stereotype.[17]

Other studies have found that women with high self-esteem hold less traditional attitudes than those with low self-esteem. Perhaps the latter lack the necessary confidence to adopt nontraditional roles in society or to advocate them for other women. Androgynous women and men, who are likely to be high in self-esteem, tend to hold less traditional attitudes toward women. However, feminine women and masculine men, whose sex role identity agrees with gender stereotypes, tend to hold more traditional attitudes.[18]

Situational characteristics also influence the manifestation of gender stereotypes in work settings. Over time, being supervised by a woman or simply working with women seems to affect attitudes toward them. In a study of the entry of women to the traditionally male field of firefighting, the longer men had worked with women firefighters, the less traditional their attitudes toward women in general and the more positive their evaluation of women firefighters. However, beliefs concerning preferential treatment for women as a group were unequivocal: while men were ready to accept women as individuals, they insisted that women be treated as individuals. Researchers at the U.S. Coast Guard Academy, from which at least one-half of Coast Guard officers graduate, found that male cadets' attitudes toward women were more positive after legislation mandating that women be integrated into the military services had been implemented than before. Thus male attitudes toward women workers are affected by personal experience with women on the job, whether it is in an office, firehouse, or ship. Men who have interacted with women peers longer are less likely to characterize them according to gender stereotypes.[19]

The Coast Guard Academy findings beg the rhetorical question, "Why were senior military officials so opposed to the inclusion of women in combat roles after the Persian Gulf war?" Was their upbringing, as influenced by parents, school, and the mass media, responsible? Would they have felt differently if they had been exposed to the military Barbie doll in their childhood? Why didn't their advanced age "broaden their knowledge base" about women's actual versus stereotypical characteristics in ways suggested by the study described above? Did their religious beliefs argue against acceptance of women as peers? Or was it simply because they had had little opportunity to work with women at their advanced level in the military hierarchy? We should not read too much into the views of only three top military officials, but provocative questions are certainly raised about how such views are developed and reinforced.

The sex ratio of a group (i.e., its ratio of women to men or vice versa) is another situational factor that affects whether gender stereotyping occurs. Based on her examination of male-female work relationships in a large industrial corporation, Rosabeth Kanter identified four types of groups of varying sex ratio that can exist in work settings. Although Kanter focused her analysis on small groups, which could be either work groups or groups of individuals who hold the same job such as manager, her analysis can be extended to groups of all sizes. *Uniform* groups, consisting of all males or all females, represent one extreme. By definition, there are no male-female issues in uniform groups. *Balanced* groups, consisting of approximately equal numbers of men and women, represent the other extreme. Attributes other than sex influence how individuals interact in balanced groups.[20]

Between these two extremes are skewed and tilted groups. *Skewed* groups have a ratio of one sex to another ranging from about 85:15 to almost 100:0. Members of the sex in abundance in skewed groups are called "dominants," because they are seen to control the group and its culture, and members of the other sex are called "tokens," because they are more often treated as representatives of their sex than as individuals. *Tilted* groups have less of an abundance of one sex over the other, with the ratio ranging from about 65:35 to about 85:15. In tilted groups, dominants become simply a majority and tokens a minority. Minority members may become allies with each other and have more of an effect on group culture in tilted than in skewed groups. They are distinguishable from each other, as well as different from the majority type.

In conclusion, several personal and situational factors influence the tendency for individuals to engage in gender stereotyping of others in work settings. Personal factors include personality characteristics such as sex-role identity and self-esteem, and demographic characteristics such as age and education, whereas situational factors include the extent of prior experience with opposite-sex peers and the sex ratio of the group. These two types of factors may interact to have additional effects.

Skewed Groups: Tokens and Dominants

Many researchers have examined the effects of being similar or dissimilar to others in a work setting on job satisfaction, commitment, absenteeism, turnover, adaptation, innovation, and other indicators of individuals' comfort levels and performance. For example, one study found that the greater the difference in sex and race between an individual and others in a work unit, the lower the individual's "attachment" to the organization. Kanter's theory of sex ratios provides a possible explanation for such results: As individuals become demographically dissimilar to their peers, they may find themselves in a skewed group being treated as tokens by the numerically dominant members.[21]

Since women have entered the management profession in large numbers, the overall proportions of women and men in managerial ranks have shifted from being skewed to being balanced. However, particularly at upper levels, the proportion of women to men managers in many organizations remains skewed. Thus the dynamics of such groups apply to many of the interactions that occur between women and men in management. In addition, even if a group currently has a tilted or balanced sex ratio, most of its members are likely to have belonged to a skewed group at one time. By examining the properties of skewed groups, we can better comprehend how such individuals' past experiences in groups may have shaped their responses to their present work situations.

Kanter chose the term *tokens* for the underrepresented members in a skewed group to highlight the special characteristics associated with being in that position.[22] Tokens do not merely differ from other group members along some particular dimension. They are categorized on the basis of an easily recognizable characteristic, such as sex, race, ethnic group, or age, characteristics that carry a set of assumptions about the token's traits and expected behavior. Tokens exist only in small numbers, and the rest of the group puts them in the position of representing their category, whether they want to or not. A token rarely becomes "just another member of the group." Although organizations sometimes deliberately set up token or display situations, any time people are in a group where others of their category are not usually found, they may find themselves tokens.

The special treatment that tokens receive in skewed groups is detrimental to their performance in several ways. First, because they are highly visible, tokens face additional performance pressures. Second, the differences between tokens and dominants tend to be exaggerated. Third, the characteristics of tokens are often distorted or misperceived because of the dominants' tendency to stereotype them. Let's examine each of these, considering the experience of token women in skewed groups as an example.

Tokens are subject to *performance pressures* because they get attention that individual members of the dominant group don't get, simply because they are different. Such attention could be seen as an advantage, and dominants often envy the attention that tokens receive. However, many token women have reported that they have to work twice as hard as men in their groups to have their competence recognized. The token woman has no trouble in having her presence noticed, but she does experience difficulty in having her achievements noticed. The organization also may attempt to show its enlightenment by displaying token women in ways that deny their individuality. At such occasions, women are singled out for the fact that they are female rather than for their particular accomplishments. The reaction of tokens to the different types of attention they receive is particularly noticed. While dominants may display disaffection with the company and get away with it, tokens display disaffection at greater risk.

Token women react to such performance pressures in several different ways. They may try to overachieve relative to their peers, a strategy that is unlikely to work for women who are less than exceptional performers. Trying to capitalize on their rarity as tokens and turning it to their advantage is also unlikely to succeed because it risks the displeasure of dominants. Finally, token women may seek to be "socially invisible" by avoiding events at which their token status would provide visibility and making little attempt to have their accomplishments known.

But this strategy results in limited recognition of their competence and the reduced likelihood of their receiving the rewards that could go with such recognition. It seems that no matter what coping strategy they adopt, token women face performance pressures that men in the dominant group do not face.

By their very presence, tokens also make dominants more aware of what they have in common, while at the same time posing a threat to that commonality. For example, if "boys will be boys," dominant males are even more so when token females are present. They may try to highlight what they can do in personal, sexual, and business affairs as men, in contrast to what the women can do. They also do not want women around at all times, choosing to exclude them from certain secretive activities. This process is called *boundary heightening*. It is seen publicly in the existence of exclusive clubs that are open only to men and at which boyish locker-room antics are reported to reign supreme. In work organizations, it is seen in male-oriented social functions that women are discouraged from attending.

Token women are left with few choices for responding to boundary heightening activities by men. They may accept isolation, opting for friendly but distant relations with the male members except at times when they are excluded. Or they may try to become insiders by defining themselves as exceptional members of their sex and turning against other women who attempt to join the group.

Token women also risk being classified according to the feminine gender stereotype, whether or not their personal characteristics are consistent with the stereotype. This process is called *role encapsulation*. Dominants' stereotypes of token women force them into playing limited roles. Such roles benefit men by providing them a familiar context for viewing women, thereby allowing them to make use of familiar forms of behavior. For example, when professional women are mistakenly taken to be secretaries, they are stereotyped as conforming to a traditionally subordinate female role. They may be further stereotyped by being assigned secretary-like functions in groups or by being given jobs that reflect their presumed feminine capabilities and concerns, such as equal employment opportunity or corporate social responsibility jobs.

Token women have few options for responding to role encapsulation. They may accept a stereotypical role, which could limit their participation in situations and lead to eliciting programmed male responses. If they try to fight being categorized, they risk being classified as "iron maidens" and face rejection by the group. Or token women may try to act in ways that are contrary to the feminine gender stereotype, no matter what personal style of behavior is most natural to them.

Kanter based her conclusions on her analysis of an environment in which men vastly outnumbered women in positions of authority. She assumed that her theories would apply equally well to women in male-dominated groups other than the ranks of management and to men in female-dominated groups. However, others have questioned the applicability of her theories to all types of skewed groups. According to most research evidence compiled since Kanter originally advanced her theories, token men do not experience the same negative consequences of numerical imbalance as token women. Instead, the visibility that token men receive can work to their advantage. For example, a study of police patrol teams and hospital nursing units found that token policewomen reacted with annoyance or resignation to their increased visibility, whereas token male nurses enjoyed the extra attention. Most token male nurses felt that patients attributed a higher status to them than female nurses, even when they said they were not physicians. Most also thought that physicians took them more seriously and gave them more responsibility than female nurses. In contrast, 42% of the token policewomen felt that they were the "black sheep" of their teams.[23]

Why do token men have different experiences than token women? Perhaps the negative effects for men of being tokens are offset by their being the higher-status individuals in our society, as male nurses suspected that patients felt. If this is the case, adding men to a group raises its status while adding women lowers its status. However, status is an intangible factor. A more concrete reason may be that most people know that workers in male-dominated occupations outearn those in female-dominated occupations. Thus the entry of women into male-dominated occupations may draw particularly negative reactions from men because they fear a loss in pay if women enter their fields in significant numbers. However, women in lower-paid, female-dominated occupations may be more accepting of men in work groups, even though they are tokens, because the entry of men into their fields may mean an increase in pay.

In conclusion, the sex ratio of a group has a powerful effect on the dynamics of work relationships among its members. I have placed special emphasis on the relationship between dominants and tokens in skewed groups, because this relationship is particularly relevant to the experiences of women and men in management. Tokens face a set of work conditions that differ from those of their numerically dominant colleagues and are particularly negative when the tokens are women in a male-dominated work setting and occupation. Although token or dominant status alone does not determine how one interacts with others, it does have an important influence on interactions between women and men in management ranks and in other types of groups.

Implications

At the beginning of this chapter, I posed the question of why women and men sometimes feel awkward and uncomfortable in working with each other and at other times feel perfectly at ease. Our review suggests that gender stereotyping contributes to awkwardness and discomfort. When gender stereotyping enters into a work relationship, the male's perception of the female is influenced more by the feminine stereotype than by her actual traits and behaviors and/or the female's perception of the male is influenced more by the masculine stereotype than by his actual traits and behaviors. As a result, groups may be prevented from developing the best solutions to problems because input from valuable members is ignored.

How can organizations reduce the effects of gender stereotyping among peers? One approach would be to rely on the effects of situational factors. In some situations, gender stereotyping diminishes without any managerial action required. This happens when employees gain experience over time in working with opposite-sex peers and also when they work with greater numbers of opposite-sex peers at a given time. The first token in a skewed group is the one who suffers most from performance pressures, boundary heightening, and role encapsulation; later tokens suffer less from these types of responses. Also, dominants who have been in a skewed group longer are less likely to stereotype tokens than new dominants in the group. So, if the numbers of men and women in a group are shifting in the direction of being more balanced, management may simply wait for the shift to happen. However, it is unfair to the individuals who are presently being stereotyped for management to take such a passive approach and hope that stereotyping will disappear on its own.

Organizations can proactively try to reduce the effects of gender stereotyping by improving the flow of information within their boundaries. Information about the qualifications and achievements of *all* group members should be made known, not just those with token or minority status. When these are identified in a formal written communication that is made public, distortion of the capabilities of token members and exaggeration of the differences between tokens and dominants are reduced.[24]

In the same vein, when an individual is promoted, it is important that people are made aware in writing of the specific skills, expertise, and accomplishments of the person that relate directly to the promotion. Again, this should take place for *all* individuals who are promoted, not just tokens or minorities, to avoid drawing attention to any particular type of group members. These formal actions reduce the potential for stereotyping due to insufficient or inaccurate information. In addition, management should be aware of what "the grapevine" is saying about why people are evaluated favorably or promoted and try to ensure that rumors flowing through the informal network of the organization are consistent with the facts distributed through formal channels.

Organizations can also make employees aware of their tendencies to stereotype others and seek to modify extreme tendencies through training. For example, all employees could be asked to complete a questionnaire that assesses belief in gender stereotypes. Those who are strongly inclined to stereotype could then be required to attend a special workshop that would provide them a common frame of reference in evaluating and working with others. Participants could be asked to evaluate hypothetical male and female employees that exhibited either stereotypical or nonstereotypical traits in different situations. Their ratings would be compared with the "correct" answers that evaluated employees in a gender-neutral fashion. Informal group discussion would then focus on any differences between the "correct" ratings and ratings based on gender stereotypes. Such discussion could enhance interest in the workshop while allowing different views of acceptable standards to emerge. "Frame of reference" training has been found to be effective in promoting consistency in individuals' evaluations of others, and it could be useful in modifying adherence to gender stereotypes.[25]

Organizations may also influence the extent of gender stereotyping by intentionally structuring work groups' membership and activities. Although problems associated with token-dominant dynamics in groups might be solved by simply adding minority members and eliminating the presence of tokens, this approach does more harm than good. Adding members to groups based on sex or some other visible characteristic unrelated to performance results in their success being seen as due to being in the right place at the right time, rather than having the right skills and expertise.[26]

Instead, management should reduce the uncertainty that group members feel about their activities and the qualifications of other members. For example, when a new group is formed, distribution of a written memo describing the group's task and the qualifications of each member for addressing the task discourages the tendency to stereotype due to insufficient or inaccurate information. The application of gender stereotypes may be further discouraged by structuring work in a way that requires group members to coordinate their efforts. When group members are dependent on each other and have to make mutual adjustments to accomplish work, they gain valuable experience in working with others and are less likely to engage in stereotyping.

Should formal work groups ever be comprised entirely of individuals who are minority members in a work setting, such as an all-female group in a male-dominated organization? Although such groups can provide valuable support for their members, members of other groups in the organization are likely to engage in boundary heightening in their interactions with an all-minority group in ways that inhibit its functioning. Thus such groups (at least on a formal basis) should be avoided if possible, as long as new members are not added or excluded solely because of their majority or minority status.

All of these recommendations assume that the basic problem to be solved in cross-sex work relationships is gender stereotyping. However, sometimes people feel awkward and uncomfortable in working with members of the opposite sex simply because of a lack of experience, not because of stereotyping. As they are gaining experience, such individuals can be assisted through training in basic social skills to help them to work with opposite-sex coworkers.[27]

In addition, individuals with token status are not powerless in their relationship with dominants. Tokens can do much to build their power and influence in groups, for example, by establishing themselves as indispensable to the group in some way. Tokens who develop special areas of expertise are more likely to receive attention because of their competence than because of their token status. They may also cultivate their skills at diagnosing power issues so that they are aware of how they may have the greatest impact on decisions in a given situation. Depending on their diagnosis, they may seek to influence the assumptions and objectives on which decisions are based, the alternatives to be considered, and/or the information available about alternatives.

Tokens may also build their power base through the ability to demonstrate self-confidence, take risks, and verbally advance their causes. Such skills are required not only of tokens but also of dominant group members to be successful.[28]

In conclusion, it may be tempting for management to claim that gender stereotyping is beyond its control and therefore to do nothing about it. Although organizations cannot ban gender stereotyping from the workplace, they have too much to lose from its negative effects to ignore the issue altogether. They will gain from taking steps both to reduce the likelihood that gender stereotyping will occur and to alleviate its effects when it does.

Gender stereotyping hinders the working relationships between males and females. What kind of effect it has depends on factors such as the personal characteristics of individuals, their experience in working with members of the opposite sex, and the proportions of men and women in occupations, jobs, and work groups. Managers can take actions to prevent the negative effects of these phenomena or to alleviate such effects when they occur. However, people have some say about whether such events interfere with their working relationships. Both men and women have the capability of recognizing that they have used gender stereotypes in the past and of discontinuing their further usage. They also can choose to refrain from engaging in dysfunctional token-dominant dynamics. Ultimately, men and women jointly determine through their attitudes and their actions whether they have good or poor work relationships, and whether they employ stereotypes such as those con- veyed in the poem at the beginning of this chapter.

Notes

1. N. Josefowitz, "Impressions from an Office," in *Is This Where I Was Going?* (New York: Warner Books, 1983). Reprinted with permission by the author.

2. M. Thompson, "Military Brass Backs Combat Ban for Women," *Hartford Courant, 154* (No. 170, 19 June 1991): A1, A7. © Knight-Ridder Newspapers.

3. K. L. Dion, "Sex, Gender, and Groups: Selected Issues," in *Women, Gender, and Social Psychology*, ed. V. E. O'Leary, R. K. Unger, and B. S. Wallston (Hillsdale, NJ: Lawrence Erlbaum, 1985); K. M. Bartol and D. C. Martin, "Women and Men in Task Groups," in *The Social Psychology of Female-Male Relations: A Critical Analysis of Central Concepts*, ed. R. D. Ashmore and F. K. Del Boca (Orlando, FL: Academic Press, 1986).

4. W. Wood, "Meta-Analytic Review of Sex Differences in Group Performance," *Psychological Bulletin, 102* (1987): 53-71; A. H. Eagly, *Sex Differences in Social Behavior: A Social-Role Interpretation* (Hillsdale, NJ: Lawrence Erlbaum, 1987), pp. 108-113; L.

L. Carli, *Are Women More Social and Men More Task Oriented? A Meta-Analytic Review of Sex Differences in Group Interaction, Reward Allocation, Coalition Formation, and Cooperation in the Prisoner's Dilemma Game*, Unpublished manuscript (Amherst: University of Massachusetts, 1982); L. R. Anderson and P. N. Blanchard, "Sex Differences in Task and Social-Emotional Behavior," *Basic and Applied Social Psychology*, 3 (1982): 109-139.

5. W. Wood and S. J. Karten, "Sex Differences in Interaction Style as a Product of Perceived Sex Differences in Competence," *Journal of Personality and Social Psychology*, 50 (1986): 341-347.

6. A. H. Eagly and S. J. Karau, "Gender and the Emergence of Leaders: A Meta-Analysis," *Journal of Personality and Social Psychology*, 60 (1991): 685-710.

7. C. Radecki and J. Jennings (Walstedt), "Sex as a Status Variable in Work Settings: Female and Male Reports of Dominance Behavior," *Journal of Applied Social Psychology*, 10 (1980): 71-85; M. A. Baker, "Gender and Verbal Communication in Professional Settings: A Review Of Research," *Management Communication Quarterly*, 5 (1991): 36-63; E. Aries, "Gender and Communication," in *Sex and Gender*, ed. P. Shaver and C. Hendrick (Newbury Park, CA: Sage, 1987); D. Tannen, Chapter 7, "Who's Interrupting? Issues of Dominance and Control," in *You Just Don't Understand: Women and Men in Conversation* (New York: Morrow, 1990).

8. E. I. Megargee, "Influence of Sex Roles on the Manifestation of Leadership," *Journal of Applied Psychology*, 53 (1969): 377-382.

9. R. A. Fleischer and J. M. Chertkoff, "Effects of Dominance and Sex on Leader Selection in Dyadic Work Groups," *Journal of Personality and Social Psychology*, 50 (1986): 94-99.

10. R. A. Webber, "Changes in Perception and Behavior in Mixed Gender Teams," *Human Resource Management*, 26 (No. 4, 1987): 455-467.

11. S. E. Snodgrass, "Women's Intuition: The Effect of Subordinate Role on Interpersonal Sensitivity," *Journal of Personality and Social Psychology*, 49 (1985): 146-155.

12. M. S. Horner, "Sex Differences in Achievement Motivation and Performance in Competitive and Noncompetitive Situations" (Unpublished doctoral dissertation, University of Michigan, 1968).

13. V. F. Nieva and B. A. Gutek, Chapter 8, "View of Women's Achievements," in *Women and Work: A Psychological Perspective* (New York: Praeger, 1981).

14. J. A. Kelly, H. E. Wildman, and J. R. Urey, "Gender and Sex Role Differences in Group Decision-Making Social Interactions: A Behavioral Analysis," *Journal of Applied Social Psychology*, 12 (1982): 112-127; J. R. Goktepe and C. E. Schneier, "Role of Sex, Gender Roles, and Attraction in Predicting Emergent Leaders," *Journal of Applied Psychology*, 74 (1989): 165-167; N. Porter, F. L. Geis, E. Cooper, and E. Newman, "Androgyny and Leadership in Mixed-Sex Groups," *Journal of Personality and Social Psychology*, 49 (1985): 808-823; J. L. Hegstrom and W. I. Griffith, "Dominance, Sex, and Leader Emergence," *Sex Roles*, 27 (1992): 209-220.

15. V. F. Nieva and B. A. Gutek, "Sex Effects on Evaluation," *Academy of Management Review*, 5 (1980): 267-276; J. Swim, E. Borgida, G. Maruyama, and D. G. Myers, "Joan McKay Versus John McKay: Do Gender Stereotypes Bias Evaluations?" *Psychological Bulletin*, 105 (1989): 409-429.

16. G. H. Dobbins, R. L. Cardy, and D. M. Truxillo, "The Effects of Purpose of Appraisal and Individual Differences in Stereotypes of Women on Sex Differences

in Performance Ratings: A Laboratory and Field Study," *Journal of Applied Psychology*, 73 (1988): 551-558.

17. D. D. Baker and D. E. Terpstra, "Locus of Control and Self-Esteem Versus Demographic Factors as Predictors of Attitudes Toward Women," *Basic and Applied Social Psychology*, 7 (1986): 163-172.

18. B. G. Harrison, R. F. Guy, and S. L. Lupfer, "Locus of Control and Self-Esteem as Correlates of Role Orientation in Traditional and Nontraditional Women," *Sex Roles*, 7 (1981): 1175-1187; S. J. Motowidlo, "Sex Role Orientation and Behavior in a Work Setting," *Journal of Personality and Social Psychology*, 42 (1982): 935-945; M. Collins, L. K. Waters, and C. W. Waters, "Relationships Between Sex-Role Orientation and Attitudes Toward Women as Managers," *Psychological Reports*, 45 (1979): 828-830.

19. H. F. Ezell, C. A. Odewahn, and J. D. Sherman, "The Effects of Having Been Supervised by a Woman on Perceptions of Female Managerial Competence," *Personnel Psychology*, 34 (1981): 291-299; J. M. Craig and R. R. Jacobs, "The Effect of Working with Women on Male Attitudes Toward Female Firefighters," *Basic and Applied Social Psychology*, 6 (1985): 61-74; G. Stevens and S. Gardner, "But Can She Command a Ship? Acceptance of Women by Peers at the Coast Guard Academy," *Sex Roles*, 16 (1987): 181-188.

20. R. M. Kanter, "Some Effects of Proportions on Group Life: Skewed Sex Ratios and Responses to Token Women," *American Journal of Sociology*, 82 (1977): 965-990; R. M. Kanter, Chapter 8, "Numbers: Minorities and Majorities," in *Men and Women of the Corporation* (New York: Basic Books, 1977).

21. J. Pfeffer, "Organizational Demography," in *Research in Organizational Behavior*, vol. 5, ed. L. L. Cummings and B. M. Staw (Greenwich, CT: JAI Press, 1983); A. S. Tsui, T. Egan, and C. O'Reilly III, "Being Different: Relational Demography and Organizational Attachment," in *Proceedings: Annual Meeting of the Academy of Management*, ed. J. L. Wall and L. R. Jauch (Miami Beach, 1991).

22. Kanter, "Some Effects of Proportions on Group Life"; Kanter, Chapter 8, "Numbers: Minorities and Majorities."

23. J. D. Yoder, "Rethinking Tokenism: Looking Beyond Numbers," *Gender & Society*, 5 (1991): 178-192; E. M. Ott, "Effects of the Male-Female Ratio at Work: Policewomen and Male Nurses," *Psychology of Women Quarterly*, 13 (1989): 41-57; C. L. Williams, *Gender Differences at Work: Women and Men in Nontraditional Occupations* (Berkeley: University of California Press, 1989).

24. L. Falkenberg, "Improving the Accuracy of Stereotypes Within the Workplace," *Journal of Management*, 16 (1990): 107-118.

25. Dobbins et al., "The Effects of Purpose of Appraisal and Individual Differences in Stereotypes"; H. J. Bernardin and M. R. Buckley, "Strategies in Rater Training," *Academy of Management Review*, 6 (1981): 205-212.

26. Falkenberg, "Improving the Accuracy of Stereotypes Within the Workplace."

27. R. L. Dipboye, "Some Neglected Variables in Research on Discrimination in Appraisals," *Academy of Management Review*, 10 (1985): 116-127.

28. G. T. Fairhurst and B. K. Snavely, "Majority and Token Minority Group Relationships: Power Acquisition and Communication," *Academy of Management Review*, 8 (1983): 292-300.

5

Dealing With Sexuality in the Workplace

The Case of the Tattooed Lady

When Newscaster Liz Randolph joined WBZZ-FM radio in Pittsburgh, she was told that she was expected to join in the repartee with zany drive-time disc jockeys Jim Quinn and "Banana Don" Jefferson as part of the lead-in to the news. The Quinn and Banana Show featured the team's irreverent, fast-paced banter between top-40 music. From all reports, Randolph was able to hold her own in this daily battle of wits at the beginning. But things soon got out of control.

While Randolph was on a Caribbean cruise in February 1986, Quinn and Banana aired a series of skits titled "The Love Bloat." The skits implied that Randolph was having sex with the crew. As an example of the level of humor involved, Randolph says in one of the skits, "Oh, Captain, what a big dingy you have!"

Over the next two years, a series of on-air jokes were apparently premised on the idea that Randolph was a nymphomaniac with a preference for group sex. Listeners were told that the prisoners at Allegheny County Jail voted her Miss Congeniality after she did a story there. Jokes were aired about her involvement with the Pittsburgh Steelers, the Marine Corps, and the Naval Academy. Listeners were encouraged to call in and report where Liz Randolph's toothbrush had been found. One of these callers turned out to be an ex-boyfriend holding a grudge against her.

On January 22, 1988, just before Randolph was to do the news, the team aired a prerecorded joke, performed by a disc jockey at a sister station, that involved a supposed tattoo on her forehead and oral sex. Randolph left the studio without doing the newscast.

Randolph received psychiatric treatment, including hospitalization, for the panic attacks she suffered as a result of the on-air harassment. This fact, too, was aired. At one point, Quinn interrupted the news broadcast to announce that Randolph had seen *Couch Trip*—a film about a mental patient who becomes a talk show host—because Randolph thought it was her autobiography.

Cliff Tuttle[1]

Issues pertaining to the expression of sexuality arise in all types of organizations, from fast-and-loose radio stations to staid (on the surface) corporate offices. In this chapter, we shall discuss *sexual harassment*, or the directing of unwelcome sexual attention by one member of an organization toward another, and *organizational romances*, or the sharing of welcome sexual attention by two members of an organization. Sexual harassment is a matter of public concern with potential legal ramifications. Organizational romances are a frequent subject of public debate: How should participants and their organizations handle them? Even if they are not the participants, men and women in organizations frequently have to deal with the intermingling of work roles and sexual roles by other employees.

Sexual harassment has become a highly charged public issue. As discussed in Chapter 1, incidents such as those involving Lisa Olson and the New England Patriots, the Tailhook Association convention, and Anita Hill and later U.S. Supreme Court Justice Clarence Thomas, have received considerable publicity. Sexual harassment is primarily directed toward women, but also toward men. A study of over 20,000 federal employees in 1980 found that 42% of female employees and 15% of male employees reported having experienced some form of uninvited and unwanted sexual attention in the previous 24 months. A similar study of over 8,000 federal employees in 1987 yielded virtually identical percentages. These figures show that the public attention directed toward sexual harassment has been well-deserved.[2]

Organizational romances have been less a matter of public concern than sexual harassment, although they are often the subject of titillating television and radio talk shows. (Lisa Mainiero, author of a popular book on the topic, *Office Romance: Love, Power, and Sex in the Workplace,* reports that she receives invitations from TV talk shows just before Valentine's Day every year.[3]) Although sexual harassment is illegal, there are no laws against organizational romances. Sexual harassment usually victimizes and offends the target person. The "victim" of an organizational romance is less clear, although one or both parties may pay a price in their emotional health, task assignments, or career advancement if others are offended by the romance. In such cases, the participants are seen as bringing on their own troubles rather than being victimized by others.

We shall examine researchers' explanations for and individuals' experiences with both sexual harassment and organizational romances in the workplace. In addition, we shall discuss what organizations and individuals can do when such incidents occur. Sexuality cannot be banned from the workplace, but also cannot be ignored. Its presence has to be addressed, especially in situations where there are effects on the performance and morale of employees.

Sexual Harassment

The Issue of Definition

Most people recognize that a line needs to be drawn between acceptable and unacceptable sexually oriented behavior in the workplace. However, the question remains as to exactly what types of behavior constitute sexual harassment. In other words, where should the line be drawn?[4]

Definitions of sexual harassment generated by surveys and government agencies provide some guidance, but nothing definitive. These definitions have varied as follows: (a) An early study defined sexual harassment as "any repeated and unwanted sexual comments, looks, suggestions or physical contact that you find objectionable or offensive and causes you discomfort on your job." (b) A later study concluded that sexual harassment consists of four types of behaviors: seductive behavior (inappropriate and offensive but essentially sanction-free advances), sexual bribery (solicitation of sexual activity by promise of reward), threat (coercion of sexual activity by threat of punishment), and sexual imposition (forceful behavior or assault). (c) The U.S. Office of Personnel Management (OPM), in banning sexual harassment within the federal government, defined it as "deliberate or repeated unsolicited verbal comments, gestures, or physical contact of a sexual nature which are unwelcome." This definition was used as the basis for the 1980 and 1987 studies of federal employees. (d) The U.S. Equal Employment Opportunity Commission (EEOC) ruled in 1980 that sexual harassment would be considered an unlawful employment practice under Title VII of the 1964 Civil Rights Act. It defined sexual harassment as "unwelcome sexual advances, requests for favors, and other verbal or physical conduct of a sexual nature" when submission to or rejection of the conduct enters into employment decisions and/or the conduct interferes with work performance or creates a hostile work environment.[5]

These definitions share several key elements. Harassing behavior is regarded as unwelcome and unsolicited, and it can be either verbal (such as the unwelcome sexual comments toward Liz Randolph by the disc jockeys) or physical. However, agreement is lacking on which actions constitute harassment. The first definition includes comments, looks, suggestions, and physical contact. The OPM definition adds gestures to the first definition but leaves out looks (unless they are included with gestures). The second definition is the most precise, including behaviors that vary both in severity (with seductive behavior being less severe and sexual imposition being more severe) and in the intended consequences for the victim (with sexual bribery and threat offering specific consequences and seductive behavior and imposition being offensive in themselves without further consequences). However, the EEOC definition is the least precise, specifying advances and propositions but leaving all other offending behaviors as "other verbal and physical conduct of a sexual nature." In fact, when it issued its ruling, the EEOC correctly anticipated that its definition of sexual harassment would be regarded by many as too vague and in need of clarification. Others were left to interpret exactly what conduct is meant by it and when such conduct violates the EEOC guidelines.

The U.S. Supreme Court generally upheld the EEOC guidelines in 1986 in *Meritor Savings Bank vs. Vinson*, the first case of sexual harassment it considered. It concluded that two types of harassment are actionable under Title VII. In *quid pro quo* harassment, sexual activity is requested as a condition for gaining a job, promotion, raise, or some other job benefit. In *hostile environment* sexual harassment, one employee makes sexual requests, comments, looks, and so on toward another employee and thereby creates a hostile environment in which that employee must work, even when no economic benefits are lost as a result. However, the Supreme Court failed to define exactly what constitutes a hostile work environment.[6]

Given the uncertainty over what legally constitutes sexual harassment, individuals' own definitions assume considerable importance in determining the sexually oriented behaviors that they feel entitled to initiate and their responses to behaviors initiated by others. In fact, people vary widely in their personal definitions of sexual harassment. One study found that about 80% of adults thought that requests for dates or sexual activity, coupled with the understanding that denial would hurt the individual's job situation and compliance would help, constituted harassment, but only 20% considered positive comments of a sexual nature (e.g., "You look sexy today") to be harassment. A sample of working women included sexual propositions and touching, grabbing, or brushing, but not staring or flirting in their personal definitions of sexual harassment; they were evenly divided over whether sexual remarks, suggestive gestures, or sexual relations should be included. A study of undergraduate and graduate business students yielded similarly varied definitions. In addition, people are more likely to view certain behaviors as sexual harassment when the initiator is an individual's supervisor rather than a coworker. In general, sexual harassment is more likely to be seen in a situation when (a) coercion is present, (b) there are job consequences for the victim, (c) the harasser is at a higher hierarchical level than the victim, and (d) the harasser has behaved similarly towards the victim and other individuals over time.[7]

These definitions are influenced by individuals' personal and job characteristics. Sex has the strongest effect: Men consistently see less sexual harassment than women do. In addition, men are more likely than women to perceive the victims as contributing to their own harassment, either by provoking it or by not properly handling "normal" sexual attention. Sex role identity has a minor effect on definitions of sexual harassment, but not as great as that of sex. An individual's managerial level also influences perceptions of sexual harassment, with managers at lower levels more likely to see sexual harassment as a problem than those at middle levels. Top managers are the least likely to acknowledge sexual harassment.[8]

We see ambiguity in the definitions of sexual harassment provided by government agencies and courts and variability in individuals' own definitions of sexual harassment. What constitutes sexual harassment to some is simply the harmless expression of an individual's basically sexual nature to others. Some people are flattered by sexual attention that others find repulsive. In short, drawing a line between acceptable and unacceptable sexually oriented behavior in the workplace is not easy. Differences of opinion over where the line should be drawn make it difficult for organizations to carry out their legal obligation to discourage sexual harassment within their boundaries. In addition, the presence of sexually oriented behaviors in a work setting may affect the productivity of individuals, their work groups, and thereby the organization as a whole. To understand these effects, we will examine some explanations of sexual harassment to see how well they account for men's and women's experiences.

Explanations

Four general models have been offered as explanations for sexual harassment. According to the *sociocultural model*, sexual harassment has little to do with sexuality—it is an expression of power and hostility. In this view, individuals with the least amount of power in society, meaning women in most cultures, are the most likely to be harassed. In a patriarchal society that rewards males for aggressiveness and domineering behavior and females for passivity and compliant behavior, sexual harassment may almost be regarded as a male prerogative. Harassment under such conditions is likely to appear in the form of extreme "do it or else" behavior.[9]

The opposite view of sexual harassment is that it has everything to do with sexuality. Individuals with strong sex drives are sexually aggressive toward others due to biological necessities. Therefore, it should be neither surprising nor of particular concern that individuals exhibit such aggressiveness in work settings as well as elsewhere. It is also assumed that men and women are naturally attracted to each other and like to interact in sexually oriented ways in the workplace. This view, labeled the *natural/biological model* of sexual harassment, trivializes the issue and claims that sexual harassment represents a harmless behavior to accept, rather than a problem to solve.[10]

A third explanation, labeled the *organizational model*, suggests that certain organizational characteristics set the stage for sexual harassment. The hierarchical structure of organizations grants higher-level employees legitimate power over lower-level employees. Also, some employees, because they have gained critical expertise or information that other employees value, may have personal power over others independent of their position in the organizational hierarchy. Such situations provide the opportunity to use the promise of rewards or the threat of punishments to obtain sexual gratification from others. The reaction of the victim to the harasser will vary according to the nature and amount of the harasser's power. However, individuals who have more access to formal grievance procedures or are more capable of obtaining other jobs may be less likely to experience or tolerate sexual harassment deriving from such uses of power.[11]

In the *sex role spillover model*, the effects of sex role expectations in an organizational context are emphasized. The term *sex role spillover* refers to the carryover into the workplace of gender-based expectations that are irrelevant or inappropriate at work. Sex role spillover is most likely to occur when the sex ratio of a group is skewed in either direction, making members of the minority sex more noticeable and subject to special attention. As we saw in Chapter 4, women in male-dominated groups and men in female-dominated groups experience sex role spillover because they are assumed to be basically different from members of the dominant sex and therefore are treated differently. They may experience more harassment than individuals who stand out less in their work environments. According to this explanation, incidents of sexual harassment vary according to the sex ratio of the group.[12]

Three different sex ratios (occupation, job, and work group) are relevant to male-female work relationships. The sex ratio of an occupation is specified by the proportions of men and women who hold jobs in it nationwide. However, those figures do not necessarily reflect the sex ratio of the job. Even if the sex ratio of an occupation is skewed or tilted in one direction, the sex ratio of jobs within it in a particular organization could be skewed or tilted in the other direction. For example, there are more than three waitresses for every waiter, but some restaurants hire only waiters. Finally, the sex ratio of the individual's work group, consisting of the people with whom he or she interacts on a daily basis, may differ from the other two sex ratios. The work group may include supervisors, subordinates, and colleagues and does not necessarily consist of people in the same organizational unit.[13]

The sex ratios of the three types of groups differ in the immediacy of their impact on individuals' work experiences. The sex ratio of the occupation has the least impact on daily behavior at work, but it is part of the context in which this behavior occurs. The sex ratio of the job has some impact, but the sex ratio of the work group, the people with whom one most interacts, has the most immediate effect. In a skewed work group, the greater visibility of tokens, particularly if they are newcomers, may lead to their being scapegoats for the frustration of dominants. If they have peers who resent their presence, tokens may experience sexual harassment as a way to make them feel isolated and uncomfortable enough to resign.

Experiences

Each of these models could provide at least a partial explanation of sexual harassment in the workplace. To understand their relative merits, we need to examine experiences with sexual harassment in a variety of work situations. Data collected by both Gutek and the federal studies shed light on the underlying causes and effects of sexual harassment.

Barbara Gutek obtained data from representative samples of adult female and male workers in the Los Angeles area. She concluded that the presence of sex role spillover and the form that it takes depends on whether the person being considered is in the minority or majority and whether the person is female or male. Women in nontraditional occupations and jobs perceive their differential treatment to be harassment when the treatment is sexually oriented. Men in nontraditional occupations and jobs are less likely to see the sexual attention they receive as harassment. Women in traditional occupations and jobs whose work brings them into frequent contact with men report that the sexuality aspect of the female sex role spills over into the work role. They see aspects of sexuality as entering into their jobs, but they are less likely than nontraditionally employed women to see these aspects as harassment. Men in traditional occupations and jobs with female-dominated work groups report only the milder types of sexually-oriented behavior directed towards themselves, perhaps reflecting the fact that they are more likely to be the supervisors in such situations. Balanced occupations and jobs stimulate less sex role spillover or problems with harassment for individuals than nontraditional work.[14]

In the 1987 federal study, 42% of female and 14% of male federal employees had been harassed in the previous 24 months. Supervisors were more likely to be the harassers of female victims (29%) than of male victims (19%). In contrast, subordinates were more likely to be the harassers of male victims (10%) than of female victims (2%). These differences support the organizational model of sexual harassment. The power differential resulting from the relative positions in the organizational hierarchy of the harasser and victim appeared to contribute to the experiences of female victims more than those of male victims. The fact that more women had been harassed than men may be because more women had male supervisors than vice versa. However, it may also have reflected the fact that men have more power in American society in general, supporting the sociocultural model. Nonetheless, peers and other employees without supervisory authority over victims were the most common harassers for both sexes (69% for female victims, 77% for male victims). (Percentages add to more than 100% because some victims had been harassed by more than one type of individual.)

Women's harassers were most likely to be older, married men, whereas men's harassers were most likely to be younger, single women. This may be because females were more likely to be harassed by superiors, who tend to be older than themselves, and that males were more likely to be harassed by subordinates, who tend to be younger than themselves. Very few of the female (4%) or male (7%) victims went along with the sexual attention directed toward them, refuting the natural/biological model from the victim's perspective. These results do not reveal whether the natural/biological model would explain the harasser's motivation, because the federal studies focused on the perceptions of victims.

Other data on the experiences of federal workers do not make a convincing case for the superiority of any of the models of sexual harassment. Single, divorced, and separated employees, whether women or men, were more likely to be victims than married employees, which supports the natural/biological model if unmarried employees are assumed to be the more sexually available. However, employees who were highly dependent on their job were more likely to be victims, lending credence to the organizational model. Men and women in nontraditional jobs were more likely to be sexually harassed than others, supporting the sex role spillover model. Also, the greater the concentration of the opposite sex in the immediate work group of the employee, the greater the incidence of sexual harassment.[15]

In conclusion, men and women both define and experience sexual harassment differently. Women are inclined to see more behavior as sexual harassment and to be bothered more by it. This may be because women are harassed more by their superiors, who hold organizationally approved power over them, than men are. However, the majority of both female and male victims are harassed by their workplace peers. The sex ratio of the occupation, job, and work group also affect experiences with sexual harassment. Sex role spillover occurs more in skewed groups than in those with a balanced sex ratio. It is seen in the carryover of aspects of sexuality into the job according to the sex of the dominant group. It is also seen in the directing of unwelcome attention of all kinds, including sexual, toward the minority members of groups.

As a result, sexual harassment is an issue that sets many male and female peers at odds with each other. In the last section of this chapter, we shall discuss steps that organizations and individuals can take to try to prevent sexual harassment and deal with it when it occurs.

Organizational Romances

Sexual interest in a coworker is not always unwelcome. In some cases, it is reciprocated and serves as the basis for an organizational romance between two employees. Organizational romances are relationships between women and men working together that are characterized by mutual sexual attraction and made known to others through the participants' actions.[16]

Although most people root for lovers in principle because they like to believe that romantic relationships can have happy endings, organizational romances are controversial. Various observers have sharply disagreed over their merits and how they should be handled. Margaret Mead argued that much like the taboos against sexual expression in the family that are necessary for children to grow up safely, taboos against sexual involvements at work are necessary for men and women to work together effectively. Eliza Collins recommended that both individuals be fired, or, if the more valuable person can still be effective, the other be fired.[17]

Others have argued that people do not need protection or taboos but mutual respect for the freedom and rights of others, including the right to participate in an organizational romance. This right was defended by Mary Cunningham, who resigned from a vice-president position at Bendix in 1980 amidst considerable media attention due to allegations of her having a romantic involvement with her boss, the company chairman, that had helped her career. (She subsequently married him.) Afterwards, Cunningham stressed the value of romances that lead to marriage: "When a man and woman working in the same company cultivate a relationship that eventually leads to marriage, it enhances the couple's creativity as a unit" and helps the company's bottom line. Therefore, organizational romances may benefit as well as hinder productivity.[18]

Most individuals have to deal with both the need for intimacy and the need for accomplishment. Because the workplace is a particularly convenient setting for meeting attractive people of the opposite sex, individuals are frequently faced with situations where they have to choose which need, if not both, they will fulfill. While recognizing that romantic relationships pose problems for their organizations, they still have their own needs that may conflict, and must be reconciled, with the needs of the business.

Beliefs

I conducted a study to provide insight into the choices that the "managers of tomorrow" might make when it comes to organizational romances. Two groups of students were surveyed, undergraduate business students, most of whom expected to hold full-time jobs, and evening MBA students, most of whom already held full-time jobs. The study examined individuals' beliefs concerning the positive effects of sexual intimacy, the desirability of managerial actions to discourage it, the acceptability of sexually oriented behavior in general, and whether they would participate in an organizational romance. It also examined the difference between men's and women's beliefs and between the beliefs of undergraduates and evening MBAs.[19]

The results of the survey, summarized in Table 5.1, revealed an uneasy coexistence between sexual intimacy and work. Individuals were low in their endorsement of positive benefits that might arise from sexual intimacy at work. They strongly disagreed with the statement that sexual relations foster better communications and disagreed to a lesser extent with the statement that sexual intimacy makes for a more harmonious work environment. A relationship leading to marriage was regarded more positively, though individuals still disagreed more than they agreed with Mary Cunningham on its benefits.

Respondents believed strongly that management should try to discourage sexual propositions toward coworkers and that supervisors who direct sexual attention toward their subordinates should be reprimanded. They were more neutral about the use of reprimands when any worker, not necessarily a supervisor, directed sexual attention toward another. When sexually oriented behavior did not affect productivity, responses were also close to neutral.

Table 5.1 Beliefs Concerning Sexual Intimacy in the Workplace

	Combined (N = 351)	Male (N = 198)	Female (N = 153)
1. Sexual relations foster better communication between the workers involved.	2.05	2.33	1.68 **
2. Some sexual intimacy among coworkers can create a more harmonious work environment.	3.30	3.58	2.95 **
3. When two workers cultivate a relationship that eventually leads to marriage, it enhances their creativity as a unit and helps their company's bottom line.	3.51	3.57	3.44
4. Management should take strong steps to discourage sexual propositions toward coworkers.	5.27	4.97	5.64 **
5. Supervisors who direct sexual attention toward their subordinates should be reprimanded.	5.71	5.53	5.95 *
6. Any worker who directs sexual attention toward another should be reprimanded.	3.83	3.71	3.98
7. Companies ought to ignore sexually oriented behavior among coworkers as long as it doesn't affect productivity.	4.34	4.47	4.17
8. It is all right for someone to look for a marriage partner at work.	5.15	5.22	5.07
9. It is all right for someone to dress attractively to draw the attention of coworkers of the opposite sex.	4.71	4.98	4.37 **
10. I would be offended by a coworker flirting with the supervisor.	4.42	4.29	4.59
11. I would never get intimately involved with a coworker.	3.51	3.20	3.91 **
12. I would never get intimately involved with my supervisor.	4.43	4.13	4.82 **

SOURCE: G. N. Powell, "What Do Tomorrow's Managers Think About Sexual Intimacy in the Workplace?" *Business Horizons, 29* (No. 4, July/August 1986): 32-33.
NOTE: All statements were rated from strongly disagree (1) to strongly agree (7). Mean scores are shown, with the higher scores italicized for significant sex differences.
* $p < .01$; ** $p < .001$

Individuals showed a tolerance for some workplace attempts to satisfy needs for intimacy. Looking for a marriage partner was generally acceptable. Dressing attractively to draw attention from others was more acceptable than unacceptable. Flirting with the supervisor aroused more disapproval. Respondents were disinclined to say "never" about intimate involvements with coworkers themselves. Supervisors, though, were regarded less favorably as sexual partners than coworkers.

Overall, individuals seemed to agree that some forms of sexual intimacy are acceptable in the workplace, as long as they are not extreme and have no adverse effect on productivity. Intimate exchanges between supervisors and subordinates were regarded more negatively than those between coworkers in general. Also, individuals who already held full-time jobs responded more negatively to sexual intimacy in the workplace than those who were not yet in the work force. The undergraduates were more optimistic than the evening MBAs, believing that sexual intimacy and work can be mixed successfully.

However, there were considerable differences in the beliefs of female and male respondents. Women saw less positive value in sexual intimacy in the workplace, desired more managerial action to discourage sexually oriented behavior, regarded sexually oriented behavior by others as less acceptable, and were less inclined than men to get involved in organizational romances themselves. Since women are more likely than men to see sexual harassment in the workplace and to be concerned about it, their negative reactions should not be surprising. Given their historically lower status, women have been the ones who suffered more when sexual liaisons became public knowledge. When decisions are made to fire the least valuable person, that person is more likely to be the woman. Thus it is understandable that women disapprove of sexual intimacy entering the workplace more strongly than men. They rightfully see themselves as having the most to lose if it does.

Explanations and Experiences

Robert Quinn and Patricia Lees distinguished between three types of organizational romances.[20] One type, labeled *true love*, involves two people who have a sincere, long-term interest in each other and usually leads to marriage. This type of relationship, which Mary Cunningham wrote about, arouses the fewest objections from coworkers, particularly when it occurs between peers. In the second type, the *fling*, both participants become deeply excited and involved, but the relationship ends quickly. A fling meets with less approval from coworkers than true love, but more than the *utilitarian relationship*, which involves some trade-off between sexual adventure and ego satisfaction for one employee and job or career advancement for the other. Because this relationship violates coworkers' sense of equity in the workplace, it provokes the most extremely negative reactions.[21]

Most organizational romances are between higher-status males and lower-status females. A survey of romances in white-collar settings found that 62% involved a man in a higher position, 30% involved men and women at the same level, and only 8% involved a woman in a higher position, possibly because more men are in management positions, particularly at upper levels. This is not to say that, to quote the poem at the beginning of Chapter 4, if "she's having lunch with the boss, they must be having an affair." However, a large majority of romances involve a power differential, suggesting that the status of employees plays some role in the relationship.[22]

Other factors besides status contribute to the existence of organizational romances. Proximity is important, because working closely with others sets the stage for a romantic relationship to develop. The intensity of the work relationship, stimulated by the pursuit of similar work goals and performance of similar tasks, may create an additional feeling of excitement that fosters interpersonal attraction and leads to romance. Romances are especially common in professions where employees are expected to spend long hours on the job or engage in extensive travel together. Gutek's study suggested that the sex ratio of the occupation, job, and work group also influence the tendency for organizational romances to arise. Physical attractiveness influences work relationships in some work environments more than others, such as in female-dominated occupations and jobs with male-dominated work groups, raising the possibility that romances are more likely to flourish in such environments.[23]

Getting involved in an organizational romance is a risky endeavor, particularly for women since they are most often the lower-status individuals. When partners differ in hierarchical level, other workers may lose respect for the higher-level employee, feeling that his or her professional judgment has been clouded. The lower-level employee may begin to wonder whether his or her progress in the organization is due to competence or favoritism, and others may wonder the same. The risks to home and family if one or both employees has another romantic commitment are also high. Such concerns may prompt employees to try to hide their romance, although such attempts are typically futile. Most coworkers are sensitive to even minor changes in behavior and can sense that a romantic relationship exists whether it is publicly announced or not.

Matters become even more complicated when employees who are romantically involved with each other take on other partners in the same organization. According to employees of a trendy women's apparel manufacturer, the company's fortunes suffered when one of the firm's co-owners engaged in extramarital affairs with several employees to the knowledge of his wife, the other co-owner. In this case, involvement of a high-status male with lower-status females contributed to bitter conflict between him and an equally high-status female that eventually hurt the company's bottom line.[24]

Organizational romances invoke issues of power and dependency. The more powerful employee is the one who is giving more than he or she is getting, and therefore is less dependent on the relationship. Three kinds of dependency may be at stake. One is *task dependency*, which exists when a worker depends on another to perform his or her function effectively. A second, *career dependency*, involves individuals who desire advancement in organizations that are dependent on the consent of others. In manager-subordinate relationships, subordinates often exchange working hard (satisfying the manager's task dependency on the subordinate) for the reward of career advancement (for which the subordinate depends on the manager).

In an organizational romance, a *romantic dependency* is added to an otherwise work-oriented relationship that threatens the balance between task and career dependencies, which in turn activates a generally negative reaction from peers. Other group members, who are blocked from interacting with the two partners in the romantic domain, fear that their interactions with the partners in the task and career domains will be altered because of the romantic relationship, particularly when the partners are at different levels. They fear that task or career rewards will be handed out in exchange for sexual favors, thereby creating an inequitable situation. When the partners are at the same level, however, the effect of the relationship does not seem so troublesome.

When there is an imbalance of power in a romantic relationship, there is a high potential for exploitation of whoever is more dependent on the relationship. The higher-level employee can use the personal exchange to force the lower-level employee to increase task performance. However, the lower-level employee can use the personal exchange to argue for favorable task assignments or work conditions. Clearly there is a threat to the careers and self-image of employees as well as the morale and productivity of coworkers. Utilitarian romances present the biggest threat. When rewards are deliberately granted on the basis of personal relationships, morale is affected and the organization is rendered less effective. Although flings are also disruptive because of their effect on coworkers' perceptions of workplace inequities, these relationships are motivated by infatuation or ego rather than job or power enhancement and pass quickly. Relationships based on true love and long-term interest, particularly between peers, are the least threatening and may contribute to the couple's productivity.

True-love relationships seem the most difficult to maintain in a skewed group. Boundary heightening directed toward tokens by the dominant group makes it difficult for a dominant group member to get personally involved with a token member. Flings seem more likely to occur in a skewed group, because they are based on short-term feelings of excitement rather than perceptions of long-term compatability. Utilitarian relationships could occur in a skewed group if members of the group are at different organizational levels. However, true-love relationships seem more possible in a balanced group, where members are respected more as individuals and are less influenced by gender stereotyping or dominant-token dynamics in their relationships with others.

The discussion so far has focused on opposite-sex relationships characterized by physical intimacy. Most of what has been said also applies to same-sex, physically intimate relationships. However, gay romances have an additional level of complexity. Many gay employees fear retribution from their employers and coworkers should their sexual preferences become known. Because of homophobia in the workplace, gay couples typically are forced to keep their romances private. If unsuccessful at maintaining their privacy, they are likely to suffer additional negative consequences that heterosexual couples do not face.[25]

Nonsexual love relationships, characterized by psychological but not physical intimacy, also exist in the workplace. Employees may experience some of the feelings associated with a fling, such as an exhilarating interpersonal chemistry and a preoccupation with each other. They may also experience mutual respect and positive regard resembling the feelings associated with a true-love romance, except that the relationship is more of a strong friendship. However, even if the two employees are not physically intimate, coworkers are likely to assume that they are and react accordingly.[26]

Whether they stem from long-term interest, short-term excitement, or utilitarian reasons, organizational romances will always represent potential areas of concern for organizations. Even *perceptions* of organizational romances cause problems. Unless such issues are addressed, morale and productivity among coworkers are likely to suffer.

Implications

In the previous chapter, I posed the question of why women and men sometimes find it awkward and uncomfortable to work together and at other times have no difficulty at all. Our answer then was that gender stereotyping is the culprit. This chapter suggests two additional answers to the question. One is that either the male or female has directed unwelcome sexual attention toward the other, or unwelcome sexual attention is frequently directed by one employee towards another in their work environment. The other is that either the male or female is a participant in an organizational romance with another party, or one or both fear the potential of mutual sexual attraction entering into their own work relationship and maintain a distance from the other as a result.

Let's now consider the implications of our discussion for how organizations and the individuals involved can best deal with the various conditions described. We shall focus in turn on sexual harassment and organizational romances.

Dealing With Sexual Harassment

Unless organizations are very fortunate and no sexual harassment occurs within their boundaries, sexual harassment is a problem that they must address in some way. If they don't, they may not only be held in violation of the law but also risk losing productivity and alienating a large portion of their work force. Many cases of sexual harassment, though not all, may require managerial action. Some writers have suggested a ban on all forms of sexual expression in the workplace. However, most employees would not agree with this prescription. Some of the milder forms of sexual expression, such as flirting and dressing attractively to draw attention, are regarded more benignly than the more extreme forms of required dating or sex. Also, potentially harassing forms of behavior are reacted to and experienced differently by women and men and by members of groups with different sex ratios.

Organizations can begin to combat sexual harassment by issuing strong written policies against it and establishing formal grievance procedures to deal with allegations of harassment. The types of behaviors that are forbidden and the penalties for occurrence of those behaviors should be clearly specified. New employees should be informed of the organizational policy on sexual harassment during their initial orientation. Managers should be informed in a training program of the reasons for the policy, the variety of forms that sexual harassment can take, and what to do if they see or hear about possible cases of harassment. They should be made aware that sexual harassment would be disastrous behavior for themselves and could cost them their careers.[27]

In dealing with cases of alleged harassment, *the severity of the action taken should be based on the severity of the alleged offense and the certainty that an offense was committed.* After a complaint of sexual harassment has been directed to a designated party, organizational policy can be effectively implemented by a formal grievance procedure such as the following:

1. Interview the complainant, the accused, and possible witnesses.
2. Check personnel files for evidence that documents prior animosities between the parties, previous complaints against the accused or by the complainant, and/or sudden discrepancies in the work record of the complainant or accused.
3. Assess the severity of the offense, considering the type of behavior, intent, power position of the accused relative to the complainant, and frequency of occurrence. Actions by complainants' supervisors should be considered more severe offenses than the same actions by coworkers. Repeated incidents should be considered more severe offenses than isolated cases:
   a. Severe—forced sexual relations, sexual propositions, touching, grabbing, or brushing.
   b. Moderate—suggestive gestures, sexual remarks, sexual relations with promise of ensuing rewards.
   c. Mild—staring, flirting.
4. Assess the certainty that an offense was committed:
   a. High—solid evidence, in the form of either witnesses or documents, to support the complaint.
   b. Medium—some evidence to support the complaint.
   c. Low—no evidence to support the complaint other than the complainant's word.
5. Determine appropriate step(s) to be taken. Severe penalties are to be assessed when the alleged offense is severe and the certainty that it was committed is high. Mild actions are to be taken when the alleged offense is mild and the certainty that it was committed is low. Moderate responses are to be considered in cases that fall between these two

extremes. A combination of actions of different levels of severity may be taken. Possible actions include:

   a. Severe—dismissal, demotion, suspension, or transfer of the accused; restoration of the work record of the complainant when unjustly blemished.
   b. Moderate—warning or disciplinary notice in file of accused with provision for action if subsequent offense (dismissal, demotion, or some other action) and/or provision for removal of the notice if no subsequent offense within a specified period of time; required counseling for the accused.
   c. Mild—no record of complaint in file of accused, or record with annotation that the accusation was found groundless; no dissemination of information about the complaint; letter to the accused stressing organizational policy against sexual harassment; general announcement to all employees reminding them of organizational policy against sexual harassment.[28]

Such a procedure, if well-administered, clearly demonstrates that an organization is willing to take action to remove or minimize the incidences and effects of sexual harassment among its employees. It also acknowledges differences of opinion regarding sexual harassment by matching the sanction with the severity of the offense and the certainty that one was committed. By implementing such procedures in a clear and objective way, organizations both protect themselves from liability and increase the probability that their employees will work in an environment free of harassment.

However, no matter how well-intentioned a formal grievance procedure may be, it will have little effect unless individuals who feel that they have been harassed are willing to make formal complaints against their harassers. Many victims are reluctant to use formal procedures, probably because they have less power than their harassers and fear retaliation for a complaint. In the 1980 federal study, only 3% of female victims and 2% of male victims filed formal complaints, and one third of those who did reported that it made things worse.[29]

In addition to a formal grievance procedure, organizations should provide informal options such as third-party mediators for victims of harassment. However, informal procedures are problematic in themselves, because their purpose typically is to end the harassment rather than to establish a harasser's guilt or innocence and specify punishment if appropriate. The confidentiality usually required by such procedures does not allow identification of repeat offenders, which keeps them from being punished accordingly. In addition, victims with less power than the harasser are still vulnerable to retaliation.[30]

In the end, if they take any action at all, most victims choose to deal with the situation themselves. In fact, this may be their only recourse if there is no concrete proof that harassment has taken place.

The most effective way to end harassment is to ask or tell the harasser to stop. In the 1987 federal study, this "knock-it-off" approach made things better for 61% of female victims and 66% of male victims. Telling colleagues, or threatening to do so, is also an effective response. In contrast, going along with the offensive behavior, making a joke of it, or pretending to ignore it usually does not resolve the issue.[31]

Mary Rowe recommended that when verbal requests to stop offensive behavior have been unsuccessful, the victim write a letter to the harasser. The letter should contain (a) a detailed description of the offending behavior, when it occurred, and the circumstances under which it occurred; (b) the feelings of the victim about the behavior and the damage that has been done (e.g., "Your behavior has made me feel uncomfortable about working in this unit," "You have caused me to ask for a change in job"); and (c) what the victim would like to have happen besides an end to the harassment, such as the rewriting of an unjust evaluation that was prepared after the victim rejected sexual advances. The letter should be delivered in person with a security person or some other witness present. The harasser will usually accept the letter and say nothing. There is rarely a response in writing, and, nearly always, the harassment stops.[32]

Rowe viewed the role of the organization as encouraging employees to take such measures as a way of focusing their anger and recognizing that they can take steps to protect themselves. The organization may also wish to initiate its own action if there is significant evidence of wrongdoing, in which case it should provide assurance that people who do not wish to file formal complaints remain anonymous. If individuals feel uncomfortable about handling the issue directly, they should be provided with the opportunity to discuss the harassment with a psychologist, personnel counselor, or some other person who is discreet and supportive of victims. For example, Du Pont runs a 24-hour hotline that offers advice on personal security and sexual harassment. Callers may remain anonymous, and calling does not constitute bringing a charge. However, if a victim or witness to harassment decides to lodge a formal complaint, it is investigated immediately.[33]

When considering filing a lawsuit, individuals will gain from reviewing the strengths and weaknesses of their potential case in a legal sense before proceeding. An analysis of federal court cases involving sexual harassment below the Supreme Court level found that complainants were more likely to win their cases when (a) the harassment was severe, (b) supporting witnesses were present, (c) supporting documents were available, (d) they had complained to superiors or management prior to filing charges, and (e) management took no action on being notified of alleged harassment. If complainants had none of these factors in their favor, their odds of winning the case were less than 1%. If all five factors were in their favor, their odds of winning were almost 100%. Thus, if the odds of success are low, an individual may not wish to pursue the issue. In the same vein, if an organization has been threatened with a serious lawsuit, it will gain from reviewing the strength of its case in deciding whether to contest sexual harassment charges or to settle out of court. If its odds of success are low, the organization may prefer a settlement to the time, expense, and negative publicity associated with losing a court case.[34]

The outcome of the Liz Randolph case is instructive. She filed a suit in state court for defamation, intentional infliction of emotional distress, and invasion of privacy. The radio station claimed at the trial that the jokes directed towards her were so outrageous that no one could ever mistake them for fact. However, to the contrary, witnesses testified that they sincerely thought that Randolph was sexually loose after they heard the jokes. The jury concluded that the comments and skits constituted a pattern of unacceptable conduct and awarded Randolph almost $700,000 in damages. For WBZZ-FM, *that* was no joke.[35]

We have seen several kinds of actions that organizations may take to deal with sexual harassment. Organizations should (a) establish firm policies against sexual harassment, (b) set up and administer formal and informal grievance procedures, (c) develop a mechanism for identification of repeat offenders, (d) make sure that employees are aware of both policies and procedures, and (e) provide assistance to employees in psychologically coping with harassment and in dealing with it on their own if they so choose. Only when organizations consistently take such actions will they begin to make a dent in the problem of sexual harassment in the workplace.

Dealing With Organizational Romances

What management should do about romantic relationships between employees is less clear-cut.[36] In a survey of personnel managers, 70%

agreed with the statement, "There is really nothing the organization can do to stop romantic attractions between men and women working together." However, 61% disagreed with the statement, "The romantic interests of employees in each other should be of no concern to employers."[37] There is a wide range of opinions over how management should respond to romances, ranging from fostering norms that encourage them to firing one or both employees.

A *Business Week* survey found that the written policies of most companies specified only that married couples should not work with or for each other. Unwritten policies were more varied. Some companies looked with more disfavor on extramarital affairs than on other romances, possibly reflecting the values of the dominant people in the company or a concern for possible scandal. From a business point of view, however, extramarital affairs were seen as less worrisome than romances between single employees who also have some work relationship. Most companies transferred one or both employees when they learned of such a relationship. One company took action only if sexual harassment or a conflict of interest was involved. If the relationship had a detrimental effect on productivity or morale, then it was treated as a performance problem requiring some action. Otherwise, the company didn't interfere.[38]

There is a wide range of actions from which management may choose in responding to organizational romances. The general principle to be followed is that *the severity of the action taken should be based on the potential for offense, the severity of the alleged offense, and the certainty that an offense was committed.* The primary concern of management ought not to be who is involved with whom but whether the necessary work is getting done, and done well. If there is no actual or potential disruption to the accomplishment of work goals, then there is no need to take any action.

However, a relationship in which task-related or career-related decisions could be but have not been influenced by romantic considerations presents some threat to work. Coworkers may fear the relationship's potentially inequitable effect on decisions or suspect that it is already having an effect. As a result, their morale and productivity suffer. When the two romantic partners have committed no actual offense (assuming that simply being involved in a romance is not an offense) but the potential for an offense exists, they should be presented with two options. Either they may "cool" the relationship and demonstrate to coworkers that it has been cooled by their subsequent interactions in the presence of others, or either one or both employees may accept being transferred to equivalent positions elsewhere in the company.

When task-related or career-related decisions definitely have been influenced by romantic considerations, there is cause for greater concern. This situation calls for some kind of punitive action against *both* participants. The hierarchical level of the participants should not be allowed to affect the actions taken. This recommendation runs counter to the common practice that the lower-status person receive the brunt of punitive action. However, when both individuals are punished, rather than only the person at the lower level, the appearance of an equitable decision will have the most positive effect on morale and productivity.

Management can also contribute to a satisfactory resolution of romance-related issues by making counseling available to all individuals involved—the employees in the relationship, the managers of work areas that are disrupted by the relationship, and the coworkers in such areas. Coworkers need to have a designated neutral party with whom they can consult about a troublesome romantic relationship. As their manager may be one of the participants, they need to be able to report it without fear of reprisal to themselves.

Before going ahead and plunging into an organizational romance, Lisa Mainiero recommends that individuals weigh carefully all the potential risks and benefits. The benefits may outweigh the risks. As she puts it:

> What could be better than meeting your lover at work every day, and using the sexual energy you generate to enhance your work performance? There is some truth to the saying that when love is in the air, people feel happier and more satisfied. They also may be more motivated. Creativity, innovation, and excitement surround those involved in an office romance. What more could a manager ask? [39]

However, the risky side of an organizational romance is that if it is inappropriate for the two participants or not handled well, their careers and personal lives may suffer and they may alienate coworkers as well.

Mainiero offers several guidelines for those considering a romance at work:

1. Be aware of office norms about romance before acting.
2. Evaluate the potential risks to career advancement.
3. Don't mess around with a boss—or mentor.

4. Maintain strict boundaries between personal and professional roles.
5. Clarify at the start exactly what you want from the relationship.
6. Identify the possible areas in which partners may become competitive.
7. Anticipate possible conflict-of-interest situations.
8. Be sensitive to the reactions of colleagues and management.
9. Remember that the romance will not remain a secret for long.
10. Discuss "contingency plans" at the start of the romance.

Most of the benefits of organizational romances occur when the employees do not have other romantic commitments and work in unrelated jobs and departments in companies that do not discourage personal relationships at work. Then the success of the romances depend on the employees' willingness and ability to maximize the benefits and minimize the risks.

In conclusion, although not posing a legal threat, organizational romances represent concerns involving productivity and morale that are similar to those of sexual harassment. I have outlined steps that management can take to respond to the negative effects of both sexual harassment and organizational romances and to help the individuals affected to help themselves. In taking such steps, organizations contribute to the creation of a more comfortable, if not entirely asexual, work environment for their employees. However, in dealing with sexual harassment or attraction at work, individuals also influence their own destinies. They have the choice of whether to harass other employees or not. They also must decide whether to act on feelings of attraction toward coworkers, and if so, how to manage the interface between work roles and sexual roles.

Notes

1. C. Tuttle, "Sexual Harassment Is No Joke," reprinted by permission of the publisher from *Management Review*, August 1990, © 1990, p. 46. American Management Association, New York. All rights reserved.

2. U.S. Merit Systems Protection Board (USMSPB) *Sexual Harassment in the Federal Workplace: Is It a Problem?* (Washington, DC: Government Printing Office, 1981); U.S. Merit Systems Protection Board (USMSPB), *Sexual Harassment in the Federal Government: An Update* (Washington, DC: Government Printing Office, 1988).

3. L. A. Mainiero, *Office Romance: Love, Power, and Sex in the Workplace* (New York: Rawson Associates, 1989).

4. This section of the chapter is based primarily on G. N. Powell, "Sexual Harassment: Confronting the Issue of Definition," *Business Horizons*, 26 (No. 4, July/August 1983): 24-28.

5. Definitions in this paragraph are from (1) L. Farley, *Sexual Shakedown: The Sexual Harassment of Women on the Job* (New York: Warner Books, 1978), p. 39; (2) L. F. Fitzgerald and M. Hesson-McInnis, "The Dimensions of Sexual Harassment: A Structural Analysis," *Journal of Vocational Behavior*, 35 (1989): 309-326; (3) U.S. Office of Personnel Management, "Policy Statement and Definition of Sexual Harassment," in *Sexual Harassment in the Federal Workplace*, USMSPB, 1981, p. E-8; and (4) U.S. Equal Employment Opportunity Commission, "Guidelines on Discrimination Because of Sex," in *Sexual Harassment in the Federal Workplace*, USMSPB, 1981, p. E-10. For a review, see J. E. Gruber, "A Typology of Personal and Environmental Sexual Harassment: Research and Policy Implications for the 1990s," *Sex Roles*, 26 (1992): 447-464.

6. D. Bennett-Alexander, "Sexual Harassment in the Office," *Personnel Administrator*, 33 (No. 6, June 1988): 174-188; C. M. Koen Jr., "Sexual Harassment Claims Stem from a Hostile Work Environment," *Personnel Journal*, 69 (No. 8, August 1990): 88-99; K. E. Lewis and P. R. Johnson, "Preventing Sexual Harassment Complaints Based on Hostile Work Environments," *SAM Advanced Management Journal*, 56 (No. 2, Spring 1991): 21-32.

7. B. A. Gutek, C. Y. Nakamura, M. Gahart, and I. Handschumacher, "Sexuality and the Workplace," *Basic and Applied Social Psychology*, 1 (1980): 255-265; G. N. Powell, C. A. Benzinger, A. A. Bruno, T. N. Gibson, M. L. Pfeiffer, and T. P. Santopietro, "Sexual Harassment as Defined by Working Women" (Paper delivered at the Annual Meeting of the Academy of Management, San Diego, 1981); G. N. Powell, "Effects of Sex Role Identity and Sex on Definitions of Sexual Harassment," *Sex Roles*, 14 (1986): 9-19; P. M. Popovich, B. J. Licata, D. Nokovich, T. Martelli, and S. Zoloty, "Assessing the Incidence and Perceptions of Sexual Harassment Behaviors Among American Undergraduates," *Journal of Psychology*, 120 (1986): 387-396; USMSPB, *Sexual Harassment in the Federal Government*, 1988, pp. 13-15, figures 2-1 to 2-4; K. M. York, "Defining Sexual Harassment in Workplaces: A Policy-Capturing Approach," *Academy of Management Journal*, 32 (1990): 830-850; J. B. Pryor, "The Lay Person's Understanding of Sexual Harassment," *Sex Roles*, 13 (1985): 273-286.

8. Gutek et al., "Sexuality and the Workplace"; USMSPB, *Sexual Harassment in the Federal Government*, 1988, pp. 16-17; S. Kenig and J. Ryan, "Sex Differences in Level of Tolerance and Attribution of Blame for Sexual Harassment on a University Campus," *Sex Roles*, 15 (1986): 535-549; I. W. Jensen and B. A. Gutek, "Attributions and Assignment of Responsibility in Sexual Harassment," *Journal of Social Issues*, 38 (No. 4, 1982): 121-136; Powell, "Effects of Sex Role Identity and Sex on Definitions of Sexual Harassment"; E. G. C. Collins and T. B. Blodgett, "Sexual Harassment: Some See It . . . Some Won't," *Harvard Business Review*, 59 (No. 2, March/April 1981): 76-95.

9. S. S. Tangri, M. R. Burt, and L. B. Johnson, "Sexual Harassment at Work: Three Explanatory Models," *Journal of Social Issues*, 38 (No. 4, 1982): 33-54.

10. Tangri et al., "Sexual Harassment at Work."

11. Tangri et al., "Sexual Harassment at Work."; R. A. Thacker and G. R. Ferris, "Understanding Sexual Harassment in the Workplace: The Influence of Power and Politics Within the Dyadic Interaction of Harasser and Target," *Human Resource Management Review*, 1 (1991): 23-37.

12. B. A. Gutek and V. Dunwoody, "Understanding Sex in the Workplace," in *Women and Work: An Annual Review*, vol. 2, ed. A. H. Stromberg, L. Larwood, and B. A. Gutek (Newbury Park, CA: Sage, 1987); C. L. Williams, *Gender Differences at Work: Women and Men in Nontraditional Occupations* (Berkeley: University of California Press, 1989); N. DiTomaso, "Sexuality in the Workplace: Discrimination and Harassment," in *The Sexuality of Organization*, ed. J. Hearn, D. L. Sheppard, P. Tancred-Sheriff, and G. Burrell (London: Sage, 1989).

13. B. A. Gutek and B. Morasch, "Sex-Ratios, Sex-Role Spillover, and Sexual Harassment of Women at Work," *Journal of Social Issues*, 38 (No. 4, 1982): 55-74; U.S. Department of Labor, Bureau of Labor Statistics, *Employment and Earnings*, 39 (No. 1, January 1992), pp. 185-190, table 22.

14. B. A. Gutek, Chapter 8, "Explanations for Sexuality in the Workplace: Unequal Sex Ratios and Sex Role Spillover," in *Sex and the Workplace* (San Francisco: Jossey-Bass, 1985); B. A. Gutek, A. G. Cohen, and A. M. Konrad, "Predicting Social-Sexual Behavior at Work: A Contact Hypothesis," *Academy of Management Journal*, 33 (1990): 560-577; A. M. Konrad and B. A. Gutek, "Impact of Work Experiences on Attitudes toward Sexual Harassment," *Administrative Science Quarterly*, 31 (1986): 422-438; B. A. Gutek and A. G. Cohen, "Sex Ratios, Sex Role Spillover, and Sex at Work: A Comparison of Men's and Women's Experiences," *Human Relations*, 40 (1987): 97-115; Gutek and Morasch, "Sex-Ratios, Sex-Role Spillover, and Sexual Harassment of Women at Work."

15. USMSPB, *Sexual Harassment in the Federal Government*, 1988; USMSPB, *Sexual Harassment in the Federal Workplace*, 1981; Tangri et al., "Sexual Harassment at Work"; T. C. Fain and D. L. Anderton, "Sexual Harassment: Organizational Context and Diffuse Status," *Sex Roles*, 17 (1987): 291-311.

16. L. A. Mainiero, "A Review and Analysis of Power Dynamics in Organizational Romances," *Academy of Management Review*, 11 (1986): 750-762.

17. M. Mead, "A Proposal: We Need Taboos on Sexuality at Work," in *Sexuality in Organizations*, ed. D. A. Neugarten and J. M. Shafritz, (Oak Park, IL: Moore Publishing, 1980); E. G. C. Collins, "Managers and Lovers," *Harvard Business Review*, 61 (No. 5, September/October 1983): 142-153.

18. P. Horn and J. Horn, *Sex in the Office* (Reading, MA: Addison-Wesley, 1982); "Bendix Officer Leaves Her Job After Rumors On Promotion," *Hartford Courant*, 143 (No. 284, 10 October 1980): C9; Statement by Mary Cunningham, *Hartford Courant*, 145 (No. 128, 8 May 1982), p. A2.

19. G. N. Powell, "What Do Tomorrow's Managers Think about Sexual Intimacy in the Workplace?" *Business Horizons*, 29 (No. 4, July/August 1986): 30-35.

20. R. E. Quinn and P. L. Lees, "Attraction and Harassment: Dynamics of Sexual Politics in the Workplace," *Organizational Dynamics*, 13 (No. 2, Autumn 1984): 35-46.

21. An earlier version of this section of the chapter appeared in G. N. Powell and L. A. Mainiero, "What Managers Need to Know about Office Romances," *Leadership & Organization Development Journal*, 11 (No. 1, 1990): i-iii.

22. C. I. Anderson and P. L. Hunsaker, "Why There's Romancing at the Office and Why It's Everybody's Problem," *Personnel*, 62 (No. 2, February 1985): 57-63.

23. Gutek, *Sex and the Workplace*, Chapter 8.

24. P. Waldman, "Esprit's Fortunes Sag As Couple at the Helm Battle Over Its Image," *Wall Street Journal*, 211 (No. 57, 24 March 1988): 1, 17.

25. Mainiero, *Office Romance*, p. 190.

26. R. E. Quinn, S. Lobel, and A. Warfield, "The Dynamics of Non-Sexual Love: An Exploration of Psychological Intimacy in Cross-Gender Work Relationships" (Paper delivered at the Annual Meeting of the Academy of Management, San Francisco, 1990).

27. Lewis and Johnson, "Preventing Sexual Harassment Claims Based on Hostile Work Environments"; T. L. Leap and E. R. Gray, "Corporate Responsibility in Cases of Sexual Harassment," *Business Horizons, 23* (No. 10, October 1980): 58-65; P. Linenberger and T. J. Keaveny, "Sexual Harassment: The Employer's Legal Obligations," *Personnel, 58* (No. 6, November/December 1981): 60-68; C. Backhouse and L. Cohen, Chapter 10, "Action Plans for Management and Unions," in *Sexual Harassment on the Job* (Englewood Cliffs, NJ: Prentice Hall, 1981).

28. Powell, "Sexual Harassment."

29. USMSPB, *Sexual Harassment in the Federal Workplace*, 1981, p. 71; J. A. Livingston, "Responses to Sexual Harassment on the Job," *Journal of Social Issues, 38* (No. 4, 1982): 5-22.

30. S. Riger, "Gender Dilemmas in Sexual Harassment Policies and Procedures," *American Psychologist, 46* (1991): 497-505.

31. USMSPB, *Sexual Harassment in the Federal Government*, 1988, figure 3-2, p. 26.

32. M. P. Rowe, "Dealing with Sexual Harassment," *Harvard Business Review, 59* (No. 3, May/June 1981): 42-46.

33. A. Deutschman, "Dealing with Sexual Harassment," *Fortune, 124* (No. 11, 4 November 1991): 145-146.

34. D. E. Terpstra and D. D. Baker, "Outcomes of Federal Court Decisions on Sexual Harassment," *Academy of Management Journal, 35* (1992): 181-190.

35. Tuttle, "Sexual Harassment Is No Joke."

36. An earlier version of the recommendations for management in this section of the chapter appeared in Powell and Mainiero, "What Managers Need to Know about Office Romances."

37. R. C. Ford and F. S. McLaughlin, "Should Cupid Come to the Workplace?" *Personnel Administrator, 32* (No. 10, October 1987): 100-110.

38. "Romance in the Workplace: Corporate Rules for the Game of Love," *Business Week*, No. 2847 (18 June 1984): 70-71.

39. Mainiero, Chapter 15, "Living Love in the Office," in *Office Romance*, p. 259.

6

Managing People

Vive What?

Views about the existence of differences between female and male managers:

1. Vive la différence!
   Marilyn Loden[1]

2. Vive la no différence!
   Douglas W. Bray[2]

In 1965, *Harvard Business Review*, which then billed itself as "The Magazine of Thoughtful Businessmen," published results from a survey of male and female executives' attitudes toward women in management in an article entitled, "Are Women Executives People?" The article posed the general questions of whether women executives act like people, whether they think of themselves as people, and whether the business community was treating them like people. These are curious questions from today's vantage point, but we must remember that women held a much smaller proportion of management positions at the time. The first two are questions that we might expect dominants to ask about tokens, and the third is about dominant-token relationships.[3]

The survey results suggested that women were saying, "Treat us like people"; men were saying to women, "Act like people"; and successful women were saying to other women, "Think of yourselves as people." Most women executives believed that women should be treated on an individual basis rather than as a uniform group. However, although few men (6%) were strongly opposed to women in management, a large proportion (41%) regarded the idea with some disfavor. They believed not only that women were special but also that they had a special place, which was outside the ranks of management. Older men tended to be more accepting of women in managerial roles than younger men, and men who had been superiors or peers of women managers thought more favorably of them than men who had only worked for women. However, few men thought that they would be comfortable in working for a woman manager, and even fewer thought that men in general would be comfortable in such a situation.

Respondents to the survey gave several reasons for the negative attitudes toward female executives. According to a large proportion of both male and female executives, women themselves were partially responsible for the negative attitudes because they had accepted their exclusion from managerial ranks without major protest. Cultural prejudice against women working outside the home was also cited as a reason. Also, many men did not want to contend with women as well as other men for the keenly competitive managerial jobs. Over half of the male executives believed that the rationale for excluding women from management was basically sound. In contrast, women executives were more positive in their beliefs about women's capabilities and encouraged them to shed their traditional roles to make use of these capabilities in the workplace.

When women are treated like people, on a case-by-case basis rather than as a category, they are more likely to think of themselves as people, not just as women, and to act naturally. On the other hand, women who act like unique individuals rather than representatives of their sex and ask for no special treatment are more likely to be treated like people. In the opinions of the executives surveyed in 1965, change was needed in how both women and men were thinking and acting for women to be successful in management. Otherwise, women would continue to be at a disadvantage in entering and being promoted within the ranks of management.

In the next 20 years, the composition of the managerial ranks changed considerably. The proportion of female managers more than doubled between 1965 and 1985, increasing from 15% to 36%. Between 1965 and 1985, the number of female managers quadrupled, whereas the number of male managers increased by only one-quarter. Two thirds of the managers added to the work force since 1965 were women.

Attitudes about whether women belong in management also changed, particularly among male executives. In a 1985 replication of the 1965 *HBR* survey, only 5% of male executives viewed the idea of women managers with some disfavor. In fact, male executives were more positive about how women executives were being accepted in business than the women themselves. The proportion of men who thought that a woman must be exceptional to succeed in business dropped from 90% in 1965 to 59% in 1985, whereas this proportion remained at about 85% for women. Similarly, the proportion of men who thought that the business community will never wholly accept women executives fell from 61% in 1965 to 20% in 1985, whereas this proportion fell only from 47% to 40% for women. As in 1965, younger male executives expressed less favorable attitudes toward women managers than older male executives. However, men thought that women's prospects would inevitably improve with the passage of time. Women were more skeptical and wondered exactly when that improvement would take place, if at all. Although men reported that things were better for women in management, women executives saw continued resistance to their progress.[4] This difference in views remains in place today.

The increase in female managers has led to several kinds of situations occurring with greater frequency in organizations. More employees than ever before have had a female boss at some time. Many employees have become used to working for a woman, having had two or more female bosses in their careers. Most middle managers now have female as well as male lower-level managers as their subordinates. At the same time, more lower-level managers than ever before have a female middle manager as their boss. However, the proportion of women in top management positions remains extremely low.

The changing sex composition of the managerial ranks gives us reason to question the universality of prevailing theories of management. Until relatively recently, most studies of how managers manage and what works well and not so well for them were based on observations of male managers. A classic 1974 compendium of research results, *Handbook of Leadership*, discovered few studies that exclusively examined female managers or even included female managers in their samples.[5] When female managers were present in organizations being studied, they were usually excluded from the analysis because their inclusion might lead to distorted results. It was as if female managers were less real, or less worthy of observation, than male managers.

Management researchers no longer automatically exclude female managers from their samples. The most recent edition of *Handbook of Leadership* now devotes a chapter to women and leadership.[6] Nonetheless, many of the existing theories of management were developed with male managers in mind. Do these theories apply equally as well to female managers, or should female managers be described with models of their own? Male and female managers could differ in their basic behavioral tendencies and internal responses to work situations, or they could be quite similar.

Besides examining the behavioral tendencies of female and male managers, we need to examine subordinates' preferences for and responses to female versus male managers. Few managers are likely to adopt and maintain a style of leadership that does not yield the desired responses from their employees. Subordinates who engage in gender stereotyping are likely to have different expectations of female and male managers and thus reinforce different behaviors from them.

Managerial stereotypes also need to be reconsidered. Much as the masculine stereotype has provided a model of the "good boy" and the feminine stereotype of the "good girl," a managerial stereotype (influenced by the fact that most managers over time have been male) has provided a model of the "good manager." The overall proportions of female and male managers have changed considerably in recent years, but not so at the upper levels of the managerial ranks. Thus we have reason to wonder whether the stereotypes that people have of good managers have changed or remain the same. We also need to examine the relationship between stereotypes of good managers and what actually makes managers effective.

In this chapter, we shall examine both the stereotypes and realities of management today. First, we shall examine how managerial stereotypes compare with gender stereotypes and whether they have changed over time. Second, we shall investigate whether female and male managers differ in their responses to managerial situations, the responses they elicit from subordinates, or their overall effectiveness as leaders. Finally, we shall consider whether masculinity is actually associated with more effective management or whether androgyny, femininity, or something else should serve as the new model for effective management in today's changed work environment.

Managerial Stereotypes

Studies of the relationship between sex, managerial stereotypes, and gender stereotypes were first conducted in the early 1970s. Virginia Schein compiled a list of 92 characteristics of individuals that differentiated between people's beliefs about women and men, thereby forming the basis for gender stereotypes. She then asked a sample of middle managers to describe how well each of the characteristics fit either women in general, men in general, or successful middle managers. Both female and male executives believed that successful middle managers possessed an abundance of characteristics that were more associated with men in general than with women in general.[7]

Replications of Schein's studies have yielded essentially the same reactions from men but different reactions from women. Although the correspondence between men's descriptions of women and successful managers increases considerably when they described women *managers*, male managers and students continue to describe men as more similar to successful managers than are women. However, female managers and students no longer sex-type the managerial job. They now see the same association between each sex and the managerial role. Women's stereotypes of women have changed, but not their stereotypes of managers.[8]

Tony Butterfield and I took a different approach to the analysis of managerial stereotypes. In the mid-1970s, the concept of androgyny began receiving attention as a standard of psychological health that seemed more flexible for both men and women than the double standards of masculinity and femininity. Androgyny and more effective behavior had been linked in a variety of nonwork situations. We reasoned that if the more effective *person* is androgynous, the more effective *manager* might be androgynous as well. Also, the proportion of female managers had risen to 22% in 1977 from a figure of 15% in 1965. As more women became managers, it was possible that traditional masculine standards for management were being replaced with more androgynous standards. Therefore, we hypothesized that the "good manager" would now be seen as androgynous.[9]

We administered a questionnaire containing the Original Bem Sex-Role Inventory (BSRI) to a sample of undergraduate business students and part-time evening MBA students. As you recall from Chapter 2, the Original BSRI contains 20 masculine items, 20 feminine items, and 20 filler items. Each individual completed the questionnaire twice, describing how much each phrase applied to both him/herself and a good manager.

The good-manager descriptions from this study are summarized in the first column of Table 6.1. Contrary to our hypothesis, individuals overwhelmingly preferred a masculine manager. About 70% of both women and men and both graduate and undergraduate students described a good manager in predominantly masculine terms. Less than 20% of all individuals described a good manager as androgynous. Virtually no one preferred a feminine good manager. Men and women did not significantly differ in their descriptions of a good manager. I obtained similar results in a separate study of actual managers' stereotypes of a good manager.[10]

Two developments in later years led us to believe that we might obtain different results if we conducted our study again. Sandra Bem released a "new, improved" BSRI, called the Short BSRI, that eliminated half of the previous items while retaining masculine and feminine items of similar desirability. We expected that individuals would rate the good manager as no different in masculinity but much higher in femininity on the new instrument, thereby leading to a more androgynous view of the good manager. Also, the proportion of women in management positions had continued to rise, reaching 34% by 1984. In Kanter's terms, this proportion had shifted from skewed in 1965 to tilted in 1977 to on the borderline of being balanced in 1984. We thought that with women comprising more than one-third of all managers, the image of good managers as masculine may have finally been dispelled.

Consequently, we conducted a replication of the original study eight years later, using the Short BSRI with a new sample of undergraduate business students and part-time evening MBA students. Once again, we hypothesized that the good manager would be seen as androgynous. And, once again, our hypothesis was rejected. As we see in the second column of Table 6.1, about 70% of both women and men and both graduate and undergraduate students again described a good manager in predominantly masculine terms. Even when we reanalyzed our original data using only the items on the Short BSRI, over 60% of all students still saw a good manager as masculine.[11]

In summary, men, but no longer women, describe successful managers as more like men than women. However, men and women at different career stages, including practicing managers, part-time MBA students on the verge of careers as managers, and undergraduate business

Table 6.1 Descriptions of a Good Manager

Questionnaire: Date of Data Collection	Original BSRI 1976-1977 (percentage)	Short BSRI 1984-1985 (percentage)
Undergraduates		
Men		
Androgynous	16	25
Masculine	70	69
Feminine	1	1
Undifferentiated	13	5
Women		
Androgynous	18	20
Masculine	67	76
Feminine	2	2
Undifferentiated	13	2
Part-Time Graduates		
Men		
Androgynous	21	19
Masculine	72	67
Feminine	2	1
Undifferentiated	5	13
Women		
Androgynous	10	25
Masculine	80	67
Feminine	0	0
Undifferentiated	10	8
Totals		
Androgynous	16	22
Masculine	72	70
Feminine	1	1
Undifferentiated	11	7

SOURCE: G. N. Powell and D. A. Butterfield, "The 'Good Manager:' Did Androgyny Fare Better in the 1980s?" *Group & Organization Studies*, 14 (1989): 216-233.
NOTE: The totals were obtained by weighting undergraduate males, undergraduate females, part-time graduate males, and part-time graduate females equally.

students, continue to describe good managers as higher in stereotypically masculine traits than stereotypically feminine traits.

Stereotypes could be influenced by the perspective taken on the managerial role. A study asked undergraduate students to take either a worker's perspective, describing a manager that they would like to work for as their immediate supervisor, or a management perspective, describing a manager that they would want working for them if they were company owners. Masculine traits were seen as more desirable in managers by company owners than by workers. In contrast, feminine traits were seen as more desirable in managers by workers than by company owners. These results suggest the merits of an androgynous managerial style. Masculine traits may enhance the impression of effectiveness and appeal more to a manager's superiors. However, feminine traits, by contributing to a supportive work climate, may appeal more to a manager's subordinates. A predominance of one set of traits over the other could result in pressures for change from either superiors or subordinates.[12]

Survey results regarding managerial stereotypes raise as many questions as they answer. The first question pertains to their dependence on sex ratios in the management ranks. If the proportion of women managers continues to rise, will there be some point at which stereotypes of managers no longer agree with the masculine gender stereotype? Not necessarily. Our review of gender stereotypes in Chapter 2 showed that, even though they have been demonstrated repeatedly to have little to do with actual sex differences, support for them has diminished little over time. Managerial stereotypes, at least from a management perspective, have stayed essentially the same despite the considerable increase in women managers in recent years. We have little reason to believe that the stereotypes will change if even more women become managers. Besides, the upper levels of management remain a male bastion despite the overall increase in the proportion of women managers. If stereotypes of managers are influenced at all by sex ratios, they may be influenced most by the sex ratio of top executives. Unless this sex ratio changes, the stereotypes may remain the same. Furthermore, women could bring similar qualities to the managerial job as men and thereby not necessitate a change in managerial stereotypes.

A second question raised by managerial stereotypes pertains to the nature of their effect. Should we be concerned with managerial stereotypes at all, or should we be concerned only with the reality of what makes a manager good or bad? Our answer to this question is that the stereotypes as well as the realities of management are important. Further results that Tony Butterfield and I obtained shed light on the possible effects of managerial stereotypes.

In both of our studies described above, undergraduate business students exhibited stereotypical sex differences in their self-descriptions, with males seeing themselves as higher in masculinity and lower in femininity than females. Female and male undergraduates agreed on a description of the good manager as highly masculine. As a result, the undergraduate women saw effective managers as most unlike themselves. In contrast, there were few sex differences in the self-descriptions of part-time evening MBA students. Male MBAs described themselves in similar terms as male undergraduates. However, female MBAs saw themselves as more masculine and less feminine, and thereby more like a good manager, than female undergraduates.

Why do women's self-descriptions, but not those of men, differ according to student status? Undergraduate women who do not fit the stereotype of a good manager may hold back in developing their management skills and be diverted from the pursuit of managerial careers. Women who fit the stereotype may be the ones who apply to graduate business programs and most likely be accepted for admission. In addition, many organizations exert strong pressures on their members to conform to ways acceptable to other members, particularly those in power. As long as women remain in the minority in management circles, they may be expected to behave as men are. Thus a masculine stereotype of the good manager is self-reinforcing and inhibits the expression of femininity by women in or aspiring to management positions. However, males are more socialized from the onset to fit the stereotype of a good manager. Men who are close to attaining management positions are unlikely to differ substantially from those who are at earlier career stages.

A third question raised by managerial stereotypes pertains to their applicability to countries other than the United States. The results that have been reported so far represent *American* stereotypes of managers. Schein found similar results in Great Britain, Germany, Japan, China, and Ireland as she did for American men: Men are seen as more similar to successful managers than women are. However, such stereotypes need not hold back women managers on international assignments. For example, when North American women are sent on assignments to Asia, they are primarily seen as foreigners, not as local people. As a result, the rules governing the behavior of local women do not apply to foreign women, including local norms that limit the access of women to management positions. Asians apparently see female expatriates as foreigners who happen to be women, rather than women who happen to be foreigners. As a result, stereotypes favoring local men over local women for managerial roles do not seem to restrict the success of women as managers in international assignments.[13]

The fourth and final question raised by managerial stereotypes pertains to their applicability to the practice of management. Stereotypes are known to die hard, even when facts do not substantiate them, but they are not necessarily wrong. Do the stereotypes that men are better managers, still held by American men but not American women, and that better managers are masculine, accurately reflect what makes for a good manager, or do these stereotypes only reflect the fact that most managers have been men and that most men have been expected to live up to the masculine stereotype?

The remainder of the chapter shall be devoted to this question. First, we need to examine whether sex differences are actually exhibited within the ranks of management. If men and women behave similarly once they become managers, even if they differed beforehand, the stereotype that men make better managers would not be supported. However, subordinates could differ in their responses to female and male managers, thereby influencing their managers' overall effectiveness. Thus we also need to examine subordinates' responses to female and male managers.

Do Female and Male Managers Differ?

Do female and male managers differ in the personal qualities they bring to their jobs? Women and men certainly differ in their success within the ranks of management, with male managers holding positions at higher managerial levels and receiving higher salaries than female managers. However, this may be due simply to the average male manager being older and more experienced than the average female manager. After all, managerial careers invariably start at the bottom, and the influx of women managers since the early 1970s has occurred mostly at the lower managerial levels.[14]

Few writers have advocated the existence of biologically based sex differences that affect the capability of women versus men to manage effectively. Instead, most research now focuses on differences in the early socialization experiences of females and males that set up expectations for participation in the work force. However, very different conclusions are reached about whether or how sex differences in socialization experiences contribute to sex differences in the managerial ranks.[15]

1. No Differences. One conclusion is that women who pursue the nontraditional career of manager reject their gender stereotype and have goals, motives, personalities, and behaviors that are similar to those of men who pursue managerial careers. This may be due to (a) self-selection, with men and women who decide on managerial careers sharing similar traits and behavioral tendencies; (b) organizational selection, with managers of both sexes being chosen according to similar criteria; (c) organizational socialization, with female and male managers being similarly socialized into proper role behavior early in their careers; and/or (d) organizational structure, with managers who hold positions with similar status and power behaving similarly. A team of researchers at the Center for Creative Leadership concluded, "The basis for claiming differences between executive women and executive men—whether used to exclude or encourage women into these ranks—is suspect at best.[16]

2. Stereotypical Differences Favoring Men. Another theory maintains that female and male managers differ in ways predicted by gender stereotypes as a result of early socialization experiences that leave men better suited as managers. For example, Margaret Hennig and Anne Jardim concluded that men are better prepared to be managers because of such factors as their greater participation in team sports during their formative years. They claimed that men "bring to the management setting a clearer, stronger and more definite understanding of where they see themselves going, what they will have to do, how they will have to act, and what they must take into account if they are to achieve the objectives they set for themselves." Although Hennig and Jardim saw women as lacking essential managerial skills and traits coming out of childhood, they believed that women could still be successful as managers and compete on an equal footing with men if they developed the skills they lacked in earlier years.[17] In addition, negative attitudes toward female managers, particularly if they are tokens, may restrict the range of acceptable behavior for them and limit their approaches to managerial situations, thereby harming their ultimate effectiveness.

3. Stereotypical Differences Favoring Women. Some writers have argued that female and male managers differ in accordance with gender stereotypes, but that femininity is particularly needed by managers in today's work world. For example, on conducting a survey of International Women's Forum members and men with similar backgrounds, Judy Rosener concluded:

> The first female executives, because they were breaking new ground, adhered to many of the "rules of conduct" that spelled success for

men. Now a second wave of women is making its way into top management, not by adopting the style and habits that have proved successful for men but by drawing on the skills and attitudes they developed from their shared experience as women. These second-generation managerial women are drawing on what is unique to their socialization as women and creating a different path to the top. They are seeking and finding opportunities in fast-changing and growing organizations to show that they can achieve results—in a different way. They are succeeding because of—not in spite of—certain characteristics generally considered to be "feminine" and inappropriate in leaders.[18]

Rosener labeled the leadership style more associated with women as "interactive leadership," because leaders who exhibit it actively promote positive interactions with subordinates by encouraging participation, sharing power and information, and stimulating excitement about work. In contrast, she labeled the leadership style more associated with men as "command-and-control leadership." Marilyn Loden similarly concluded that female managers, because of biology and socialization, are more capable than male managers of exhibiting "feminine leadership," which organizations need more than ever; hence, her conclusion at the beginning of the chapter: "Vive la différence!" [19]

4. *Nonstereotypical Differences.* Yet another conclusion is that female and male managers differ in ways opposite to gender stereotypes because women managers have had to be exceptional to compensate for early socialization experiences that are different from those of men. For example, a survey of American Management Association (AMA) members found that female managers were more committed to their careers, as opposed to their home lives or other interests, than male managers with equivalent ages, salaries, educations, and managerial levels. To hold managerial positions, women may have greater barriers to overcome than men, both in their internal predispositions and in others' expectations for them, and thereby require a stronger sense of commitment to their careers. Men, in contrast, who have greater expectations for success than women, could find themselves in managerial jobs in response to such pressures even if they possess less commitment to their careers than women in equivalent positions.[20]

We shall review the extent of support for each of these competing points of view by considering five types of differences that may exist between female and male managers. The first pertains to personal traits or attributes that are brought to jobs. The second concerns behavioral responses to others, particularly subordinates, and overall leader effectiveness. The third pertains to work values and commitment to jobs, organizations, and careers. The fourth deals with experiences with stress. The fifth concerns subordinates' responses to female and male managers. Table 6.2 summarizes the findings of the review. Let's begin our analysis by examining sex differences in managerial traits.

Managerial Traits

Many studies have examined sex differences in the personal traits of managers, including their personalities, sex role identities, motivation, background, abilities, and even their physical attributes. For example, one study found that managers were significantly taller than nonmanagers, regardless of their sex, in two different organizations. The researchers speculated that taller individuals may be held in higher esteem by others. Also, tall children may have more expected of them than short children; when they meet these expectations, they may be more competent performers as a result. Your 5'5" author, who is probably biased, thinks that such conclusions may be "stretching" the point of the research (although they could explain why he is writing about management instead of practicing it). However, perceptions and expectations of others play an important role in determining who is selected for high status positions such as manager.[21]

One of the most extensive research studies ever conducted of managers and their personal characteristics took place in the Bell System through its parent, the American Telephone and Telegraph Company (AT&T). Prior to the court-ordered 1984 divestiture of its regional operating companies, the Bell System was the nation's largest business enterprise. The study originated with the assessment of 422 lower-level managers in the 1950s, a time when nearly all Bell managers were white males. These managers were considered to be representative of those managers from whom Bell's future middle- and upper-level managers would come. In the late 1970s and early 1980s, AT&T initiated a new study of 344 lower-level managers, nearly half of whom were women and about one-third were members of minority groups.[22]

The second group went through three days of assessment center exercises. Extensive comparisons were made in terms of background, work interests, personality, motivation, abilities, and overall management potential. Women had advantages in administrative ability (seen in their

Table 6.2 Sex Differences in Managers: Selected Results

Dimension	Results
Traits	
AT&T study	Offsetting sex differences in traits led to no sex difference in overall management potential.
Other studies	No difference in personality and motivation in most studies. Nonstereotypical difference in other studies: Female motivational profile is closer to that associated with successful managers.
Behavior	
Task style	Stereotypical difference in laboratory studies. No difference for actual managers.
Interpersonal style	Stereotypical difference in laboratory studies. No difference for actual managers.
Democratic versus autocratic style	Stereotypical difference.
Response to poor performer	Stereotypical difference: Males use norm of equity, whereas females use norm of equality.
Influence strategies	Stereotypical difference: Males use a wider range of strategies, more positive strategies, and less negative strategies. This difference diminishes when women managers have high self-confidence.
Effectiveness	No difference.
Values	No difference.
Commitment	No difference.
Stress	No difference for workers in general.
Subordinates' responses	Stereotypical difference in responses to managers in laboratory studies in which situation traditionally favors males. No difference in responses to actual managers.

being more creative in finding solutions to business problems), interpersonal skills and sensitivity, written communication skills, energy, and inner work standards (seen in a high concern for the quality of their own work regardless of what others thought of it). Men had advantages in company loyalty (particularly from being flexible in their goals), motivation to advance within the company, and attentiveness to power structures. The greatest sex difference was that of masculinity/femininity: Men were more likely to have traditionally masculine interests, whereas women were more likely to have traditionally feminine interests. There were no sex differences in intellectual ability, leadership ability, oral communication skills, or stability of performance.

Putting together all the information available to them and taking these trade-offs into account, the assessors judged women and men as having similar management potential. Forty-five percent of the women and 39% of the men were judged to have the potential to attain middle management in the Bell System within 10 years. Hence the conclusion at the beginning of this chapter by Douglas Bray, who directed the AT&T studies until he was succeeded by Ann Howard in 1983: "Vive la no différence!"

The AT&T study also compared assessments of the three most prevalent race and ethnic groups: white, Hispanic, and African American managers. Differences according to race and ethnicity were more pervasive than sex differences in the assessment center exercises. Fortyeight percent of white managers, 46% of Hispanic managers, and 25% of African American managers were judged to have the potential to reach middle management within 10 years. However, the sexes demonstrated distinctions within the different race and ethnic groups in overall management potential. Among white and African American managers, 10% more women than men received high ratings; among Hispanic managers, 37% more men than women received high ratings.

Other research on managers' personality and motivation generally has found few sex differences. Both male and female managers are high in their motivation to manage. Many researchers have found that women and men managers score essentially the same on psychological tests of needs and motives that are supposed to predict managerial success.[23]

When differences have been found in the relative strength of motives possessed by female and male managers, they have generally favored women and been contrary to gender stereotypes. In one study, women managers had higher needs for both achievement and power than men managers. When the need for socialized power (satisfied by serving the organization or others) was separated from the need for personalized power (satisfied by controlling and exploiting others), women were higher than men in the former and similar in the latter. In a study of nearly 2,000 managers that was similar to the AT&T study in scope but examined managers from different organizations, Susan Donnell and Jay Hall found that women managers reported lower basic needs and higher needs for self-actualization. Women were seen as exhibiting a more mature and higher-achieving motivational profile than the male managers, being more concerned with opportunities for growth, autonomy, and challenge and less concerned with work environment and pay.[24]

These results support the notion that women managers possess superior traits to their male counterparts. Women with a high need for socialized power may have once looked elsewhere such as to teaching careers to fulfill that need, but now look to managerial opportunities that are more open to them. Female managers may conform more closely than male managers to the ideal motivational profile originally developed with male managers in mind.

In summary, studies of sex differences in managerial traits offer some support for each of the views of sex differences among managers described earlier. The AT&T study found sex differences in some traits but not others, some stereotypical and others not. Certain differences favored women and others men. However, the AT&T assessors found no sex difference in overall management potential. Other research has generally supported either a no-differences view or a nonstereotypical-differences view of sex differences among managers.

Managerial Behavior and Effectiveness

Most studies of sex differences in managerial or leader behavior have examined two aspects of leadership style. The first, which may be called *task style* or task accomplishment, refers to the extent to which the manager initiates work activity, organizes it, and defines the way work is to be done. For example, a manager who reorganizes a department, develops a description of the function of each department member, formulates department and individual goals, assigns projects, and gives details on how projects should be conducted may be considered high in task style.[25]

The second, commonly called *interpersonal style* or maintenance of interpersonal relationships, refers to the extent to which the manager engages in activities that tend to the morale and welfare of people in the work setting. For example, a manager who expresses appreciation to subordinates for work performed well, is concerned about their job and work satisfaction, and seeks to build their self-esteem may be considered high in interpersonal style. Individuals' task and interpersonal styles of leadership are typically regarded as independent dimensions.

That is, a manager may be high in both task and interpersonal style, low in both, or high in one but not the other.

A third aspect of leadership style that has been frequently studied is the extent to which the leader exhibits *democratic leadership*, which allows subordinates to participate in decision making, versus *autocratic leadership*, which discourages such participation. These are generally considered to be opposite styles.

Although a meta-analysis found sex differences in each of these three dimensions of leadership style, the size of the sex difference and the circumstances under which it appeared varied. Small differences were found in task style and interpersonal style. Male leaders tended to be higher in task style and lower in interpersonal style than female leaders. However, these sex differences appeared only for individuals who participated in laboratory experiments and for nonleaders who were assessed on how they would behave if they were actually leaders. There were no sex differences in the task and interpersonal styles of actual managers. In contrast, a more pronounced sex difference was found in individuals' democratic versus autocratic leadership style. Women tended to be more democratic, less autocratic leaders than men, a difference that appeared for individuals in all settings and circumstances—actual managers, nonmanagers, and subjects in laboratory experiments. These results offer support for both a no-differences and stereotypical-sex-differences view of sex differences among managers.[26]

A separate meta-analysis found no sex difference in overall leader effectiveness. However, men fared better in male-dominated work environments such as the military, whereas women fared better in female-dominated work settings such as schools. These results support a no-differences view overall, but a stereotypical-differences view within work environments dominated by either females or males.[27]

Task style, interpersonal style, and democratic versus autocratic leadership style represent global measures of managerial behavior. Sex differences in more specific managerial behaviors are also of interest. For example, managers differ in how they react to subordinates' performance. When they are confronted with excellent or poor performers, they go through a two-step process in determining a response. First, they attribute the performance to one of four causes: ability, effort, the degree of difficulty of the task, or luck. Second, they decide on reward or punishment based on their causal attributions, which may differ when considering the performance of women versus men and people of color versus white people. Attributions range from "What's skill for the male is luck for the female" to "Those who are number two (i.e., women and people of color) try harder."[28]

Male and female leaders seem to differ in their responses to poor performers. In laboratory studies, male leaders' responses were based more on a norm of equity. They were inclined to punish subordinates who performed poorly because of lack of effort and to provide extra training to subordinates who performed poorly because of lack of ability. In contrast, the responses of female leaders were based more on a norm of equality. They were equally likely to punish or to train subordinates who performed poorly regardless of whether the performance was attributed to lack of effort or lack of ability. They also tended to be less punitive and more supportive of female subordinates. Male leaders may have preferred an equity orientation because they were socialized to value achievement, performance, and contributions to team accomplishment. Female leaders may have preferred an equality orientation because they were socialized to minimize status differences and to strive for group harmony. However, a study of actual managers that was not restricted to responses to poor performers found that women rated performance and allocated pay *more* equitably than did men.[29]

Other researchers investigated the effect of managers' self-confidence and sex on their use of general influence strategies to direct and facilitate the work of subordinates. Managers may use positive strategies emphasizing praise and rewards, negative strategies emphasizing criticism and threats, or neutral strategies emphasizing information and general interest in workers and their performance. A leader who is high in interpersonal style would be expected to use more positive than negative influence strategies. However, a leader who is high in task style could favor any of these strategies.[30]

Women, who exhibited lower self-confidence than men, tended to make fewer attempts to influence subordinates' performance; they used a more limited range of influence strategies, fewer positive strategies, and more negative strategies than men. Although the self-confidence of men was not affected by prior supervisory experience, the self-confidence of women was very much related to their prior experience as managers. Females reported levels of self-confidence commensurate with their experience, whereas males reported that they felt capable of being effective supervisors regardless of their previous experience at it. Women with high self-confidence differed less from men in their use of influence strategies than women with low self-confidence, suggesting that sex differences in influence strategies disappear as women gain experience and thereby self-confidence in managerial positions.

Other sex differences in managerial behavior may also reflect differences in self-confidence. For example, direct observations of managers at all levels in one study revealed that female managers were twice as accessible to others as their male counterparts. Criteria for accessibility included open and closed office-door policies, use of secretaries to screen out potential interruptions, and encouragement of telephoning at home on evenings and weekends. Women managers experienced greater difficulty in saying no to others, possibly stemming from their undervaluing themselves and the importance of their own time. Most female managers rarely if ever closed their office doors, while most men closed their doors when they needed to work. Accessibility is not good or bad in itself. Managers can contribute to their subordinates' satisfaction and growth by being truly accessible and gaining rapport with them, but the need to say no to subordinates' requests for time when appropriate is also an important consideration.[31]

Our review of sex differences in managerial behavior has been necessarily selective, since it is beyond the scope of this book to report the results of all studies. Overall, it portrays a mixed pattern of results. Men and women are similar in their overall effectiveness as leaders. Sex differences are inconsistent in global dimensions of behavior demonstrated by actual managers, who exhibit a stereotypical sex difference in democratic versus autocratic leadership style but not in task style or interpersonal style. Stereotypical differences in specific behaviors such as responses to poorly performing subordinates, influence strategies, and accessibility to others are more evident. However, these differences could reflect men's higher self-confidence as managers.[32] When women managers are tokens in their work environments, their treatment by dominants does not give them reason to feel confident in themselves. As male dominants become more comfortable with female tokens or as women move from having token status to occupying a larger proportion of managerial positions, women managers as a group have their competence doubted less and probably gain in self-confidence. The research on influence strategies suggests that, as women managers gain managerial experience and grow in self-confidence, they become similar to men in their responses to subordinates.

Managerial Values and Commitment

The values of managers, especially top executives, usually receive attention only when a corporate scandal takes place. Personal values have considerable influence on how managers handle the responsibilities of their jobs. Values may influence perceptions of others, solutions to problems, and the sense of what constitutes individual and organizational success. Values also influence what managers believe to be ethical and unethical behavior and whether they accept or resist organizational pressures and goals. Most evidence suggests that similarities outweigh differences in the value systems of male and female managers. With few exceptions, sex differences have not been found in the work values and personal business ethics of managers.[33]

The sense of commitment that managers bring to their work is also important, at least as far as their organizations are concerned. Commitment to job, work, organization, and career versus home or family life have all been examined in research studies. We shall simply consider commitment in general, since each suggests a greater involvement in work in spite of fine differences among them. More committed managers might be expected to work longer hours when the need arises, to relocate when the organization wishes, and to place a greater importance on the interests of the organization than on personal interests when the two are in conflict. Managers who are less committed may be more likely to emphasize their family-related and leisure interests, believe that "a job is a job," and balk when they are asked to do anything that is outside of their normal routines. Although excessive commitment could result in overzealous or unethical behavior, organizations are likely to be more effective when their managers are more committed. Clearly it is desirable for organizations to identify, hire, promote, and otherwise reward more committed managers.[34]

Thus the question of whether female or male managers, or neither, are the more committed managers is of considerable interest. Gender stereotypes suggest that women lack the high level of commitment essential for a successful managerial career. However, a meta-analysis found no sex differences between the commitment of women and men in either professional or nonprofessional jobs. Instead, commitment is best explained by variables other than a person's sex. For example, the personal influences of age, education, and the possession of higher-order growth needs are positively linked to commitment. Favorable job circumstances such as higher job satisfaction, more meaningful work, and greater utilization of skills are also positively related to commitment.[35]

Family characteristics such as being married and having children could contribute to a sex difference in managerial commitment. Although the commitment of working men in general does not appear to be affected by family considerations, the commitment of working women in general is more affected by such concerns. However, this effect may be small among managers because fewer female managers than male managers, especially in the executive ranks, are married or have children.[36]

The degree of sex-role conflict felt by the woman manager may be more important than the family situation itself in determining her level of commitment. Sex-role conflict can be caused by pressures from others as well as an overload from family responsibilities. Working women, who as a whole feel greater sex role conflict than working men, may be less committed to their jobs, organizations, and careers. However, married working women with nontraditional attitudes toward sex roles in general are more committed to their jobs than those with traditional attitudes. Women managers in particular, by assuming leadership roles in organizations, have rejected gender stereotypes. They may also be less inclined to feel sex role conflict than other women, perhaps because they are less affected by family considerations than other women or because they have worked hard to overcome such conflict. The excitement of their jobs may stimulate a strong sense of commitment that overrides the negative effect of sex-role conflict.[37]

In summary, the commitment of male and female managers seems to be affected by the same set of factors, such as family characteristics and sex-role conflict. Although these factors could lead to a sex difference in managerial commitment, job circumstances and personal factors other than sex are more likely to influence a manager's level of commitment.

Managerial Stress

Early studies of stress in managers as well as people in other occupations were conducted using male subjects. These studies found that individuals who held more taxing jobs, such as that of manager, were particularly prone to Type A behavior. As you recall, Type A behavior was described in Chapter 2 as consisting of extreme levels of competitiveness, aggressiveness, striving for achievement, haste, impatience, and feelings of being under pressures of time and responsibility. Type

A behavior increases the risk of coronary heart disease. Male managers also were found to engage in high consumption of alcohol, tranquilizers, and sleeping pills and to experience exhaustion, to be overweight, to lack exercise, to have high blood pressure, and to have family problems.[38]

More recent research using female subjects has shown that those with higher occupational levels and more demanding jobs than other women are more prone to Type A behavior and suffer from the same symptoms of stress as male managers. A study of top female executives in the United Kingdom found that the women generally did not report high incidences of physical ill health, although a quarter of them experienced migraine headaches. Rather, over half of the executives reported experiencing psychological maladies (tiredness, irritation, and anxiety). Their rates of smoking and consumption of stress-relieving drugs and alcohol were high. Similar to male managers, most of the female executives did not like to admit that they suffered from some form of stress-related illness and attempted to hide it from colleagues. They felt that they could not afford to be ill.[39]

Managerial work is stressful. Managers frequently experience work overload, both in qualitative terms by having difficult work to do, not having the necessary training, or having to meet performance standards that are too high, and in quantitative terms by having too much work to do, too many different things to do, or insufficient time to complete their work. They are responsible for many decisions but often have little latitude in making them. They have to deal with competing pressures that cannot all be satisfied, insecurity about their career progress, and ambiguity about their roles, objectives, and scope of responsibilities. Having responsibility for people versus responsibility for things is also a source of managerial stress. Since managers gain a large portion of their self-satisfaction and their identity in work, their work and nonwork lives become interdependent. Stress experienced on the job spills over into nonwork life and may contribute to stress in it as well. The stress caused by having an unsatisfactory home life may in turn contribute to the level of stress felt in the managerial role. As a result, managers often experience a vicious cycle of escalating stress in all areas of life once major stress is experienced in one area.[40]

Stress is a negative by-product of both commitment and motivation. Managers who feel a high degree of commitment work extra hours, relocate when their organization wishes, and make other personal adjustments that are more in the organization's best interest than their own.

This pattern of putting the organization first takes its toll in the form of added stress. Both female and male managers who are more committed to their jobs are more likely to exhibit Type A behavior. A high need for power, seen as preferable for managers in general, has also been linked to Type A behavior in women but not in men.[41]

Although women and men are affected by common stressors such as the demands of the managerial job, women have to deal with a unique set of stressors that men encounter less often, such as discrimination, gender stereotyping, social isolation, and the conflicting demands of family and work life. Discrimination is a major obstacle to women's advancement and thereby a key source of stress. Although women managers have not let gender stereotyping keep them from attaining management positions, they may experience stress by having to deal with individuals whose reactions to them are based on stereotypes. Social isolation resulting from being placed in the token category also contributes to stress. For married women, the conflicting demands of family and career cause stress when they are expected to provide the primary care for their children while pursuing their careers. A supportive husband who participates equally in child care and household duties can help to alleviate this stress.[42]

The home traditionally has been depicted as a sanctuary in which male breadwinners can recuperate from their stressful experiences at work; however, it can be a source of stress for men as well. In addition, men may experience unique stress from trying to live up to the demands of the masculine stereotype. For example, they may feel stress caused by role overload from trying to maintain their image as successful achievers and providers, pressure and conflict from attempts to exercise leadership, and frustration and dissatisfaction if they are not progressing as rapidly as expected in their careers. However, the consequence of male managers' trying to live up to the masculine stereotype is seen in their tendency to experience physical illness and nonwork problems rather than in their career progress. The masculine stereotype does not place as great a constraint on men's careers and achievements as the feminine stereotype places on those of women.[43]

Due to the difficulty of obtaining access to appropriate samples, the stress-related experiences of female and male managers have seldom been examined in the same study. A meta-analysis found no sex difference in occupational stress for workers from different occupations, but it did not find sufficient studies to determine whether a sex difference exists for managers in particular. Thus we do not know whether female and male managers experience different levels of suffering from stress symptoms. However, female and male managers could differ in their exposure to stressors and in their coping responses to stress. Female managers could experience greater stressors than male managers but not show it. Just as women in general take more health-related actions that prevent major illnesses from occurring than men in general, women managers could compensate for experiencing greater stressors by taking better care of themselves than men managers. The research evidence is also inconclusive on this point. It is not clear whether there are differences in the ways in which women and men cope with stress in general or in the effects of their coping strategies.[44]

However, it is clear that the managerial role tends to promote Type A behavior in both women and men, and that women and men managers exhibit many of the same symptoms of stress. Thus, attaining a managerial position seems to be a mixed blessing. The managerial role may be a source of considerable satisfaction for its male and female occupants, but it is also a source of considerable stress.

Subordinates' Responses

Even if male and female managers did not differ in any respect, subordinates could still have different preferences for working with them or respond to them differently. In the 1965 and 1985 *Harvard Business Review* surveys described earlier, agreement with the statement "I would feel comfortable working for a woman" increased from 27% to 47% for male executives and from 75% to 82% for female executives. Since individuals were not asked how comfortable they would feel working for a man, it should not be assumed that they felt totally comfortable with that prospect either. Nonetheless, it was striking that over half of male executives and almost one-fifth of female executives surveyed in 1985 reported anticipated discomfort at the prospect of working for a woman. In the same vein, a survey of employed adult Americans found that almost half preferred a boss of a specific sex. Among those workers who expressed a preference, 85% of men and 65% of women said they would rather work for a male boss.[45]

In Chapter 4, we discussed differences in individuals' tendencies to see women and men in terms of gender stereotypes. Individuals who prefer their managers to be men may be making heavy use of gender stereotypes. However, discomfort in working for women may reflect fear of the unknown as well as traditional attitudes and is likely to be alleviated by the actual experience of working for or with women managers.[46]

A meta-analysis of laboratory studies of sex differences in evaluations of leaders found a small tendency for female leaders to be evaluated less favorably than male leaders. However, this tendency was more pronounced under specific circumstances. Female leaders were particularly devalued relative to male leaders when they (1) used an autocratic leadership style, (2) occupied a male-dominated leader role, and (3) were evaluated by male subjects. Female and male leaders were evaluated in a more equivalent fashion when they (1) used an interpersonal or democratic leadership style, (2) occupied a female-dominated leader role or one with a balanced sex ratio, and (3) were evaluated by female subjects. These findings suggest that, at least in laboratory studies, gender stereotyping especially influences evaluations when the leadership style or situation invokes traditional male norms.[47]

In contrast, studies of actual managers and their subordinates have typically found that subordinates express similar satisfaction with male and female managers.[48] A comparison of two studies conducted at the United States Military Academy at West Point, one "in the laboratory" and the other "in the field," vividly demonstrates how conclusions can differ according to the method of study.

In one study, cadets worked in groups on tasks that were designed for the purpose of a behavioral experiment. Half of the groups were assigned male leaders and half had female leaders. Also, half of the groups were assigned male followers with traditional attitudes toward women and half were assigned male followers with liberal attitudes toward women. (Female cadets were scarce at West Point at the time.) After the experiment was completed, followers evaluated their leader's performance, group performance, and group morale. In the other study, conducted 2 years later, male and female cadets completed a questionnaire assessing their attitudes toward women during a new-cadet orientation program. After later completing a 6-week summer training program, they evaluated the performance of their squad or platoon leader as well as group performance and morale. In this study, 11% of the cadets had a female leader.[49]

The two West Point studies yielded substantially different results. In the laboratory study, groups with male leaders performed more effectively than groups with female leaders. Followers who held traditional attitudes toward women made less favorable judgments about female leaders than male leaders, and followers with liberal attitudes toward women made more favorable judgments about female leaders than male leaders. In the field study, male and female leaders were seen as similar in effectiveness by their followers. Also, followers did not differ in their judgments of male or female leaders depending on whether they possessed traditional or liberal attitudes toward women. Thus the laboratory study yielded results supporting followers' use of gender stereotypes in responding to their leaders, whereas the field study did not obtain such results. The researchers concluded:

> The long term duration and intensity of leader-follower interactions may be a key difference accounting for the results of the present study and prior laboratory research. In the present study, leaders and followers interacted on a 24-hour per day basis over a period of several weeks; they got to know one another quite well. In contrast, the previous studies yielding bias effects have been based on either short term laboratory interactions or totally hypothetical situations in which subjects responded to written scenarios concerning the actions of male or female managers. [The effect of gender stereotypes] may wane over time as people are compelled to judge women based on long-term performance and face-to-face interaction.[50]

Little research has been conducted on the effect of the sex of subordinates on their responses to actual leaders. A separate West Point study suggested that female subordinates give more positive ratings of leader behavior than male subordinates. This could result from their receiving more favorable treatment from leaders, with their generally favorable evaluations of leaders reflecting this preferential treatment. However, female subordinates could use different standards than male subordinates in evaluating leaders.[51]

Overall, subordinates do not appear to respond differently to male and female leaders for whom they have actually worked. Results supporting the influence of gender stereotypes on subordinates' responses to leaders have been obtained primarily from laboratory studies in situations that have traditionally favored males rather than field studies. Once subordinates have experienced both female and male managers, the effects of gender stereotypes tend to disappear and managers are treated more as individuals than as representatives of their sex. However, general tendencies to prefer male managers to female managers are present in many American workers.

Conclusion

The title of this section posed the question, "Do female and male managers differ?" The research evidence suggests the answer, "They differ in some ways and at some times, but, for the most part, they do not differ."

Women and men do not differ in their effectiveness as leaders, although some situations favor women and others favor men. In the three global measures of managerial behavior, a sex difference is present in the tendency to exhibit democratic versus autocratic leadership; sex differences in task and interpersonal style are confined to laboratory studies and not present in the leadership styles of actual managers. Specific behavioral differences, such as responses to poorly performing subordinates or influence strategies, tend to favor male managers. However, as one study suggested, these differences may be caused by the initially lower self-confidence of women managers and alleviated by the acquisition of management experience.

Most studies have found little evidence of sex differences in managerial traits. Although the AT&T study found several sex differences in traits, they offset each other in the determination of overall management potential. Sex differences in motivational profiles found in other studies tend to favor female managers. Results suggest an absence of sex differences in values, commitment, and symptoms of stress experienced. Female managers appear to be faced with greater stressors, but they may cope with stressors better than male managers. Actual male and female managers also provoke similar responses in subordinates. Overall, few sex differences favoring either men or women have been found.

Thus beliefs about the inferiority of women managers that lead many people to prefer male managers reflect gender stereotyping on their part but not reality. The stereotype that men make better managers is simply not true.

However, as we reject this stereotype, we should not necessarily conclude that female and male managers are completely interchangeable. The leadership roles that women and men hold in organizations typically provide clear guidelines for acceptable behavior. Managers become socialized into their roles early in their careers. In addition, they are selected by their organizations to fill leadership roles (and select themselves into these roles) because they are seen as meeting a specific set of attitudinal and behavioral criteria. These factors decrease the likelihood that women and men will differ substantially in their leadership styles, even if they are initially inclined to act differently as leaders. Given the strong pressures on women to conform to standards based on a stereotypically masculine view of managerial effectiveness, the finding that women tend to exhibit more democratic and less autocratic leadership than men is noteworthy.[52]

Implications: Are Better Managers Masculine?

The other stereotype about management that warrants our attention is that better managers are masculine. Unlike the stereotype that men make better managers, this stereotype has received little critical examination because management research has generally been blind to issues regarding the socialization of managers. Until recent years, virtually all theories of effective management have been based on observations of male managers. Although these theories make judgments about the effectiveness of managerial traits and behaviors, they do not recognize that men, who still comprise the majority of managers, are also judged in our society according to their adherence to the masculine gender stereotype. Thus it is not surprising that masculinity remains prevalent in the ranks of management.

The fact that managers tend to be masculine does not necessarily mean that *better* managers are masculine. Management theories have varied over the years, and no universal agreement has been reached on which theory is best. However, most theories have made reference to feminine as well as masculine characteristics. Let's briefly review some of the major theories of management.

Great-man theories were among the earliest management theories. They were developed in the belief that knowledge about the personalities of individuals who have influenced the course of Western civilization provides insight into what makes a great leader. The leaders typically examined were men such as Winston Churchill, Thomas Jefferson, and Alexander the Great. Women such as Joan of Arc, Queen Elizabeth I, and Catherine the Great who also have strongly influenced Western civilization were ignored in the development of these theories. The bias of these theories is captured best by their label; they receive little serious attention today.[53]

Trait theories of leadership assume that effective leaders are endowed with personal qualities that differentiate them from other people. These qualities may include traits associated with the masculine gender stereotype such as initiative, decisiveness, and self-confidence; traits associated with the feminine stereotype such as sociability, tactfulness, and nurturance; and traits not associated with either stereotype such as intelligence, physical energy, and fluency of speech. Given that all individuals do not have these qualities, only those who actually possess them are presumed fit to be leaders. A recent review concluded that leaders differ from nonleaders on six basic traits: drive (including achievement motivation, ambition, energy, tenacity, and initiative), the desire to lead, honesty/integrity, self-confidence, cognitive ability, and knowledge of the business. The implications of trait theories for how leaders should act in their roles, other than to be honest, learn the business, and get a good night's sleep before coming to work, are limited. Trait theories are more intended to provide guidance for the selection and training of future leaders.[54]

Behavioral theories, which focus on the specific behaviors used by managers to influence their subordinates' actions, currently receive the greatest amount of attention. Most behavioral theories distinguish between two types of managerial behavior, task style and interpersonal style. Other behavioral theories particularly focus on how decisions are made, rather than how subordinates are treated in general, and distinguish between autocratic and democratic leadership.[55]

Some behavioral theories regard one type or a certain combination of behaviors as best in all situations. For example, the Managerial Grid Theory proposes that the best manager is one who is high in both task style and interpersonal style in all situations. Other behavioral theories, also called *situational theories*, regard different types of behavior as appropriate for different situations. For example, Bob Tannenbaum and Warren Schmidt recommended that managers be more autocratic or more democratic in decision making according to such factors as their own knowledge and values, subordinates' motivation and previous experiences with managers, and time pressures. Also, Paul Hersey and Ken Blanchard's Situational Leadership Theory recommends that the manager adopt high task/low interpersonal, high task/high interpersonal, low task/high interpersonal, and low task/low interpersonal styles in that order as subordinates move from low to high in maturity.[56]

The linkage between gender stereotypes and behavioral theories of leadership is obvious. Task-oriented behaviors by the leader such as setting goals and initiating work activity are those most associated with the masculine stereotype, whereas interpersonally oriented behaviors such as showing consideration toward subordinates and demonstrating concern for their satisfaction are considered feminine. Also, the masculine stereotype implies a greater emphasis on dominance and control, that is, more autocratic and less democratic leadership, than the feminine stereotype.[57]

None of the behavioral theories suggests that better managers are masculine (i.e., high task/low interpersonal in style or autocratic in decision making) or feminine (i.e., low task/high interpersonal in style or democratic in decision making) except in special situations. The Managerial Grid Theory suggests that better managers are androgynous by advocating a combination of high task and high interpersonal style. Although they did not offer their own theory of leadership, Donnell and Hall reached the same conclusion. High managerial achievers successfully integrated their concerns for task and people, average achievers concentrated on the task at the expense of the people performing it, and low achievers showed little concern for either task or people. In sex-role identity terms, high achievers were androgynous, average achievers were masculine, and low achievers were undifferentiated. Donnell and Hall provided a possible explanation for why the ranks of management are filled with individuals who exhibit predominantly masculine behaviors, even though such behaviors are seldom exclusively recommended. These individuals may be the organization's average managers, who perform well enough to retain their positions but not well enough to be considered excellent performers.[58]

When a high task/high interpersonal behavioral style has been advocated for managers, the rationale has usually been that subordinates need both their work structured for them and concern shown for their feelings, ideas, and job satisfaction. *Androgynous leadership*, defined by Alice Sargent as "a style that blends behaviors previously deemed to belong exclusively to men or women," has been proposed for somewhat different reasons. Sargent offered three reasons why managers should be androgynous. One is that women, whom she assumed to have different qualities than men, are entering the profession of management in increasing numbers. Therefore management theory and practice should expand its definition of what makes a good manager beyond the masculine behaviors preferred by males to include the feminine behaviors preferred by the newest members of the managerial ranks. This reason relied on assumptions about the applicability of gender stereotypes to male and female managers that we questioned earlier in the chapter.[59]

The second reason offered in support of androgynous leadership is that androgyny is the best route to fulfillment in managers' personal lives and makes them happier people. If androgyny is also adopted as a standard for managerial behavior, androgynous managers will be able to better integrate their personal and professional lives. We reviewed the controversy over the advantages of androgyny for individuals in Chapter 2. Before androgyny is accepted as the ideal state of being, we need to be sure that androgynous individuals are truly better off in life.

Third, androgynous leadership is seen as particularly appropriate for the climate in which organizations currently operate. Sargent argued that workers increasingly seek fulfillment rather than just a paycheck from their work and that more motivated and committed employees are needed to take advantage of improved technology. Also, in a low-growth economy with shrinking or unchanging capital resources, organizations must focus on the contributions of their human resources if they are to improve their efficiency and work output.

This latter justification for androgynous leadership has been used for other purposes as well. Behavioral theories of leadership offer such reasoning to justify managers' showing concern for people as well as concern for the task. Other writers have concluded that one of the management principles that distinguishes successful American corporations from not-so-successful ones in today's fast-changing and increasingly competitive economy is "productivity through people," or a focus on the increased productivity possible when workers are treated in a way that encourages them to be highly involved in and committed to their work.[60]

In addition, writers advocating greater use of *feminine leadership*, or leadership styles traditionally associated with women, have used similar reasoning. For example, Loden concluded that American corporations face a crisis due to the changing nature of the world economy and the American worker. Because today's worker resents autocratic management practices, management structures based on teams and participative management are necessary for organizations to compete effectively in the global economy. They need to make greater use of a feminine leadership model, relying on team structures and collaborative decision making, rather than a masculine leadership model that relies on hierarchical structures and autocratic decision making. Loden did not advocate complete rejection of the traditional masculine approach to managing, but argued for an organizational climate that recognizes and encourages *both* approaches.[61]

Thus we reject another managerial stereotype. It makes no more sense for us to believe that better managers are masculine than it does to believe that men make better managers. Both the feminine manager, who exhibits the leadership qualities that seem necessary for corporations to compete in the global economy, and the androgynous manager, who incorporates concern for both task and people in a balanced approach to managerial situations, seem preferable to the masculine manager in today's work environment. As suggested in our discussion of managerial stereotypes, the traits displayed by the androgynous manager may appeal to both superiors and subordinates, although for different reasons. The masculine manager, who focuses solely on the work to be done and ignores the feelings and attitudes of subordinates, seems appropriate only when subordinates are extremely immature and unwilling to accept responsibility, an attitude that probably should not be reinforced by organizations that wish to remain competitive. Neither managerial stereotype is warranted, if either ever was.

As I pointed out before, stereotypes are not necessarily wrong. They are resistant to change, however, even when they are not substantiated by facts. Hopefully the stereotypes that have been perpetuated about management will die soon. Women do not deserve the burden of having to prove that members of their sex belong as managers. In addition, despite management traditions, neither women nor men deserve the burden of having to live up to the masculine stereotype in their managerial roles.

In many settings, individuals cannot deviate from traditional standards of behavior without taking considerable personal risk. They need organizational support to make the change. Organizations will be far better off if they encourage their managers to be flexible in responding to management situations and not restrict themselves to the masculine leadership model. The difference between such organizations and their less successful competitors will then be captured by the expression, "Vive la différence!"

Notes

1. M. Loden, *Feminine Leadership, or How to Succeed in Business Without Being One of the Boys* (New York: Times Books, 1985), p. 79.

2. D. W. Bray, "Ten Important Lessons about Management Success" (Presentation delivered at the Human Resources Meeting of the General Signal Company, Cambridge, MA, 1988).

3. G. W. Bowman, N. B. Worthy, and S. A. Greyser, "Are Women Executives People?" *Harvard Business Review, 43* (No. 4, July/August 1965): 15-28, 164-178.

4. C. D. Sutton and K. K. Moore, "Executive Women—20 Years Later," *Harvard Business Review, 63* (No. 5, September/October 1985): 43-66.

5. R. M. Stogdill, *Handbook of Leadership* (New York: Free Press, 1974).

6. B. M. Bass, Chapter 32, "Women and Leadership," in *Bass and Stogdill's Handbook of Leadership,* 3rd ed. (New York: Free Press, 1990).

7. V. E. Schein, "The Relationship Between Sex Role Stereotypes and Requisite Management Characteristics," *Journal of Applied Psychology, 57* (1973): 95-100; V. E. Schein, "Relationship Between Sex Role Stereotypes and Requisite Management Characteristics Among Female Managers," *Journal of Applied Psychology, 60* (1975): 340-344.

8. M. E. Heilman, C. J. Block, R. F. Martell, and M. C. Simon, "Has Anything Changed? Current Characterizations of Men, Women, and Managers," *Journal of Applied Psychology, 74* (1989): 935-942; O. C. Brenner, J. Tomkiewicz, and V. E. Schein, "The Relationship Between Sex Role Stereotypes and Requisite Management Characteristics Revisited," *Academy of Management Journal, 32* (1989): 662-669; V. E. Schein, R. Mueller, and C. Jacobson, "The Relationship Between Sex Role Stereotypes and Requisite Management Characteristics Among College Students," *Sex Roles, 20* (1989): 103-110.

9. G. N. Powell and D. A. Butterfield, "The 'Good Manager': Masculine or Androgynous?" *Academy of Management Journal, 22* (1979): 395-403.

10. G. N. Powell, Unpublished analysis of data from actual managers.

11. G. N. Powell and D. A. Butterfield, "The 'Good Manager': Did Androgyny Fare Better in the 1980s?" *Group & Organization Studies, 14* (1989): 216-233.

12. A. Cann and W. D. Siegfried, Jr., "Sex Stereotypes and the leadership Role," *Sex Roles, 17* (1987): 401-408.

13. V. E. Schein, "Sex Role Stereotyping" (Presentation delivered at the Annual Meeting of the Academy of Management, Las Vegas, 1992); V. E. Schein and R. Mueller, "Sex Role Stereotyping and Requisite Management Characteristics: A Cross Cultural Look," *Journal of Organizational Behavior* (in press); N. J. Adler, "Pacific Basin Managers: A *Gaijin,* Not a Woman," in *Women in Management Worldwide,* ed. N. J. Adler and D. N. Izraeli (Armonk, NY: Sharpe, 1988).

14. An earlier and much abbreviated version of this section of the chapter appeared in G. N. Powell, "One More Time: Do Female and Male Managers Differ?" *Academy of Management Executive, 4* (No. 3, August 1990): 68-75.

15. G. N. Powell, "Gender and Leadership" (Presentation delivered at the Annual Meeting of the Academy of Management, Las Vegas, 1992); A. H. Eagly and B. T. Johnson, "Gender and Leadership Style: A Meta-Analysis," *Psychological Bulletin, 108* (1990): 233-256.

16. A. M. Morrison, R. P. White, E. Van Velsor, and the Center for Creative Leadership, *Breaking the Glass Ceiling: Can Women Reach the Top of America's Largest Corporations?,* updated ed. (Reading, MA: Addison-Wesley, 1992), p. 49.

17. M. Hennig and A. Jardim, Chapter 2, "Patterns of Difference and Their Implications," in *The Managerial Woman* (New York: Anchor Press/ Doubleday, 1977), p. 63.

18. J. B. Rosener, "Ways Women Lead," *Harvard Business Review*, 68 (No. 6, November/December 1990), pp. 119-120.

19. Loden, Chapter 4, "The Case for Feminine Leadership," in *Feminine Leadership*. A similar argument was made in J. Grant, "Women as Managers: What They Can Offer to Organizations," *Organizational Dynamics*, 16 (No. 3, Winter 1988): 56-63.

20. G. N. Powell, B. Z. Posner, and W. H. Schmidt, "Sex Effects in Managerial Value Systems," *Human Relations*, 37 (1984): 909-921.

21. D. B. Egolf and L. E. Corder, "Height Differences of Low and High Job Status, Female and Male Corporate Employees," *Sex Roles*, 24 (1991): 365-373.

22. A. Howard and D. W. Bray, *Managerial Lives in Transition: Advancing Age and Changing Times* (New York: Guilford, 1988).

23. R. L. Dipboye, "Problems and Progress of Women in Management," in *Working Women: Past, Present, Future*, ed. K. S. Koziara, M. H. Moskow, and L. D. Tanner (Washington, DC: Bureau of National Affairs, 1987); A. Harlan and C. L. Weiss, "Sex Differences in Factors Affecting Managerial Career Advancement," in *Women in the Workplace*, ed. P. A. Wallace (Boston: Auburn House, 1982); J. B. Miner, "Motivation to Manage Among Women: Studies of Business Managers and Educational Administrators," *Journal of Vocational Behavior*, 5 (1974): 197-208.

24. L. H. Chusmir, "Motivation of Managers: Is Gender a Factor?" *Psychology of Women Quarterly*, 9 (1985): 153-159; L. H. Chusmir and B. Parker, "Dimensions of Need for Power: Personalized vs. Socialized Power in Female and Male Managers," *Sex Roles*, 11 (1984): 759-769; S. M. Donnell and J. Hall, "Men and Women as Managers: A Significant Case of No Significant Difference," *Organizational Dynamics*, 8 (No. 4, Spring 1980): 60-77.

25. Eagly and Johnson, "Gender and Leadership Style."

26. Eagly and Johnson, "Gender and Leadership Style."

27. A. H. Eagly, "Gender and Leadership" (Presentation delivered at the Annual Meeting of the American Psychological Association, San Francisco, 1991).

28. S. G. Green and T. R. Mitchell, "Attributional Processes of Leaders in Leader-Member Interactions," *Organizational Behavior and Human Performance*, 23 (1979): 429-458; K. Deaux and T. Emswiller, "Explanations of Successful Performance on Sex-Linked Tasks: What Is Skill For the Male Is Luck For the Female," *Journal of Personality and Social Psychology*, 29 (1974): 80-85; S. Feldman-Summers and S. B. Kiesler, "Those Who Are Number Two Try Harder: The Effect of Sex on Attributions of Causality," *Journal of Personality and Social Psychology*, 30 (1974): 846-855; K. L. Yarkin, J. P. Town, and B. S. Wallston, "Blacks and Women Must Try Harder: Stimulus Persons' Race and Sex Attributions of Causality," *Personality and Social Psychology Bulletin*, 8 (1982): 21-24.

29. G. H. Dobbins, "Effects of Gender on Leaders' Responses to Poor Performers: An Attributional Interpretation," *Academy of Management Journal*, 28 (1985): 587-598; G. H. Dobbins, "Equity vs. Equality: Sex Differences in Leadership," *Sex Roles*, 15 (1986): 513-525; G. H. Dobbins, E. C. Pence, J. A. Orban, and J. A. Sgro, "The Effects of Sex of the Leader and Sex of the Subordinate on the Use of Organizational Control Policy," *Organizational Behavior and Human Performance*, 32 (1983): 325-343; G. B. Northcraft, V. Huber, and M. A. Neale, "Sex Effects in Performance-Related Judgments," *Human Performance*, 1 (1988): 161-175.

30. D. Instone, B. Major, and B. B. Bunker, "Gender, Self Confidence, and Social Influence Strategies: An Organizational Simulation," *Journal of Personality and Social Psychology, 44* (1983): 322-333.

31. N. Josefowitz, "Management Men and Women: Closed vs. Open Doors," *Harvard Business Review, 58* (No. 4, September/October 1980): 57-62.

32. M. C. White, G. De Sanctis, and M. D. Crino, "Achievement, Self-Confidence, Personality Traits, and Leadership Ability: A Review of Literature on Sex Differences," *Psychological Reports, 48* (1981): 547-569. For an opposing view regarding sex differences in managerial self-confidence, see L. H. Chusmir, C. S. Koberg, and M. D. Stecher, "Self-Confidence of Managers in Work and Social Situations: A Look at Gender Differences," *Sex Roles, 26* (1992): 497-512.

33. Powell et al., "Sex Effects in Managerial Value Systems"; C. Mottaz, "Gender Differences in Work Satisfaction, Work-Related Rewards and Values, and the Determinants of Work Satisfaction," *Human Relations, 39* (1986): 359-378; L. H. Chusmir and B. Parker, "Gender and Situational Differences in Managers' Values: A Look at Work and Home Lives," *Journal of Business Research, 23* (1991): 325-335; G. E. Stevens, "The Personal Business Ethics of Male and Female Managers: A Comparative Study" (Paper delivered at the Annual Meeting of the Academy of Management, Dallas, 1983). For an exception, see O. C. Brenner, A. P. Blazini, and J. H. Greenhaus, "An Examination of Race and Sex Differences in Managerial Work Values," *Journal of Vocational Behavior, 32* (1988): 336-344.

34. G. N. Powell, B. Z. Posner, and W. H. Schmidt, "Women: The More Committed Managers?" *Management Review, 74* (No. 6, June 1985): 43-45; D. M. Randall, "Commitment and the Organization: The Organization Man Revisited," *Academy of Management Review, 12* (1987): 460-471.

35. F. F. Aven, Jr., B. Parker, and G. M. McEvoy, "Gender and Attitudinal Commitment to Organizations: A Meta-Analysis," *Journal of Business Research* (in press); L. H. Chusmir, "Job Commitment and the Organizational Woman," *Academy of Management Review, 7* (1982): 595-602.

36. Korn/Ferry International, *Profile of Senior Women Executives* (New York: Korn/Ferry International, 1982); Sutton and Moore, "Executive Women—20 Years Later."

37. Chusmir, "Job Commitment and the Organizational Woman"; M. Kim and C. Cammann, "Effects of Family-Related Variables and Sex Differences on Job Involvement" (Paper delivered at the Annual Meeting of the Academy of Management, Chicago, 1986); C. S. Koberg and L. H. Chusmir, "Impact of Sex Role Conflict on Job-Related Attitudes," *Journal of Human Behavior and Learning, 4* (No. 3, 1987): 50-59.

38. R. J. Burke and T. Weir, "The Type A Experience: Occupational and Life Demands, Satisfaction and Well Being," *Journal of Human Stress, 6* (No. 4, 1980): 28-38; C. L. Cooper and M. J. Davidson, "The High Cost of Stress on Women Managers," *Organizational Dynamics, 10* (No. 4, Spring 1982): 44-53.

39. K. E. Kelly and B. K. Houston, "Type A Behavior in Employed Women: Relation to Work, Marital, and Leisure Variables, Social Support, Stress, Tension, and Health," *Journal of Personality and Social Psychology, 49* (1985): 1067-1079; Cooper and Davidson, "The High Cost of Stress on Women Managers."

40. J. M. Ivancevich and M. T. Matteson, Chapter 1, "The Nature of Stress," and Chapter 5, "Physical Environment and Individual Level Stressors," in *Stress and Work: A Managerial Perspective* (Dallas: Scott, Foresman, 1980).

41. J. A. Hood and L. H. Chusmir, "Factors Determining Type A Behavior Among Employed Women and Men" (Paper delivered at the Annual Meeting of the Academy of Management, Chicago, 1986).

42. D. L. Nelson and J. C. Quick, "Professional Women: Are Distress and Disease Inevitable?" *Academy of Management Review, 10* (1985): 206-218; A. P. Brief, R. S. Schuler, and M. Van Sell, Chapter 7, "Working Women and Stress," in *Managing Job Stress* (Boston: Little, Brown, 1981).

43. G. K. Baruch, L. Biener, and R. C. Barnett, "Women and Gender in Research on Work and Family Stress," *American Psychologist, 42* (1987): 130-136; Brief, Schuler, and Van Sell, Chapter 7, "Working Women and Stress," in *Managing Job Stress.*

44. J. J. Martocchio and A. M. O'Leary, "A Note on Stress: A Meta-Analysis of the Relationship Between Sex and Occupational Status," *Proceedings: Annual Meeting of the Academy of Management,* ed. F. Hoy (Anaheim, 1988); T. D. Jick and L. F. Mitz, "Sex Differences in Work Stress," *Academy of Management Review, 10* (1985): 408-420.

45. Bowman, Worthy, and Greyser, "Are Women Executives People?"; Sutton and Moore, "Executive Women—20 Years Later"; M. B. Rubner, "More Workers Prefer a Man in Charge," *American Demographics, 13* (No. 6, June 1991): 11.

46. H. F. Ezell, C. A. Odewahn, and J. D. Sherman, "The Effects of Having Been Supervised by a Woman on Perceptions of Female Managerial Competence," *Personnel Psychology, 34* (1981): 291-299; Bowman, Worthy, and Greyser, "Are Women Executives People?"

47. A. H. Eagly, M. G. Makhijani, and B. G. Klonsky, "Gender and the Evaluation of Leaders: A Meta-Analysis," *Psychological Bulletin, 111* (1992): 3-22.

48. Bass, Chapter 32, "Women and Leadership," in *Bass and Stogdill's Handbook of Leadership;* K. M. Bartol and D. C. Martin, "Women and Men in Task Groups," in *The Social Psychology of Female-Male Relations: A Critical Analysis of Central Concepts,* ed. R. D. Ashmore and F. K. Del Boca (Orlando, FL: Academic Press, 1986).

49. R. W. Rice, L. R. Bender, and A. G. Vitters, "Leader Sex, Follower Attitudes Toward Women, and Leadership Effectiveness: A Laboratory Experiment," *Organizational Behavior and Human Performance, 25* (1980): 46-78; J. Adams, R. W. Rice, and D. Instone, "Follower Attitudes Toward Women and Judgments Concerning Performance by Female and Male Leaders," *Academy of Management Journal, 27* (1984): 636-643.

50. Adams, Rice, and Instone, "Follower Attitudes Toward Women," pp. 641-642.

51. R. W. Rice, D. Instone, and J. Adams, "Leader Sex, Leader Success, and Leadership Process: Two Field Studies," *Journal of Applied Psychology, 69* (1984): 12-31.

52. L. M. Calvert and V. J. Ramsey, "Bringing Women's Voice to Research on Women in Management," *Journal of Management Inquiry, 1* (1992): 79-88; Powell, "Gender and Leadership"; Eagly and Johnson, "Gender and Leadership Style."

53. Bass, Chapter 3, "An Introduction to Theories and Models of Leadership," in *Bass and Stogdill's Handbook of Leadership.*

54. S. A. Kirkpatrick and E. A. Locke, "Leadership: Do Traits Matter?" *Academy of Management Executive, 5* (No. 2, May 1991): 48-60.

55. Eagly and Johnson, "Gender and Leadership Style."

56. R. R. Blake and J. S. Mouton, *The Managerial Grid* (Houston: Gulf, 1964); R. Tannenbaum and W. H. Schmidt, "How to Choose a Leadership Pattern," *Harvard Business Review, 36* (No. 2, March/April 1958): 95-102; P. Hersey and K. H. Blanchard, *Management of Organizational Behavior: Utilizing Human Resources,* 4th ed. (Englewood Cliffs, NJ: Prentice Hall, 1982).

57. A. Cann and W. D. Siegfried, "Gender Stereotypes and Dimensions of Effective Leader Behavior," *Sex Roles*, 23 (1990): 413-419.

58. Donnell and Hall, "Men and Women as Managers."

59. A. G. Sargent, "Prologue" and Chapter 6, "New Models of Effective Managers in the 1980s," in *The Androgynous Manager* (New York: AMACOM, 1981), p. 2. For a review of research on androgynous leadership, see K. Korabik, "Androgyny and Leadership Style," *Journal of Business Ethics*, 9 (1990): 9-18.

60. T. J. Peters and R. H. Waterman, Jr., *In Search of Excellence: Lessons from America's Best-Run Companies* (New York: Harper & Row, 1982).

61. Loden, *Feminine Leadership*.

7

Getting Ahead—In Career and Life

Gary N. Powell and Lisa A. Mainiero

The Two-Career Carousel

Imagine that three of America's beloved old sitcoms were modernized to reflect the predicaments facing today's urban young professionals. In the new versions, Ozzie and Harriet Nelson (*The Adventures of Ozzie and Harriet*), Ward and June Cleaver (*Leave It to Beaver*), and Jim and Margaret Anderson (*Father Knows Best*) would be newly married yuppies. The wives, of course, would have careers outside the home.

Harriet would have an MBA degree and would be employed in the marketing division of a *Fortune* 500 corporation; June would have a law degree and would be an associate with a large law firm; and Margaret would be a field producer with a television news program.

Instead of hilarious situations about a casserole that burns the evening the boss is coming to dinner or tiffs with the neighbors, the new plots would deal with Ozzie's reaction to Harriet's bigger salary, June's insistence that she postpone having children until she becomes a partner in the firm, and Margaret's disruptive transfer to London.

The new reality also means extinction for one of the most enduring domestic scenes in middle-class mythology:

The big guy comes home after a hard day at the office. Exhausted, he collapses in his favorite chair. The little woman, who much earlier completed her housewifely duties and is refreshed and attentive, gives him an adoring kiss, mixes him a drink, brings him the newspaper—

pipe and slippers are optional—and asks him how his day was. Sometimes, she surprises him by putting the kids to bed early and preparing a romantic, candlelight dinner for the two of them.

Fade out and flash forward. Now, they *both* are wiped out from
work, although it is unlikely that they arrive at the apartment at the
same time. He is probably working late on a report, and she may be
flying to Seattle on business. If they are both in town, chances are they
will take a brief nap, jog or visit the health club, then eat at a trendy
neighborhood restaurant—taking recreational drugs or talking shop to
keep from falling asleep at the table—before heading home and crash-
ing to a TV talk show monologue.

Paul Galloway[1]

Galloway's humor conveys what may be called the old and new stereotypes of women's and men's careers. Women and men had vastly different career patterns under the old stereotype: women were homemakers and men were breadwinners. The new stereotype portrays women
and men as having similar career patterns: both members of a couple
"win bread" and, with the help of the babysitter or day care program,
also "make home" in their spare time. We know that the old stereotype
is no longer appropriate, but should it be replaced with the new one?
Are there no longer any differences between men's and women's career
patterns, or do some differences remain? If so, what are they?[2]

Unfortunately, we cannot rely on theories of career development that
have been proposed in the management literature for answers to these
questions. Similar to theories of what makes for an effective manager,
most theories of how individuals' careers evolve and what helps or
hinders them in getting ahead in organizations have been derived from
observations of men. If data on women's and men's careers had been
compared, there would be some concrete basis for describing their
career patterns as similar or different. However, because such comparisons have seldom been made, most conclusions about sex differences
in career patterns are speculative rather than factual.

The overemphasis on men's careers is not as easily remedied as the
overemphasis on men's management styles. Managerial behavior yields
a variety of short-term results that may be measured and evaluated, en-
abling researchers to reach conclusions about the effectiveness of female

and male managers fairly easily. Careers, in contrast, may cover a span of over 60 years from childhood's first impressions of occupations to aspirations to first jobs to retirement. To establish whether men and women differ in their basic career patterns, we would need to compare their career decisions, strategies, and progress over time. Such research would yield meaningful results only if the necessary data were available and if the external factors that affected individuals' careers either remained constant over the duration of careers or changed in a manner that similarly affected women and men. However, neither of these conditions has been met during the last 60 years.

Until the 1970s, researchers were rarely interested in women's careers; even if they had been inclined to collect the necessary data, few women were in the ranks of management before the 1970s, rendering statistical comparison of the careers of successful women and men impractical. Furthermore, social and governmental pressures forced many organizations beginning in the late 1960s to initiate affirmative action programs. Proportions of women and men in various jobs became closely monitored rather than ignored or taken for granted as before, and corrective actions were often attempted, though they were seldom entirely successful. As a result, the forces that influenced the development of men's and women's careers changed.

Thus it has been nearly impossible in recent years for anyone to discover whether women's and men's careers are best described by the same or by separate theories and concepts. Longitudinal studies, more difficult to conduct than studies with shorter time perspectives, are essential for reaching definitive conclusions about the patterns of women's and men's careers. An absence of social changes that differentially affected the sexes over the course of these studies would also contribute to the usefulness of their results. In the meantime, what is available for us to consider is a relatively small amount of research evidence and a relatively large amount of speculation based on limited observations over a narrow period of time.

In this chapter, we shall review both the speculation and the facts about women's and men's careers. Many career theorists in the past started with men's careers and then treated women's careers as special cases. We shall turn things around by examining effects in the opposite direction: That is, our study shall start with the factors that influence women's careers and then suggest implications for men's careers as well. First, the ways in which various theories of career development have addressed the topic of sex differences will be examined. Second, a model will be presented, based on observations of women's careers, that may serve as a basis for understanding career development issues faced by both sexes. Third, in light of the model, the research evidence on the personal, organizational, and societal factors that influence career patterns will be reviewed. Finally, we shall examine the implications of our review for organizations in aiding their employees' pursuit of careers and for individuals in pursuing their own careers.

Theories of Career Development

Most theories of career development raise and address, even if only in passing, the question of sex differences. Women's careers are typically depicted as vastly different from men's, although reasons for the perceived sex differences depend on whether the theorist has been more interested in men's or women's careers. Some theorists have argued that men's and women's abilities, interests, and proper roles in society are basically different. Others have maintained that the life experiences that shape women's and men's careers are basically different. Still others have claimed that although the career development of women is not fundamentally different from the career development of men, women's careers are a great deal more complex.

Theories Emphasizing Men's Careers

The primary career models that characterize adult development typically have viewed anomalies associated with women over the life span as "developmental deficiencies" that require added explanation.[3] For example, Donald Super, author of one of the first formal theories of career development, regarded woman's role as homemaker as a biological and social necessity. He argued that women's careers, career orientations, and career motivations are fundamentally different from those of men because the woman's role as childbearer makes her the focal point of the home and gives homemaking a central place in her career. In support of this argument, he quoted Kate Meuller, author of the 1954 book *Educating Women for a Changing World*:

> Girls will be girls, or at least 90 percent of them will be girls, and the other 10 percent may find themselves in *Who's Who*. . . . The significant thing is the far more uniform and standardized pattern of feminine

interests than of masculine. John may want to be a lawyer, physician, engineer, farmer, statistician, radio announcer, but Mary, nine times out of ten, can see no further than her marriage. She wants a little job that will put her immediately into the company of men.[4]

Super proposed that people experience four distinct psychological stages in their careers: exploration, establishment, maintenance, and decline, resulting in four career patterns for men and seven career patterns for women. For men, they were (a) *stable*, life-long occupation begun immediately after schooling; (b) *conventional*, a progression from initial to trial to stable employment; (c) *unstable*, failure to establish stable employment at first attempt and change to a career in which the individual may or may not permanently establish himself; and (d) *multiple-trial*, frequent change of employment with no one type sufficiently prolonged to justify calling the person established in a career. Career patterns for women included (a) *stable homemaking*, marriage at the completion of schooling or shortly thereafter with no significant work experience; (b) *conventional*, marriage and full-time homemaking ends what starts as the conventional career pattern for men; (c) *stable working*, work as the life career in lieu of marriage (followed by Meuller's 10% of women); (d) *double-track*, continuing to work after marriage —a "double career"; (e) *interrupted*, a sequence of working, homemaking, and then working while or instead of homemaking; (f) *unstable*, irregular switching between working and homemaking; and (g) *multiple-trial*, a pattern of unrelated jobs as for men.

Super assumed that the same stages of career development were applicable to both sexes when childbearing and homemaking tasks for women were taken into account, an assumption that was not supported by later research.[5] He deserves some credit for recognizing that women as well as men had careers outside the home, at a time when the media conveyed an image of women as exclusively homemakers. He also deserves credit for acknowledging that he did not have data on women's careers and was therefore speculating. However, Super's theory was primarily based on gender stereotypes, as evidenced by his citation of Mueller (being in *Who's Who* and being female are incompatible; women want a "little" job to place themselves in the company of men). He reflected the prevailing bias of his times, a bias that many people still hold, that women's central role as homemaker is based on a biological fact. Although society prescribed this role for women for a long time, however, no biological fact stops the husband from being a full-time homemaker and the wife from pursuing a full-time career.

Other models of career development proposed at about the same time conveyed a similar bias. For example, in investigating individuals' occupational choices, Eli Ginzberg and his colleagues restricted their primary sample to males because "in our society the role of work has heightened significance for the male members. This does not deny that many women have strong occupational drives, but it [the decision to study males only] was based on the assumption that for most women marriage, rather than a job, forms the center of life." Sons within upper-middle-class families who were either Protestant or Catholic, had both parents alive and living together, and judged to be free of any physical, emotional, or intellectual handicap were chosen to be interviewed for the study, because such boys were felt to have minimum constraints on their occupational choices. To offer some comparison with the males, 10 female college students were also interviewed. Neither group was a good representative sample.[6]

Nonetheless, Ginzberg et al. concluded that their assumptions about women's versus men's career interests were supported by their study. The males considered marriage an eventuality that did not affect their choice of occupation. In contrast, the females were reported not to have any clear picture of the type of life they would lead because it would be largely determined by whether they married, when they married, whom they married, when they had children and how many, and the attitudes of their husbands toward their working. Three types of female career patterns were identified: work-oriented, marriage-oriented, and a combination of work and marriage in which marriage dominated. In contrast, males were depicted as solely work-oriented. As Super had done, Ginzberg et al. concluded that the career development process of women and men was equivalent except that marriage was more important than work in the career planning of most women.

More recent theories of career development have not been as obvious in their endorsement of gender stereotypes. Nevertheless, many allegedly general theories have still been consciously or unconsciously based on data about men's career patterns, with those of women treated as special cases to which theories should be carefully applied. For example, Edgar Schein identified the stages of the career cycle as growth, fantasy, and exploration (age 0-21), entry into the world of work (16-25), basic training (16-25), full membership in early career (17-30), full membership in midcareer (25+), midcareer crisis (35-45), late career in nonleadership role (40-retirement) or leadership role (unspecified), decline and disengagement (40-retirement), and retirement. Schein listed general issues to be confronted and specific tasks to be completed for each stage. His discussion of the similarity or difference between men's and women's careers was limited to one sentence: "Since much of the research has been done on men, there is likely to be some male-oriented bias in the stages and crises which have been identified." He then identified what were first called "stages and tasks of the [male] biosocial cycle" and then simply "stages and tasks of the biosocial cycle." The only other specific mention women received was as contributing to the increase in dual-career families through their increased participation in the work force, with dual-career issues seen as calling for some form of accommodation by one or both job holders.[7] We shall discuss these issues at length later in the chapter.

Daniel Levinson, in *The Seasons of a Man's Life*, presented a model of adult development that received considerable attention. He identified specific stages and developmental tasks associated with early adulthood (e.g., early adult transition, entering the adult world, age 30 transition, settling down), middle adulthood (e.g., mid-life transition, entering middle adulthood, age 50 transition, culmination of middle adulthood), and late adulthood. Although the back cover of the paperback edition of *Seasons* said that it "explores and explains the specific periods of personal development through which *all* human beings must pass—and which together form a common pattern underlying *all* human lives," Levinson based his theory-building effort on in-depth interviews with a sample of 40 men. His rationale for including only men is described as follows:

> Ultimately, it is essential to study the adult development of both genders if we are to understand either. The challenge of development is at least as great for women as for men. . . . Despite my strong desire to include women, I decided finally against it. A study of twenty men and twenty women would do justice to neither group. The differences between women and men are sufficiently great so that they would have to become a major focus of analysis. . . . In all candor, however, I must admit to a more personal reason for the choice: I chose men partly because I wanted so deeply to understand my own adult development.[8]

Here we see the familiar (and in this case admitted) bias of a male researcher toward examining only men's careers, although this time justified for personal reasons. Later studies of women's lives concluded that they follow essentially the same stages that Levinson ascribed to men.[9]

Theories Emphasizing Women's Careers

From the time of Freud's early writings, researchers have attempted to understand the developmental patterns that characterize individuals' lives. In recent years, some of these attempts have turned exclusively to the study of women. Questions about the applicability of models that have concentrated solely on men have been raised by a number of authors, who propose that women's lives present unique challenges and stresses not accounted for in most of the career development literature.

Theorists have taken either of two approaches to the study of women's adult and career development: (a) they have specifically attempted to redress the historical emphasis on men in commonly accepted developmental models, or (b) they have attempted to develop unique theories that focus on women's development exclusively.

Following the first approach, Judith Bardwick identified the "seasons of a woman's life" by reexamining Levinson's model of male adult development in the context of women. She noted that women continually place an emphasis on relationships as well as career development, which affects their adherence to Levinson's stages and the developmental tasks he assigned to each stage. For example, in the early adult transition stage (ages 17-28), although they are aware of the need to decide on career goals, women focus on marriage and forming adult commitments. At the end of the settling down stage (ages 36-40), while men's primary concern according to Levinson is "becoming one's own man," women's unique childbearing status frames their life choices. Middle adulthood (ages 40-50) then becomes a time of great promise for women. While men who have been successful achievers give up their preoccupations with themselves, women who have sacrificed their needs in relationships become more independent, allowing a more concentrated effort on career and self-identity issues.[10]

In the same vein, Carol Gilligan offered an alternative explanation for stages of moral development originally proposed by Lawrence Kohlberg by including a value on connectedness and interdependence in women. She argued that male developmental patterns focus on values of justice and fairness. Men's development begins with separation and individuality, emphasizes achievement and accomplishments, eventually explores intimacy and connections with others, and finally views others as equally important to the self. For women, the developmental pattern is reversed. It begins with the assumption of connectedness and inter-dependence, gradually explores means of separation and individuality, allows women to achieve and chart accomplishments as individuals, and then gradually allows women to view their contributions as of equal importance to that of others. To Gilligan, women were not "less devel-oped" morally than men, but experienced life and its possibilities in fundamentally different ways from men.[11]

New theories that stress the special and unique features of women's careers bear little on the traditional approaches to career development. For example, Helen Astin presented a model of women's and men's career development that focused on how socialization experiences and constraints on workplace opportunities shape individuals' work expec-tations (i.e., perceptions of what types of work are accessible and can best satisfy developmental needs), which in turn influence later career choices. Women's socialization experiences direct them to consider only a particular set of occupational career choices; the constraints on oppor-tunities that are placed on them further shape their expectations for achievement in those careers. Because men are not subject to the same constraints and expectations, their career and adult development dif-fers from that of women.[12] You will recall similar reasoning in our discussion of occupational aspirations and expectations in Chapter 3.

In contrast, Barbara Gutek and Laurie Larwood argued that theories of women's and men's career development must be separate, for vari-ous reasons: Men and women have different expectations regarding the appropriateness of jobs for them. Women are faced with more con-straints in the workplace, particularly the use of gender stereotypes in hiring and promotion decisions and in performance evaluations. Whereas family life is often treated as an external irrelevancy in models of men's careers, it is an important consideration for women. Husbands and wives do not accommodate themselves to each other's careers to the same extent; wives generally are more willing to move or otherwise adapt to their husbands' careers. Also, as typically practiced by individu-als, the mother role requires more time and effort than the father role.[13]

Gutek and Larwood identified five elements that a theory of women's career development should possess: career preparation, opportunities available, marriage, pregnancy and children, and timing. The situation seen as most likely to lead to career success is one in which the woman is prepared in adolescence to anticipate a career, finds that opportuni-ties necessary for her career are available, embarks on her career at the same age as a man, remains committed to working whether or not she marries or has children, and returns to her career as rapidly as possible if she has children. The traditional situation for women is the exact opposite; the adolescent woman does not anticipate a career, sees few interesting career possibilities available, and psychologically prepares for being a housewife. If she holds a job at the time of marriage, it is one that is started and ended easily and requires little training. She leaves the job after marriage if her husband's income is sufficient, or after pregnancy for as long as economically possible. If she reenters the work force, it is when she is older and is at a disadvantage because of both her age and lack of prior job experience.

Other justifications have been offered for separate theories of women's career development. When traditional standards of career success are used, it is easy to assess women who choose to forge a career that combines achievement and nurturance as failing professionally. However, a view of women's development that places a value on the number and variety of experiences over the life span paints a more positive picture. The more diverse the experience, the better the chances of using prior knowledge for adaptations to later crises. In addition, it may be easier to discuss what a woman's conception of a career *is not*—a lock-step progression of jobs at increasingly higher levels directed by a goal of upward mobility and career success no matter what the personal cost —than what it *is*.[14]

Thus, we have seen a shift away from a reliance on gender stereotypes in theories of career development. Super and Ginzberg et al. presented stereotypes as facts. For Super, the "fact" that women's careers were centered around homemaking was based on his general observations and opinions. For Ginzberg et al., the "fact" that most women placed marriage before career was initially stated as an assumption and then as supported by interviews with only 10 college women. Some general theorists have not reached the same stereotypical conclusions while acknowledging the complexities of women's careers.[15] When they have proposed any sex difference in career patterns at all, they have referred to the effects of such factors as differential socialization experiences, family status, and workplace opportunities rather than to gender stereotypes. Still, in many cases, supposedly general theories of career development have been primarily based on observations of men.

The theorists reviewed would agree that men's and women's career patterns tend to be strikingly different, but for different reasons. Early theorists such as Super and Ginzberg et al. would cite women's natural

inclination towards homemaking as their primary vocation. Later theorists such as Astin and the team of Gutek and Larwood would claim a
difference in the social forces and opportunities that shape women's
and men's careers.

However, if the issues identified by the theories that emphasize
women's careers serve as any guide, then two themes become clear: (a)
women's career and life development involve a complex panorama of
choices and constraints; and (b) issues of balance, connectedness, and
interdependence *in addition to* issues of achievement and individuality
permeate women's lives. We shall return to these themes as we further
consider both women's and men's career development.

Crosscurrents in the River of Time

In order to understand the current nature of women's and men's
careers, we need a theory that can account for the ways in which women's
and men's career patterns are both similar and different. A career pattern may be considered the cumulative result of the positions held by
an individual (including nonwork activities) and the transitions made
from one position to another. If there were sex differences in career
patterns, we would expect to find them in the effects of various factors
on the positions held and transitions made by men and women. As a
means of working towards a theory of career development, let's more
closely examine the themes that appear likely to influence the shape of
women's career patterns.

Our approach to women's career development does not represent
radically new thought. Instead, it incorporates the various influences
on women's careers that have been previously identified in theories and
research. In this section of the chapter, I will describe the four primary
ingredients of this approach and how they relate to each other. Then,
we will consider men's careers.

There seems to be two types of concerns that influence the lives of
women who are working, contemplating working, or temporarily not
working: (a) concerns about career and personal achievements at work
(called "concern for career" for short) and (b) concerns about family
and personal relationships outside of work (called "concern for relationships" or "concern for others" for short). At any point in time, women
may place primary emphasis on career and personal achievements at
work, place primary emphasis on family and personal relationships

outside of work, or try to strike some kind of balance between the two. They are likely to be concerned both with career and others at all times, but they place different degrees of emphasis on career versus others in their actions and decisions at different times. Thus, the placing of primary emphasis on career and the placing of primary emphasis on relationships with others may be considered as opposite ends of the same continuum.

Some women reject the idea of such a continuum and try to be "super-women," simultaneously pursuing success in both career and relation-ships with a vengeance. Although they may experience high levels of success in both spheres of life, superwomen also experience high levels of stress. Leisure time, during which they relax while pursuing their own interests, is a luxury they cannot afford. Eventually many super-women recognize the difficulty of being "super" in all areas of their lives at once and cut back in their emphasis on either career or relation-ships. Only then do they accept the notion of trade-offs that this con-tinuum implies.[16]

As a result of where they fall on this continuum, and also as a result of personal, organizational, and societal factors that act as constraints on their choices, women experience various degrees of success in their careers and in their relationships with others. The term *success* is used here to make a point about what does and should constitute success for individuals, especially in the realm of career:

> If the "traditional" model of career success, based primarily on observations of men, has emphasized objective measures and focused primarily on work life, surely a "nontraditional" model of career success, based primarily on observations of women, should emphasize subjective measures and include consideration of nonwork as well as work life.

This is not to say that men define their career success solely through objective measures or women by subjective measures. Instead, we suggest an expansion of the concept of career success to include con-cepts that have been associated more with how contemporary women view success than with how men traditionally have been regarded to view career success.

Career success is the more familiar concept. In the past, it typically has been measured by "objective" variables such as salary, title, or the position within the organizational hierarchy. Measuring career suc-cess only by objective variables that emphasize "getting ahead" in an organization has been associated with a traditionally male definition of success. That definition now appears dated in the light of corporate mergers, downsizing, lessened job security, and changes to career paths in many organizations that truncate traditional modes of achievement.

But success also may be measured by "subjective" variables such as satisfaction with the present job or with future prospects at work (e.g., perceived opportunities for advancement, perceived opportunities to hold onto a desirable job). We believe that women may focus more on measures of satisfaction that represent *how they are feeling* about their careers, rather than what their careers actually look like. In attempting to strike a balance between their relationships with others and their personal achievements at work, women seek some level of personal or subjective satisfaction in *both* realms. By so doing, they may be better equipped to cope with corporate mergers, downsizing, and the like than individuals who are preoccupied with objective measures of career success.

The notion of "success" in relationships with others is adopted to provide a concept that is analogous to career success. Marital status, number of children, number of close friends, and frequency of personal contacts with others could be used as objective measures of success. However, using only such variables would be absurd. Subjective measures such as *satisfaction with relationships*, which focuses on their perceived quality, are more telling than the objective characteristics of those same relationships. In the same vein, *satisfaction with career*, defined in terms of its perceived quality, may be more important than objective career achievements as measured by promotions, salary increments, and the like.

So far, we have identified three ingredients of our approach to women's careers: (a) emphasis on career versus relationships with others, (b) success in career, and (c) success in relationships with others. The fourth ingredient is time. Although it may seem trite to say, time exists in women's lives in the past, present, and future. Successes in career and in relationships with others experienced in the past influence present satisfaction levels, which in turn incorporate satisfaction with what the future is expected to look like. Individual women may choose to defer present satisfaction in one realm (e.g., relationships with others) to focus on another realm (e.g., career) in anticipation of greater satisfaction in the first realm at a later date. Thus, timing considerations need to be included in our approach.

Figure 7.1 represents these four ingredients. Imagine that as individuals grow older, they move from left to right along the time dimension in the figure at a steady rate. One can view time as flowing like a river, as non-management-oriented writers such as Hermann Hesse have. The phrase "the river of time," used by David Brin as the title of a short story and collection of stories, seems apt for our use.[17]

At any point in time, a woman places a particular degree of emphasis on career versus relationships with others in her actions and decisions. She may place a greater emphasis on career or on relationships, or she may strive to achieve a balance between the two. If she emphasizes one sphere of activity at present, this emphasis may be part of a life plan that anticipates later emphasis on the other sphere. One can imagine concern for career as a current that pushes a woman toward the "upper bank" of the river of time in Figure 7.1, and concern for others as pushing her toward the "lower bank" of the river. The two types of concerns then act as "crosscurrents in the river of time."

Also, at any point in time, individuals achieve particular levels of success in career and in relationships. These success levels are represented in Figure 7.1 along the opposite banks of the river of time. Success in career can be depicted by a dimension that rises from the upper bank of the river, whereas success in relationships rises from the lower bank of the river.

In summary, this approach depicts individual women as (a) placing themselves somewhere along a continuum reflecting emphasis on career versus relationships and (b) experiencing levels of success in both career and relationships at any point in time. It *does not* depict women as occupying specific career or life stages at specific points in time. Because theories emphasizing women's careers suggest that their lives cannot be pinned down so precisely, this approach does not attempt to do so.

What does this approach have to say about men's careers? Simply that men's careers may be depicted by the same nontraditional model. Contrary to assumptions made by early models of men's careers such as those proposed by Super and Ginzberg et al., not all men are exclusively career-driven without concern for the impact on their family and relationships with others outside of the workplace.[18] Just as women do, individual men place themselves somewhere along the same continuum that reflects their emphasis on career versus relationships. They also experience some degree of success in both career and relationships at any point in time.

If men's and women's careers can be described by the same model, does this mean that they have similar careers? Not necessarily. Individuals base their actions in part on what they see as their *potential* for

"Success" in Career

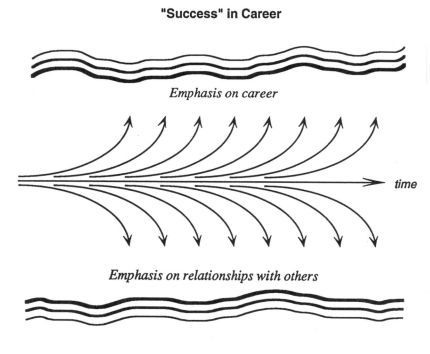

Emphasis on career

time

Emphasis on relationships with others

"Success" in Relationships With Others

Figure 7.1. Crosscurrents in the River of Time
NOTE: Vantage point is that of "looking down" on the river of time.

success in career and relationships. If women see less potential for career success than men due to personal, organizational, or societal factors, they will be less inclined to emphasize their careers in their actions. Even if women see the same potential for career success as men, they will be hindered in achieving it if such factors place greater career constraints on them. As a result, women's career patterns, although governed by the same processes, may be considerably different from those of men.

Factors That Influence Career Development

This section of the chapter will examine the prominent personal, organizational, and societal factors that pull women toward and away from each side of the river of time as they address the multiple and conflicting demands and challenges in their lives. It will conclude with consideration of how the same factors affect men.

Personal Factors

Personal factors have a considerable effect on women's success in both career and relationships with others. They influence and also reflect where emphasis is placed. Two types of personal factors will be discussed. The first pertains to the woman as a member of a family unit and includes career interruptions, dual-career demands, and parenting demands. The second considers a woman as an individual and includes work motivation and career choices.

Career Interruptions, Dual-Career Demands, and Parenting Demands. Women are more likely than men to take a "slow burn" path to career success. They may end up at the same level as men with similar personal characteristics, but they take a longer time to reach it because they make more accommodations to family and personal life along the way. However, when women make decisions that lead to gaps in their employment history, their later advancement and earnings are likely to suffer.[19]

The most often cited reason for women's career interruptions is to satisfy the demands of dual-career parenting. Family considerations are different for women and men, especially in the managerial ranks. As noted in Chapter 6, fewer female managers than male managers are married or have children. Looking at the ranks of *top* management, over 90% of male top executives are married and have children, whereas less than half of female top executives are married and have children. This may be because spouses of male managers are less likely to work outside the home and more likely to handle the bulk of family responsibilities than spouses of female managers. Some female executives may avoid having families, if they see the alternative as requiring them to be "superwomen."[20]

Being required to juggle concerns for work and family has its benefits for women. By simultaneously playing different life roles, a woman may be more able to escape from the negative aspects of any one role. As discussed in Chapter 2, employment generally has a positive effect on women's mental and physical health, especially if they have positive feelings about it. Similarly, employed women with families derive more satisfaction from their jobs than do other women. However, "jugglers" are typically starved for time and feel under a great deal of pressure.[21]

Both female and male jugglers are likely to experience work-family conflict. Such conflict may come about because work interferes with family, such as when unusually long hours at work prevent a person from devoting the usual time or energy to family responsibilities, or because family interferes with work, such as when a child's overnight illness leads to tardiness or reduced functioning at work.

Three types of work-family conflict may occur for individuals: time-based, strain-based, and behavior-based.[22] *Time-based conflict* results from the limited time that is available to handle both work and family roles. Time spent working generally cannot be devoted to family activities and vice versa. Parents experience more time-based conflict than non-parents, parents of younger children (who are particularly demanding) more than parents of older children, and parents of large families more than parents of small families. Also, men who are married to manage-rial/professional women experience more of this conflict than those who are married to nonmanagerial/nonprofessional women, probably because they are expected to handle a greater share of the family responsibilities than they would otherwise.

Strain-based conflict results when strain in one role "spills over" into the other role. Family strains may decrease performance at work and thereby negatively affect career success. Or strain at work may affect one's behavior as a parent or spouse. This type of conflict occurs in married couples most when the husband and wife disagree about their responsibility for family roles or about the wife's employment status. Working women who have husbands with nontraditional attitudes are less affected by it.

Behavior-based conflict occurs when incompatible behaviors are required for work and family roles, such as aggressiveness and objectivity at work and warmth and nurturance at home. Managers who are carrying out the masculine stereotype at work, whether female or male, may feel caught between the emotional detachment exhibited at work and the openness expected at home. "Shifting gears" from one role to another is required to avoid this type of conflict.

Issues about the *timing* of parenthood further complicate women's career decisions. Mothers may follow either of two patterns in the timing of parenthood: a sequential pattern, by pursuing either a career or motherhood first, or a simultaneous pattern, by having children and a career at the same time. In one study, over 70% of mothers used one of three sequential patterns: (a) motherhood follows employment, where the mother starts her career and then stops it with the birth of her first child; (b) employment brackets motherhood, where the mother interrupts her career, spends full time at home with the children, and then resumes her career after the children have grown; and (c) employment follows motherhood, where the mother completes her full-time parenting role before she begins her career.[23]

Decisions about the timing of parenthood have a profound effect on women's lives due to the inescapable reality of the biological time clock regarding motherhood. This issue contributes to a significant difference between men's and women's careers. Few men see marriage or family as a *constraint* on the emphasis they place on their careers or on their career success. Men may *choose* to accommodate competing priorities between work, family, and career decisions. Women, however, primarily handle the bulk of family responsibilities, even when both members of the couple have full-time jobs. Therefore motherhood almost necessitates some type of accommodation in a woman's career.[24]

Work Motivation and Career Choices. Multiple and conflicting role demands, combined with stresses concerning the timing of parenthood, often lead to women making different career choices than do men. Astin suggested that basic work motivation is the same for men and women, but that they make different choices because their early socialization and later opportunities are different. If women do not see alternatives for child care available to them and they wish to have a family, they may choose careers that allow for greater flexibility (such as the opportunity to work part-time) so that they can meet the demands of both roles. Rather than marking a difference in work motivation between the sexes, this reflects the relative complexity of the social context in which women live.[25]

Accordingly, women do not seem to have less work or career motivation than men as much as a different perspective concerning what a career means. They take more of a holistic approach to their lives than men, with images of balance between work and relationships affecting their career decisions and choices. Because the structure of opportunity does not facilitate women's achieving the balance they seek, many are required to make trade-offs between their husband's needs, family demands, and their own work motivation.

Organizational Factors

Organizational factors have a strong impact on the career success of women as well as their success in relationships with others. In particular, four types of organizational factors influence women's careers: (a) practices regarding alternative work schedules and family supports; (b) initial staffing decisions; (c) career pathing and promotion decisions; and (d) mentoring, networking, and feedback practices. The latter three types of factors contribute to a race difference in career development, with African American managers experiencing more restricted advancement opportunities and lower levels of career satisfaction, as well as a sex difference in career development.[26]

Practices Regarding Alternative Work Schedules and Family Supports. Many organizations now offer alternative work arrangements for working parents such as job sharing, flextime, telecommuting, corporate sabbaticals, and part-time work in addition to assistance with child care arrangements such as referral services, subsidies for off-site child care, or on-site child care facilities. Such practices help women, on whom the primary burden of child care responsibilities usually rests, negotiate the demands both of a fulfilling career and a fulfilling family life. In helping women to achieve success in their relationships outside of work, these practices also help women to achieve career success by alleviating the distracting elements of family responsibilities during the work day.[27]

According to some, organizational practices regarding alternative work schedules and family supports should take women's emphasis on career versus relationships with others into account. Felice Schwartz triggered a national debate about the merits of "mommy tracks," although she did not use that term herself, when she suggested that organizations divide their female employees into two groups according to their area of emphasis. "Career-primary" women were seen to emphasize their careers, whereas "career-and-family" women were seen to seek a balance between career and relationships with others. Schwartz recommended that organizations (a) remove all constraints on career success for career-primary women such that they can be just as successful as men (who were assumed to be mostly career-primary in orientation), thereby placing them on the "fast track"; and (b) maintain constraints on the career success of career-and-family women by offering them alternative work schedules and family supports to help achieve success in relationships with others in exchange for reduced opportunities for career advancement, which would place them on the "mommy track." Such organizational practices, as well as *reflecting* women's emphasis on career versus others, would *reinforce* this emphasis by categorizing them early and making it difficult for them to opt for the other category. In particular, career-and-family women who had been held back in their careers would find it almost impossible to be reclassified and achieve the level of career success as the original career-primary women.[28]

Initial Staffing Decisions. Even career-primary women may experience difficulty in achieving career success to the same extent as equally qualified men. A more challenging initial position ordinarily leads to a more challenging managerial position, and a less stimulating one to a less mobile career path. If women's initial assignments lack challenge (which they often do) and do not lead to more central line assignments considered vital for future development, their opportunities for future advancement are restricted.[29]

Gaining line experience early in one's career enhances later career success, and gaining line experience at some point is considered desirable for movement to the upper management ranks. However, women often are hired into staff rather than line positions and subsequently find it difficult to move into a line capacity. When women are stuck in career paths that preclude line experiences, their prospects for career advancement are limited.

Laurie Larwood and Urs Gattiker confirmed this notion in a study that tracked older and younger women and men's career paths. Overall, they found that men had greater professional standing, held line positions more often, and achieved higher positions in their departments than did women. Although it was possible to track the progress in men's careers clearly, showing how first jobs related eventually to hierarchical success, this process was more tenuous and less clear for women. However, the difference between the career success of younger women and younger men was less than that between older women and older men.[30]

Larwood and Gattiker's study demonstrated that changes indeed have taken place in the career development of women and men. Whether due to conscious efforts by organizations to provide equal opportunities for both, a reduced effect of gender stereotypes over time, or a change in the emphasis placed on career or the qualifications of younger women versus older women, the sex difference in career paths and success appears to be diminishing.

Career Pathing and Promotion Decisions. Women's jobs, including initial as well as later assignments, are less likely to be in job ladders that lead to hierarchical success. As a result, women have less well defined career paths than men. Some studies have found that women managers were promoted faster than men and were more satisfied than their male counterparts, yet men achieved a higher grade or level in the hierarchy. Even when women do not differ from men on total promotions achieved in a given period of time, they often receive smaller salary increases and hold lower salaries overall than men in equivalent positions.[31]

Although women are being promoted, their promotions do not seem to be as vital and may lead to less career success in objective terms than those obtained by men. What may be taking place is "pacification by promotion." Women may be given promotions to create the appearance of increasing responsibility and opportunity, but such promotions may be essentially hollow. This could explain why (a) many women feel that they are eventually blocked in their career advancement opportunities, coming up against what has been called a "glass ceiling," and (b) many corporations experience difficulty in attracting and retaining female managers and professionals.[32]

Mentoring, Networking, and Feedback Practices. Perhaps one of the reasons for the results above lies in the informal systems of development that exist in organizations. Much ado has been made about the impact of mentoring relationships on career success. Mentors play important development roles for individuals:

> Mentors provide young adults with career-enhancing functions, such as sponsorship, coaching, facilitating exposure and visibility, and offering challenging work or protection, all of which help the younger person to establish a role in the organization, learn the ropes, and prepare for advancement. In the psychosocial sphere, the mentor offers role modeling, counseling, confirmation, and friendship, which help the young adult to develop a sense of professional identity and competence.[33]

Women need mentors to understand the realities of the male-dominated business culture as well as to be identified for promotion. However, according to most reports, women are less likely to develop these relationships than men. They may fail to recognize the importance of gaining a sponsor and naively assume that competence is the only requirement needed to get ahead in an organization. Even if they recognize the importance of having a mentor, they may lack the skills necessary or see greater barriers to gaining one. As a result, they may turn to peer instead of mentoring relationships, which provide them social support but not the career-enhancing support of individuals in power.[34]

In addition, potential mentors may be reluctant to select female protégées. Because of concerns about issues of intimacy and sexual attraction, male-female mentoring relationships may involve tension and anxiety. Identifying a comfortable level of intimacy is often problematic, and such relationships can remain superficial with their full developmental potential untapped. The mere rumor of sexual involvement can damage the careers of both individuals. As a result, some male executives prefer to groom and promote other men to leadership positions. They may also simply prefer to mentor people who are similar to themselves. These difficulties in establishing and carrying out cross-gender mentoring relationships present a major barrier to women's career success.[35]

Why not then have women mentor other women? Mentoring relationships between women have been less in evidence because, until recently, there has been a paucity of upper-level women available to serve as mentors to younger, up-and-coming women. Tokenism arguments have been advanced to explain why such women have not reached out to younger women. According to Kanter, people in token positions enjoy the specialness their position affords and view others around them as a potential threat to their achievements. Upper-level women may cherish the sense of importance their unique status brings and be reluctant to mentor younger women.[36]

Mentors are not the only source of career support for women. Women's lack of advancement to high levels of management often results from their having less fully developed informal networks than men. Women may be as adept as men in forming networks, but their networks are less effective because they are not as well integrated into the organization's dominant coalition.[37]

Women's development also may be compromised by the type and quality of feedback they receive from their immediate superiors, which is not that received by men. As indicated in Chapter 4, early reports of pro-male bias in performance evaluations were not supported by meta-analysis. However, a Navy-based study found differences in the words used to evaluate the performance of female and male naval officers, not only in the content of the evaluations but also in the amount of information imparted. Evaluations of male officers were seen as more career-enhancing than those of female officers. If women do not receive the same type of critical evaluation of their performance as do men, it is more difficult for them to improve their job skills and be prepared for promotion opportunities that arise.[38]

Societal Factors

Societal factors such as legal requirements, government programs, and social mores are behind the influence of many of the organizational and personal factors on women's career development. These factors affect women's success in both career and relationships as well as their emphasis on career versus relationships.

Both legal and social changes in recent years have caused women's work to be more highly valued. As we shall discuss in greater detail in Chapter 8, federal laws such as the Equal Pay Act, the Civil Rights Act, and a variety of executive orders prohibit sex discrimination in employment. Women have greater access to managerial positions and now populate many traditionally male-intensive occupations in greater proportions than before. However, sex-role expectations and discrimination continue to operate. Social mores still suggest that the woman must bear the primary responsibility for childraising, even if she pursues a full-time career. Despite the movement of women into many male-intensive occupations, there has been little movement of men into female-intensive occupations, probably because these occupations continue to receive the lowest wages.

Barriers remain to the successful implementation of workplace and government policies that would be considered "pro-women." Although there has been considerable change in attitudes toward the role of women in society, gender stereotypes continue to be deeply held and resistant to change. Writers such as Schwartz regard the commitment of working mothers to their careers as dissipated by parental responsibilities. And men as a group continue to suffer from stigmas associated with traditional definitions of career success. For example, male employees are often hesitant to voice family-related concerns for fear these concerns will conflict with the corporate image of the successful male. Companies often consider fathers who take paternity leave to be eccentrics who cannot possibly be serious about their careers. These attitudes represent a variation of broader social mores that continue to suggest that it is a woman's place, and not the man's responsibility, to tend to the home and children.[39]

Certainly government could do more to equalize this age-old battle between the sexes over household and family responsibilities. The requirement that most employers allow their employees to take unpaid leave to care for a newborn or adopted child or an ailing elder is a step in the right direction. However, the lack of governmental programs for child-care support continues to hinder working mothers. The growing numbers of single women with children—women whose income is critical for family survival—feel this strain most acutely. In "river of time" terms, rather than zigzagging from one bank of the river to the other, these women must navigate straight upstream against a number of strong currents. Programs aimed at helping with family circumstances are necessary to help low-income and single-parent women obtain any form of career success.[40]

Influences on Men's Career Development

So far, we have focused on the personal, organizational, and societal factors that influence women's career development. These factors influence men's career development as well.

For example, men are affected by issues of work-family conflict, including how and if such issues are resolved with their partners. The impact of career interruptions is more severe for men than women, suggesting greater discrimination against men for not following a traditional career path.[41] Even if their careers are not interrupted because of family reasons, they are influenced by the nature and timing of parenthood. Organizational practices that provide assistance with child-care arrangements enable men as well as women to concentrate more on their careers. Men's careers are also hindered by unchallenging initial assignments, lack of line experience, and unhelpful performance feedback, and enhanced by the experiences of having a mentor and being a part of a strong informal network. Social mores place pressures on men as well as women to live their lives in a restricted way that may not fully satisfy their needs for success in both career and relationships with others.

As we stated previously, the assumptions governing traditional models of men's careers do not necessarily hold for all men. It has become more acceptable for men to take family concerns into account when accepting broader-based work responsibilities. Corporate mergers and downsizing have forced both men and women to rethink the concept of career. Jobs with lower security and career paths with lower ceilings have called into question the traditional view of career success defined as climbing the corporate ladder to the top. No one—man or woman—is immune to these changes.

Implications

The approach to careers proposed in this chapter differs from earlier approaches in several fundamental ways:

1. It assumes that people's experiences, concerns, and "successes" in relationships outside of work are important considerations in how they manage their careers. Earlier approaches typically assumed that nonwork concerns are separate and distinct from work concerns and need not always be taken into account.
2. It assumes that subjective measures of career success are at least as important as objective measures in determining whether people truly are successful. Earlier approaches typically assumed that objective measures, defined by promotions, salary increments, and the like, are uppermost considerations in defining career success.
3. It assumes that stage-oriented models of career progression such as those developed by Super and Levinson do not capture the full complexity of people's lives. Previous models developed using data primarily on men typically assumed that a linear or stage progression exists that directs the flow of decisions made about work and nonwork lives.
4. It assumes that people are subject to multiple influences, factors, and constraints in making decisions regarding career and relationships with others. Earlier approaches did not attend to conflicting demands made on individuals from the work and non-work spheres of their lives, or to persistent stereotypes regarding career paths of men versus women in organizations, or to societal expectations that women will play more of a nurturing role in the family than men.

What seems to matter most to women and men in evaluating their careers and lives is whether they see themselves as successful *on their own terms.* Focusing on subjective rather than objective measures of success leads to rather unconventional implications. For example, chief executive officers are often assumed to have reached the highest level of career success that can be achieved, because their positions are literally at the top of their organizations' hierarchies. Yet are these individuals necessarily the most successful employees in their organizations? It depends on what you mean by "successful." Individuals who are the most *satisfied* with their objective career status, whatever that may be, may truly be the most successful in their careers. Satisfaction with career can be found at all levels of the organization. Many people find it by avoiding organizational hierarchies altogether and running their own businesses. In the same vein, individuals who are the most satisfied with their work and nonwork lives overall may be the most successful in life overall. Thus, our thinking about careers should incorporate subjective as well as objective measures of career success and not assume that success according to the latter necessarily leads to success according to the former.

Women's lives, and often men's, frequently involve trade-offs and temporary sacrifices. Concerns for career sometimes are deemphasized for the moment in favor of concerns for others, with the expectation that career concerns will receive primary emphasis at a later date. Similarly, concerns for others may be "placed on the back burner" at present while concerns for career are being satisfied, with the expectation that concerns for others will dominate in the future. People are also affected by the emphases that their spouses or significant others place on career and relationships with others. It will be impossible for us to fully understand such considerations unless researchers take a long-term perspective in examining careers by conducting longitudinal studies.

The "river of time" approach focuses on two types of success, in career and in relationships with others. These could be (a) positively related, with success in one realm spilling over into and contributing to success in the other; (b) negatively related, with the price of more success in one realm being less success in the other; or (c) positively related under some conditions and negatively related under other conditions. For example, success in career and success in relationships with others may be positively related for women when organizations place minimum constraints on their opportunities for career success and offer programs that help working mothers to handle their family responsibilities, and negatively related when organizations create barriers to advancement and offer no such programs.

Ordinarily, we should expect that a greater emphasis on career will lead to greater career success and a greater emphasis on relationships with others will lead to greater success in relationships. However, the size of these effects is influenced by other factors. For example, the effect of women's career emphasis on their actual career success is greater when organizations place fewer constraints on their opportunities for career success. Also, the effect of women's emphasis on relationships with others on their actual success in relationships is greater when their husbands or partners have greater involvement in family responsibilities. Furthermore, women's career success, measured objectively in terms of promotions and salary, is likely to be greater when their partners become more involved in family responsibilities and thereby allow them to devote more energy to their careers.

Much research has been conducted on how specific personal, organizational, and societal factors seem to affect careers and career-related attitudes at specific points in time. However, very little attention has been paid to the combination or interaction of these influences on decisions over the life span. Yet these factors acting in tandem affect individuals' placement in the river of time and their success in career and in relationships with others as represented along the banks of the river. A person's assessment of the potential for success on either side of the river may lead him or her to be pulled more toward one river bank (emphasis on career) or the other (emphasis on others). In turn, the potential for success on either side of the river is determined by the number and magnitude of the personal, organizational, and societal factors operating at any point in time. The richness and variability of such factors acting in combination holds the key to the study of individuals' career development.

Thus, we should consider similarities and differences between men's and women's careers from a fresh perspective. Many men as well as women have identified a greater need for balance between their home and work lives. As a result, their careers are not adequately described by the career stage models advocated by Levinson and others. The study of both men's and women's careers will benefit from a "river of time" approach that focuses on the effort to balance work and nonwork concerns over time.

Implications for Organizations

Sex differences in career patterns are diminishing, but still remain to some extent. What can organizations do to minimize their contribution to a sex difference in career patterns for their managerial employees? In general, they should follow two principles in their actions:[42]

1. They should be gender-blind in how they fill open managerial positions, except when consciously trying to offset the effects of past discrimination.
2. They should try to minimize differences in the job experiences of equally qualified male and female managers, so that artificial sex differences in career patterns and success do not arise.

Organizations make several types of decisions about individuals during their careers, including hiring decisions, salary increase decisions, promotion or transfer decisions, and task assignments. They must frequently evaluate employees' recent performance and estimate their potential performance. Any sex bias that enters into evaluations of employees could influence an organization's decision and contribute to a sex difference in career patterns.

Decisions to fill position vacancies by promoting or transferring insiders rather than by hiring outsiders may be based on several types of information about applicants, including past work experiences, performance appraisals, interviews, and assessment center results. The use of past work experiences could introduce a sex bias if individuals with uninterrupted work careers were favored over those with interrupted careers. Performance appraisals and interviews could be influenced by sex bias, although the more that is known about candidates, the lower the likelihood of sex bias. Assessment centers could also contribute to sex bias if they were not run properly; however, confirming their validity, assessment center ratings similarly predicted the later career success of men and women in the AT&T study discussed in Chapter 6. Promotion and transfer decisions should not based on policies or techniques for identifying and evaluating candidates that contribute to differential treatment of female and male candidates.[43]

Organizations should do whatever they can to equalize the job experiences of equally qualified female and male managers. This means abandoning the model of a successful career as an uninterrupted sequence of promotions to positions of greater responsibility heading toward the top ranks. All too often, any request to take time out from career for family reasons, either by a woman or a man, is seen as evidence of lack of career commitment.

More women and men are adopting a holistic approach to their careers and lives. By providing the opportunity for alternative work schedules and family supports for all employees, not just "career-and-family" women as Schwartz recommended, organizations can help women and men achieve their full potential for success. Firms that offer flexible work arrangements are not only more likely to retain their employees. They may also attract more qualified employees (even for less pay) who view the opportunity to take advantage of a flexible work arrangement as a worthwhile substitute for higher pay at another firm.[44]

We recently conducted a study of the factors that affect decisions about whether to grant alternative work arrangements to employees. The most important factor affecting decisions was the criticality of the employee's job assignment. Employees whose work was more critical to the work unit were less likely to be granted alternative work arrangements than noncritical employees. In addition, requests for alternative work arrangements were viewed more favorably when (a) they were made by nonmanagers rather than managers; (b) they were for varying the site of work between the office and home rather than for a six-month unpaid leave, which had more potential for disrupting the accomplishment of work; and (c) they were justified for reasons of elder care rather than child care. Employee sex had no effect on decisions.[45]

This pattern of results has intriguing implications. Generally it is the high-performing employees who are trusted with more critical job tasks and eventually promoted to managerial positions. In fact, eligibility for alternative work arrangements seems an appropriate reward for demonstrated performance and commitment. However, our study suggested that such employees are seen as the *least* desirable candidates for alternative work arrangements. This sends a mixed message to employees. Some may feel that they have to transfer to a job with less responsibilities or to diminish their performance in order to qualify for such arrangements. Also, employees who are trying to address child-care needs may feel discriminated against if they see elder care needs as being given greater priority. Thus, if organizations wish to reap the benefits of alternative work arrangements, they must do more than simply announce to their employees that such arrangements are available. They also need to educate their managers regarding the corporate benefits and provide incentives to managers to implement such arrangements in their own work units.

Corporations could offer "parent tracks" rather than "mommy tracks" and accurately believe that they were treating their female and male employees alike. However, if women opted for such programs more than men (as is often the case) and anyone who opted for one was held back in pursuing a future managerial career, the programs would contribute to a sex difference in access to top management positions.

Automatic restrictions should not be placed on the later career prospects of individuals who choose alternative work arrangements. Those who wish to return to the fast track should be allowed to do so once they demonstrate the necessary skills and commitment.

Thus organizations need to create both standard and flexible career paths so *all* the needs of *all* their employees may be fully met. A firm that develops a flexible as well as a core work force may find considerable advantages during downturns in the business cycle, as layoffs may be avoided in favor of "sabbaticals" for those who prefer a flexible career pattern. Organizations need to reorganize their work forces in this manner to better meet the needs of employees as well as business cycles.

There are other ways by which organizations can minimize sex differences in managers' job experiences. For example, the majority of both male and female top executives have had one or more mentors, and mentorship has been critical to their advancement and success. However, for reasons stated earlier, lower-level female managers have greater difficulty in establishing mentoring relationships than male managers at equivalent levels. This gives lower-level male managers an advantage in achieving career success.

Some companies try to overcome barriers of sex by assigning highly placed mentors to promising lower-level managers. For example, at the Bank of America, senior executives are asked to serve as mentors for three or four junior managers for a year at a time. Formal mentoring programs have also been implemented at the Jewel Companies, Aetna, Bell Labs, Merrill Lynch, Federal Express, and the U.S. General Accounting Office. However, good mentoring relationships cannot be engineered. They must emerge from the spontaneous and mutual involvement of two people who see value in relating to each other. If people feel coerced into or mismatched in mentoring relationships, the relationships are likely to flounder; one study found that protégés in informal mentorships saw their mentors as more supportive than protégés in formal mentorships. Instead, a better approach for organizations is to offer educational programs about mentoring and its role in career development, and then identify who is doing good mentoring and reward them for it.[46]

Companies also influence job experiences through the training and development programs that they encourage or require their managers to take. These programs contribute to a sex difference in job experiences if (a) men and women are systematically diagnosed to have different developmental needs and thereby go through different programs, or (b) men and women are deliberately segregated in such programs. Both of these conditions have been advocated and met in the past.[47] However, women managers do not need to be sent off by themselves for "assertiveness training" as they were in the past. Instead, they need access to advanced training and development activities, such as executive MBAs or executive leadership workshops, just as male managers do.

Programs such as the Executive Women Workshop offered by the Center for Creative Leadership (CCL) are open only to women. In addition, some companies, such as Northwestern Bell, have their own executive leadership programs for women only. Such programs are intended "to give female managers the unique opportunity to understand their individual developmental needs and establish personal and career objectives," as the CCL's catalog puts it. In general, though, women and men should be recommended for training and development programs according to their individual needs rather than their sex. Almost half of the companies regarded as "the best companies for women" rely on training and workshops to develop their high-potential managerial talent. However, many of these companies, including Bidermann Industries, General Mills, Hewitt Associates, Neiman-Marcus, and PepsiCo, have no special programs for women; they simply assign the best and brightest people regardless of sex.[48]

Top management must work actively towards removal of all constraints on career success that are not based on an individual's potential or achievement. As indicated earlier, considerable constraints remain for women, even for those regarded as "career-primary," in such areas as initial staffing assignments, feedback practices, and access to top management positions. The ultimate goal is for women's and men's careers to be as free of artificial sex-based constraints as possible. This will require further change in social mores and in the allocation of family responsibilities within households. It will also require top management to act as advocates for the career needs of their promising employees regardless of sex. In particular, organizations can do a much better job of developing women, not by giving them special treatment because of their sex, but by placing them in difficult line positions and then providing them the hard feedback and coaching that men in such positions receive. If organizations act in such a manner, women will have a better chance of attaining top management positions without cries of their having been promoted only because of affirmative action clouding their success.

In summary, organizations can contribute to the elimination of a sex difference in career patterns by refraining from sex bias in the decisions that they make about individuals and by providing the opportunities and support necessary for women and men to pursue careers to equal satisfaction. Effective mentoring may reduce the advantage that men have had over women in the pursuit of careers. Training and development programs help both male and female employees to set and achieve career goals. Child- and elder-care support and alternative work arrangements lighten the burden placed on the adult female in most families and also contribute to a reduced difference between women's and men's careers.

Implications for Individuals

Individuals enhance their careers through the career actions that they take as well as the ways in which they deal with the demands of their partners and families. Though not required for individuals to progress in their careers, establishing of career goals is consistently linked with effectiveness in occupational choice. However, in order to successfully set career goals, individuals need either external support or strong self-esteem. Due to their different socialization experiences, women have experienced less external support and lower self-esteem and thereby have been rewarded less for goal setting than men.[49]

Goal setting is not effective unless it is accompanied by career planning. Career planning may range from the more proactive strategy of acquiring skills early on seen as necessary for later career progress to the more passive strategy of working hard and hoping to be rewarded in the future. Gutek and Larwood's model of women's career development suggests strategies (taken for granted by most men) that may specifically enhance women's careers. When women embark on a work career without delay and do not let marriage or children interrupt it, they are able to compete on more equal terms with men. Unless organizations change their views of what makes for a desirable career pattern, individuals will achieve the greatest career benefits from having an uninterrupted career pattern and from beginning full-time work as soon as possible.[50]

Individuals contribute to their own career success by adopting career tactics that are carefully thought out and well timed. We have already discussed the benefits of having a mentor. Men and women may also further their careers by seeking membership in informal networks, in which they enter a world of "ties of loyalties and of dependence, favors granted and owed, mutual benefit, protection, . . . promises that must be kept if you want to be operative in the future, (and) connections with people who already *have* influence." Informal networks traditionally have been called "old boy networks" because they have been dominated by men. Until recently, there haven't been enough women managers to have separate "old girl" networks. However, as more women enter management ranks, mixed-sex and "old girl" networks are becoming more prevalent. For the same reason, women now have more opportunities to have mentors.[51]

These actions represent a more active stance taken towards one's career than simply relying on one's own competence. However, they do not substitute for building one's competence. People also gain from career tactics such as furthering their education to enhance their work-related skills and knowledge, and accepting special assignments or job transfers that broaden their experience.

In addition to actions taken unilaterally, individuals influence their success in career and relationships with others by reaching accommodations with other family members that enable them to satisfy both concerns. Dual-career couples vary in the ways in which they deal with work-family conflict. Four types of dual-career couples have been identified: superordinate partners, synchronized partners, synthetic partners, and severed partners.[52]

Superordinate partners value both work and family activities and set the goal of achieving satisfaction in both domains for both partners. They may not achieve spectacular success in their careers, since they do not devote their energies solely to career success, but they feel considerable satisfaction with their family lives and try to build a sense of interdependence among family members. They are people to whom careers are important but not the only interest in life.

Synchronized partners help each other to achieve complementary individual goals. For example, one spouse may be interested primarily in career and less in family affairs while the other spouse is primarily interested in family and less in career pursuits. Couples possessing traditional sex-role identities, with the work-oriented man being more masculine and the family-oriented woman being more feminine, fit into this category. However, the combination of a family-oriented man and a career-oriented woman or combinations based on other factors (e.g., one partner's job requires extensive travel while the other's does not) are also possible.

Synthetic partners have relationships in which one or both members feel that they have compromised their aspirations. For example, the wife may feel that she has to subordinate her career to her husband's career to carry out family responsibilities, or the husband may feel that he has to suppress his involvement in his career to devote more of himself to the family. Such couples frequently experience frustrations and survive only through makeshift agreements or periodic resolution of tensions. However, the quality of family life is insecure at best.

Severed partners possess highly incompatible values, such as a non-traditional woman with a high-career, low-family commitment married to a traditional man who expects his wife to be strongly committed to family. Such couples are the most contentious and require one member to make a considerable sacrifice in personal goals to preserve the relationship.

Although the majority of dual-career couples consist of synchronized or synthetic partners, superordinate partners are likely to achieve the greatest success in all spheres of life.

Conclusions

The time is right for a new perspective on the study of careers. The "river of time" approach provides a framework for thinking about the inherent complexities of the topic. Traditional models are too narrowly focused to do an adequate job of conceptualizing the richness of people's career decisions over time. Instead, examination of the "crosscurrents in the river of time" created by the combination of personal, organizational, and societal influences on people's lives is necessary. Once these influences are more clearly understood, organizations will be better able to contribute to their employees' "getting ahead" in career and life.

There is more to life than work. Obsession with getting ahead can lead to Type A behavior and its accompanying symptoms of ill health. However, giving little thought to career issues can lead to lack of achievement and a resulting sense of anger, frustration, or disappointment. When individuals achieve a sense of balance among career, family, and other interests in their lives, they will be able to reject old and new career stereotypes and shape their own, more fulfilling life patterns.

Notes

1. P. Galloway, "The Woes of Yuppie Love and Marriage," *Chicago Tribune*, March 26, 1985. © 1985, Chicago Tribune Company, all rights reserved, used by permission.

2. An earlier version of portions of this chapter appeared in G. N. Powell and L. A. Mainiero, "Cross-Currents in the River of Time: Conceptualizing the Complexities of Women's Careers," *Journal of Management*, 18 (No. 2, 1992): 215-237.

3. J. V. Gallos, "Exploring Women's Development: Implications for Career Theory, Practice, and Research," in *Handbook of Career Theory*, ed. M. B. Arthur, D. T. Hall, and B. S. Lawrence (Cambridge, England: Cambridge University Press, 1989).

4. D. E. Super, Chapter 5, "Career Patterns and Life Stages," in *The Psychology of Careers* (New York: Harper, 1957); K. H. Meuller, *Educating Women for a Changing World* (Minneapolis: University of Minnesota Press, 1954), quoted in Super, "Career Patterns and Life Stages," p. 76.

5. S. Ornstein and L. A. Isabella, "Age vs. Stage Models of Career Attitudes of Women: A Partial Replication and Extension," *Journal of Vocational Behavior*, 36 (1990): 1-19.

6. E. Ginzberg, S. W. Ginzburg, S. Axelrad, and J. L. Herma, *Occupational Choice: An Approach to a General Theory* (New York: Columbia University Press, 1951), p. 42.

7. E. H. Schein, *Career Dynamics: Matching Individual and Organizational Needs* (Reading, MA: Addison-Wesley, 1978), p. 27.

8. D. J. Levinson, C. N. Darrow, E. B. Klein, M. H. Levinson, and B. McKee, *The Seasons of a Man's Life*, paperback edition (New York: Ballantine, 1979), back cover and pp. 8-9.

9. Ornstein and Isabella, "Age vs. Stage Models of Career Attitudes of Women"; S. Ornstein, W. L. Cron, and J. W. Slocum Jr., "Life Stage versus Career Stage: A Comparative Test of the Theories of Levinson and Super," *Journal of Organizational Behavior*, 10 (1989): 117-133; D. J. Levinson, "A Conception of Adult Development," *American Psychologist*, 41 (1986): 3-13.

10. J. M. Bardwick, "The Seasons of a Woman's Life," in *Women's Lives: New Theory, Research, and Policy*, ed. D. G. McGuigan (Ann Arbor: University of Michigan Center for Continuing Education of Women, 1980).

11. C. Gilligan, *In a Different Voice: Psychological Theory and Women's Development* (Cambridge, MA: Harvard University Press, 1982); L. Kohlberg, "Moral Stages and Moralization: The Cognitive-Developmental Approach," in *Moral Development and Behavior: Theory, Research, and Social Issues*, ed. T. Lickona (New York: Holt, Rinehart and Winston, 1976).

12. H. S. Astin, "The Meaning of Work in Women's Lives: A Sociopsychological Model of Career Choice and Work Behavior," *The Counseling Psychologist*, 12 (1984): 117-126; comments by L. W. Harmon, L. A. Gilbert, L. F. Fitzgerald and N. E. Betz, and H. S. Farmer in the same issue.

13. B. A. Gutek and L. Larwood, "Introduction: Women's Careers Are Important and Different," in *Women's Career Development*, ed. B. A. Gutek and L. Larwood (Newbury Park, CA: Sage, 1987); L. Larwood and B. A. Gutek, "Working Toward a Theory of Women's Career Development," in *Women's Career Development*, ed. Gutek and Larwood.

14. Gallos, "Exploring Women's Development," in *Handbook of Career Theory*, ed. Arthur et al.; J. Z. Giele, "Crossovers: New Themes in Adult Roles and the Life Cycle, in *Women's Lives*, ed. McGuigan.

15. For an example, see D. T. Hall, *Careers in Organizations* (Glenview, IL: Scott, Foresman, 1976).

16. C. Tomlinson-Keasey, "The Working Lives of Terman's Gifted Women," in *The Experience and Meaning of Work in Women's Lives*, ed. H. Y. Grossman and N. L. Chester (Hillsdale, NJ: Lawrence Erlbaum, 1990).

17. H. Hesse, *Siddhartha* (New York: Bantam, 1971; original work published 1922); D. Brin, *The River of Time* (New York: Bantam Spectra, 1987).

18. J. H. Pleck, Chapter 6, "Husbands' Psychological Involvement in Work and Family," in *Working Wives/Working Husbands* (Beverly Hills, CA: Sage, 1985); R. S. Weiss, *Staying the Course: The Emotional and Social Lives of Men Who Do Well at Work* (New York: Free Press, 1990).

19. L. Bailyn, "The Slow Burn Way to the Top: Some Thoughts of the Early Years of Organizational Careers," in *Work, Family and the Career: New Frontiers in Theory and Research*, ed. C. B. Derr (New York: Praeger, 1980); J. E. Olson and I. H. Frieze, "Job Interruptions and Part-Time Work: Their Effect on the Later Income of MBAs" (Paper delivered at the Annual Meeting of the Academy of Management, New Orleans, 1987); J. P. Jacobsen and L. M. Levin, "The Effects of Intermittent Labor Force Attachment on Female Earnings" (Paper delivered at the Annual Meeting of the American Economic Association, New Orleans, 1992); J. A. Schneer and F. Reitman, "Effects of Employment Gaps on the Careers of MBAs: More Damaging for Men than for Women?" *Academy of Management Journal*, 33 (1990): 391-406.

20. Korn/Ferry International, *Profile of Senior Women Executives* (New York: Korn/Ferry International, 1982); C. D. Sutton and K. K. Moore, "Executive Women—20 Years Later," *Harvard Business Review*, 63 (No. 5, September/October 1985): 43-66.

21. F. J. Crosby, *Juggling: The Unexpected Advantages of Balancing Career and Home for Women and Their Families* (New York: Free Press, 1991); R. L. Repetti, K. A. Matthews, and I. Waldron, "Employment and Women's Health: Effects of Paid Employment on Women's Mental and Physical Health," *American Psychologist*, 44 (1989): 1394-1401; M. A. Ferber and B. O'Farrell with L. R. Allen, Chapter 3, "Linkages Between Work and Family," in *Work and Family: Policies for a Changing Work Force* (Washington, DC: National Academy Press, 1991).

22. J. H. Greenhaus and N. J. Beutell, "Sources of Conflict Between Work and Family Roles," *Academy of Management Review*, 10 (1985): 76-88.

23. P. Daniels and K. Weingarten, Chapter 4, "Mother's Hours," in *Sooner or Later: The Timing of Parenthood in Adult Lives* (New York: Norton, 1982).

24. A. Hochschild, *The Second Shift* (New York: Viking Penguin, 1989).

25. Astin, "The Meaning of Work in Women's Lives."

26. A. M. Morrison and M. A. Von Glinow, "Women and Minorities in Management," *American Psychologist*, 45 (No. 2, 1990): 200-208; J. H. Greenhaus, S. Parasuraman, and W. M. Wormley, "Effects of Race on Organizational Experiences, Job Performance Evaluations, and Career Outcomes," *Academy of Management Journal*, 33 (1990): 64-86; D. A. Thomas and C. P. Alderfer, "The Influence of Race on Career Dynamics: Theory and Research on Minority Career Experiences," in *Handbook of Career Theory*, ed. Arthur et al.; B. L. Betters-Reed and L. L. Moore, "Managing Diversity: Focusing on Women and the Whitewash Dilemma," in *Womanpower:*

Managing in Times of Demographic Turbulence, ed. U. Sekaran and F. T. L. Leong (Newbury Park, CA: Sage, 1992); S. M. Nkomo, "Race and Sex: The Forgotten Case of the Black Female Manager," in *Women's Careers: Pathways and Pitfalls,* ed. S. Rose and L. Larwood (New York: Praeger, 1988).

27. M. C. Mattis, *Flexible Work Arrangements for Managers and Professionals: New Approaches to Work in U.S. Corporations* (New York: Catalyst, 1990); E. E. Kossek and V. Nichol, "The Effects of On-Site Child Care on Employee Attitudes and Performance," *Personnel Psychology,* 45 (1992): 485-509.

28. F. N. Schwartz, "Management Women and the New Facts of Life," *Harvard Business Review,* 67 (No. 1, January/February 1990): 65-76; E. Ehrlich, "The Mommy Track," *Business Week,* No. 3096 (20 March 1989): 126-134; A. M. Konrad and K. Cannings, "Sex Segregation in the Workplace and the Mommy Track: Sex Differences in Work Commitment or Statistical Discrimination?" *Proceedings of the Annual Meeting of the Academy of Management,* ed. L. R. Jauch and J. L. Wall (San Francisco, 1990).

29. M. S. Taylor and D. R. Ilgen, "Sex Discrimination Against Women in Initial Placement Decisions: A Laboratory Investigation," *Academy of Management Journal,* 24 (1981): 859-865; J. E. Rosenbaum, Chapter 6, "The Enduring Effects of Early Jobs and Earnings," in *Career Mobility in a Corporate Hierarchy* (Orlando, FL: Academic, 1984).

30. L. Larwood and U. E. Gattiker, "A Comparison of the Career Paths Used by Successful Women and Men," in *Women's Career Development,* ed. Gutek and Larwood.

31. L. K. Stroh, J. M. Brett, and A. H. Reilly, "All the Right Stuff: A Comparison of Female and Male Managers' Career Progression," *Journal of Applied Psychology,* 77 (1992): 251-260; Y. Haberfeld, "Employment Discrimination: An Organizational Model," *Academy of Management Journal,* 35 (1992): 161-180; J. N. Baron, A. Davis-Blake, A., and W. T. Bielby, "The Structure of Opportunity: How Promotion Ladders Vary Within and Among Organizations," *Administrative Science Quarterly,* 31 (1986): 248-273; A. S. Tsui and B. A. Gutek, "A Role Set Analysis of Gender Differences in Performance, Affective Relationships, and Career Success of Industrial Middle Managers," *Academy of Management Journal,* 27 (1984): 619-635; L. P. Stewart and W. B. Gudykunst, "Differential Factors Influencing the Hierarchical Level and Number of Promotions of Males and Females Within an Organization," *Academy of Management Journal,* 25 (1982): 586-597; T. Cox, Jr. and C. V. Harquail, "Career Paths and Career Success in the Early Career Stages of Male and Female MBAs" (Paper delivered at the Annual Meeting of the Academy of Management, San Francisco, 1990); J. A. Schneer and F. Reitman, "The Importance of Gender in Mid-Career: A Longitudinal Study of MBAs" (Paper delivered at the Annual Meeting of the Academy of Management, Las Vegas, 1992). For a study that found promotion *advantages* for women and African Americans, see Y. Shenhav, "Entrance of Blacks and Women into Managerial Positions in Scientific and Engineering Occupations: A Longitudinal Analysis," *Academy of Management Journal,* 35 (1992): 889-901.

32. D. P. Flanders and P. E. Anderson, "Sex Discrimination in Employment: Theory and Practice," *Industrial and Labor Relations Review,* 26 (1973): 938-955; A. M. Morrison, R. P. White, E. Van Velsor, and the Center for Creative Leadership, *Breaking the Glass Ceiling: Can Women Reach the Top of America's Largest Corporations?,* updated ed. (Reading, MA: Addison-Wesley, 1992); M. J. Davidson and C. L. Cooper, *Shattering the Glass Ceiling: The Woman Manager* (London: Chapman, 1992); U.S. Department of Labor, *Pipelines of Progress: A Status Report on the Glass Ceiling* (Washington, DC: U.S. Department of Labor, 1992); J. Fierman, "Why Women Still Don't Hit the Top,"

Fortune, 122 (No. 3, 30 July 1990): 40-62; B. Rosen, M. Miguel, and E. Peirce, "Stemming the Exodus of Women Managers," *Human Resource Management, 28* (No. 4, Winter 1989): 475-491.

33. G. R. Roche, "Much Ado About Mentors," *Harvard Business Review, 79* (No. 1, January/February 1979): 14-28; R. A. Noe, "Women and Mentoring: A Review and Research Agenda," *Academy of Management Review, 13* (1988): 65-78; K. E. Kram and L. A. Isabella, "Mentoring Alternatives: The Role of Peer Relationships in Career Development," *Academy of Management Journal, 28* (1985): 110-132, p. 111.

34. B. R. Ragins, "Barriers to Mentoring: The Female Manager's Dilemma," *Human Relations, 42* (1989): 1-22; B. R. Ragins and J. L. Cotton, "Easier Said than Done: Gender Differences in Perceived Barriers to Gaining a Mentor," *Academy of Management Journal, 34* (1991): 939-951; C. S. Koberg, W. Boss, D. Chappell, and R. C. Ringer, "An Investigation of the Antecedents and Outcomes of Mentoring" (Paper delivered at the Annual Meeting of the Academy of Management, Las Vegas, 1992); Kram and Isabella, "Mentoring Alternatives." For an exception, see G. F. Dreher and R. A. Ash, "A Comparative Study of Mentoring Among Men and Women in Managerial, Professional, and Technical Positions," *Journal of Applied Psychology, 75* (1990): 539-546.

35. J. G. Clawson and K. E. Kram, "Managing Cross-Gender Mentoring," *Business Horizons, 27* (No. 3, May/June 1984): 22-31; M. Crary, "Managing Attraction and Intimacy at Work," *Organizational Dynamics, 15* (No. 4, Spring 1987): 26-41; B. R. Ragins and D. B. McFarlin, "Perceptions of Mentoring Roles in Cross-Gender Mentoring Relationships," *Journal of Vocational Behavior, 37* (1990): 321-339.

36. R. M. Kanter, *Men and Women of the Corporation* (New York: Basic, 1977).

37. K. Cannings and C. Montmarquette, "Managerial Momentum: A Simultaneous Model of the Career Progress of Male and Female Managers," *Industrial and Labor Relations Review, 44* (No. 2, January 1991): 212-228; D. J. Brass, "Men's and Women's Networks: A Study of Interaction Patterns and Influence in an Organization," *Academy of Management Journal, 28* (1985): 327-343; K. E. Campbell, "Gender Differences in Job-Related Networks," *Work and Occupations, 15* (No. 2, 1988): 179-200.

38. J. Swim, E. Borgida, G. Maruyama, and D. G. Myers, "Joan McKay Versus John McKay: Do Gender Stereotypes Bias Evaluations?" *Psychological Bulletin, 105* (1989): 409-429; P. J. Thomas, "Appraising the Performance of Women: Gender and the Naval Officer," in *Women's Career Development*, ed. Gutek and Larwood.

39. Schwartz, "Management Women and the New Facts of Life"; N. Norman and J. T. Tedeschi, "Paternity Leave: The Unpopular Benefit Option," *Personnel Administrator, 29* (No. 2, 1984): 39-43.

40. Mattis, *Flexible Work Arrangements for Managers and Professionals*.

41. Schneer and Reitman, "Effects of Employment Gaps on the Careers of MBAs."

42. An earlier version of this section of the chapter appeared in G. N. Powell, "One More Time: Do Female and Male Managers Differ?" *Academy of Management Executive, 4* (No. 3, 1990): 68-75.

43. M. London and S. A. Stumpf, Chapter 7, "Organizational Staffing: Promotion and Transfer Decisions," in *Managing Careers* (Reading, MA: Addison-Wesley, 1982); R. J. Ritchie and J. L. Moses, "Assessment Center Correlates of Women's Advancement into Middle Management: A 7-year Longitudinal Analysis," *Journal of Applied Psychology, 68* (1983): 227-231.

44. Schwartz, "Management Women and the New Facts of Life"; Mattis, *Flexible Work Arrangements for Managers and Professionals*; Kossek and Nichol, "The Effects of

On-Site Child Care on Employee Attitudes and Performance"; Ferber et al., Chapter 6, "New Family-Related Benefits," in *Work and Family*; C. A. Thompson, C. C. Thomas, and M. Maier, "Work-Family Conflict: Reassessing Corporate Policies and Initiatives," in *Womanpower*, ed. Sekaran and Leong; D. E. Friedman and E. Galinsky, "Work and Family Issues: A Legitimate Business Concern," in *Work, Families, and Organizations*, ed. S. Zedeck (San Francisco: Jossey-Bass, 1992).

45. G. N. Powell and L. A. Mainiero, "Decision Making Regarding Alternative Work Arrangements," Unpublished manuscript, 1991.

46. K. E. Kram, "Mentoring in the Workplace," in *Career Development in Organizations*, ed. D. T. Hall and Associates (San Francisco: Jossey-Bass, 1986); M. Murray with M. A. Owen, *Beyond the Myths and Magic of Mentoring: How to Facilitate an Effective Mentoring Program* (San Francisco: Jossey-Bass, 1991); G. T. Chao, P. M. Walz, and P. D. Gardner, "Formal and Informal Mentorships: A Comparison on Mentoring Functions and Contrast with Nonmentored Counterparts," *Personnel Psychology, 45* (1992): 619-636.

47. M. H. Brenner, "Management Development for Women," *Personnel Journal, 51* (No. 3, March 1972): 165-169. For further discussion, see M. N. Lam, "Management Training for Women: International Experiences and Lessons for Canada," *Journal of Business Ethics, 9* (1990): 385-406.

48. Center for Creative Leadership, "Executive Women Workshop," in *1992 Programs* (Greensboro, NC: Center for Creative Leadership, 1992), p. 8; B. Zeitz and L. Dusky, *The Best Companies for Women* (New York: Simon and Schuster, 1988).

49. S. D. Inderlied, "Goal Setting and the Career Development of Women," *New Directions for Education, Work, and Careers, 8* (1979): 33-41.

50. Larwood and Gutek, "Working Toward a Theory of Women's Career Development," in *Women's Career Development*, ed. Gutek and Larwood.

51. M. Hennig and A. Jardim, *The Managerial Woman* (Garden City, NY: Anchor Press/Doubleday, 1977), pp. 12, 25.

52. U. Sekaran, Chapter 3, "Quality of Life in Dual-Career Families," in *Dual-Career Families* (San Francisco: Jossey-Bass, 1986).

8

Promoting Equal Opportunity and Valuing Cultural Diversity

The Ugly Duckling

Old version: Mother Duck gives birth to half a dozen ducklings. One of them is different, but the others don't appreciate his difference and make fun of him. He goes away and later develops into a graceful swan.

New Version: Ms. Duck is a first-line supervisor. All of her employees are different because it's "Workforce 2000," but Ms. Duck doesn't appreciate this. She goes away to a seminar on valuing diversity and later develops into a graceful supervisor.

Paul Hellman[1]

Since the 1960s, organizations have been under legal pressure to refrain from sex discrimination and to counteract the effects of past discrimination. Most organizations have been required to take "affirmative action" to promote equal opportunity in employment. Employers who "act affirmatively" go beyond merely refraining from discriminatory practices and make sure that current decisions and practices enhance the employment, development, and retention of members of protected groups such as women workers. Although enforcement of equal opportunity laws has varied from one presidential administration to the next, organizations have learned that violation can be quite costly, both in terms of money and negative public relations.[2]

Organizations are under additional pressures due to the changing demographic composition of the labor force. As a report entitled *Workforce 2000: Work and Workers for the 21st Century* demonstrated, the proportions of both women and members of "minority" groups (Hispanic, Asian, Native, and African Americans and others) are steadily increasing. By the year 2000, the labor force is expected to look something like this: The proportion of women, which was 42% in 1980 and 45% in 1990, is expected to be 47%. Minority group members, who represented 17% in 1980 and 21% in 1990, will comprise 25% (men, 13%; women, 12%). White, non-Hispanic men, once the majority group in the labor force, are expected to represent only 40%; white, non-Hispanic women will constitute 35%. Organizations whose management practices are more appropriate for a homogeneous group of employees will have to make adjustments to attract and retain talented individuals from diverse groups.[3]

The term *cultural diversity* has been used to refer to workplace differences that are associated with any or all of the characteristics that may make employees dissimilar. It may be restricted to differences associated with characteristics addressed in various equal employment opportunity (EEO) laws, such as sex, race, national origin, religion, age, and whether the person has a disability. However, it may also refer to differences according to characteristics such as personality, physical appearance, sexual orientation, and marital and parental status. I shall adopt a broad definition of cultural diversity in this chapter.[4]

Bringing about changes to prevent future sex discrimination and to counteract past discrimination is not simple. *Affirmative action* or *equal opportunity* programs (the terms will be used interchangeably) that increase the chances that members of one group will be hired, promoted, or paid more are likely to be objected to as "reverse discrimination" by members of other groups. When individuals feel that they or members of their group are stigmatized as "affirmative action hires" rather than hired because of their competence, they may object to the programs as well. They may even move to other organizations that they feel accept them more as individuals.

In addition, employees who are accustomed to working with similar people may not wish or know how to work with people who are different from themselves. We noted previously that the experience of working with women managers promotes acceptance of them in that capacity. However, organizations cannot wait for such acceptance to come about on its own. If the work experiences of the first managers who are female, African American, Hispanic, or members of another

minority group are strongly negative, organizations may have a difficult time finding other such employees to fill its open managerial
positions in the future.

Are organizations then faced with a "lose-lose" situation, whereby
they will be the target of complaints (a) whether they consciously try
to reduce statistical discrepancies within their ranks according to sex,
race, and so on or ignore the discrepancies altogether; and (b) whether
they promote a culture that values employee diversity or not? Not
necessarily. Organizations may take positive steps to eliminate inequities in treatment and acceptance of different groups without alienating
members of any group, *if* they carefully choose their actions and their
implementation strategies.

In this chapter, we shall first review the various laws that restrict sex
discrimination and how they have been interpreted and applied in
practice. Next, we shall consider how the underlying culture of organizations influences whether their managers act to promote or prevent
sex discrimination and whether members of diverse groups are fully
accepted. Finally, recommendations will be offered for how organizations may best promote equality of opportunity and appreciation of
cultural diversity among their employees.

Sex Discrimination: What the Law Says

The actions of employers are governed by a vast number of federal,
state, and local statutes as well as executive orders. I shall focus our
attention on federal laws and executive orders, because they have had
the broadest impact on organizations.[5]

Title VII of the Civil Rights Act of 1964 and the Equal Pay Act of 1963
are the most significant pieces of federal equal employment opportunity (EEO) legislation. Title VII prohibits discrimination on the basis of
sex, race, color, religion, or national origin in any employment condition, including hiring, firing, promotion, transfer, compensation, and
admission to training programs. It was extended to ban discrimination
because of pregnancy, childbirth, or related conditions and to ban sexual
harassment (see Chapter 5). The Equal Pay Act makes it illegal to pay
members of one sex at a lower rate than the other if they are in jobs that
require equal skill, effort, and responsibility under similar working conditions in the same establishment.

Executive Order 11246 is the one most relevant to issues of sex discrimination. As amended, it prohibits organizations with contracts of more than $10,000 per year with the federal government from discriminating against any employee or job applicant because of sex, race, religion, color, or national origin. In addition, all organizations with 50 or more employees and federal contracts exceeding $50,000 per year are required to develop written affirmative action plans and to take steps to eliminate discrimination in hiring, firing, layoff, recall, promotion, compensation, working conditions, and facilities. An acceptable affirmative action program must include an analysis of areas in which the organization is underrepresented by women and specific goals and timetables to remedy any problems.

Several agencies are involved in the administration and enforcement of EEO laws. The Equal Employment Opportunity Commission (EEOC) is charged with administering Title VII and the Equal Pay Act. It investigates and reconciles charges of discrimination against employers, unions, and employment agencies. The Department of Justice enforces Title VII in cases involving a state or local government agency or political subdivision. The Office of Federal Contract Compliance Programs, part of the Department of Labor, is responsible for administering Executive Order 11246. Individuals may also go to court on their own behalf or on behalf of a class of employees or potential employees to seek compliance with the laws.

Since these laws and executive orders have been passed, the courts and the agencies involved have wrestled with a wide variety of issues involving claims of sex discrimination. For example, sex discrimination may be reflected in non-pay areas such as recruitment and selection procedures, promotions and factors that determine upward mobility, demotions, terminations, layoffs, employee benefits, training opportunities, subsidization of educational expenses, use of facilities, anti-nepotism policies, part-time and flexible employment policies, and union contracts. Sex discrimination may also appear in the form of unwarranted disparities between the wages paid to women and men.

Ironically, the Title VII ban on sex discrimination was proposed as a last-minute amendment by a civil rights opponent as a strategy to prevent passage of the bill. Opponents felt the the male-dominated Congress would be more reluctant to pass the legislation if sex was included. Indeed, one representative justified his opposition with the phrase, "Vive la différence!" However, women's rights advocates joined civil rights opponents to pass the amendment, and then joined civil rights advocates to pass the entire bill, amendment and all. Thus Title VII opened the door for significant gains for women in the workplace despite the wishes of the representative who offered the amendment.[6]

As a result, the EEOC has had more difficulty in clarifying and applying the Title VII ban on sex discrimination than it has in administering any other provision of the law. Since Title VII was primarily written to deal with discrimination based on race, color, national origin, and religion, the distinct problems of discrimination according to sex were not taken into account. Moreover, the EEOC has had to relate the Title VII ban on sex discrimination in compensation to the overlapping provisions of the Equal Pay Act. In the remainder of this section, we shall review the major issues regarding sex discrimination that have been the subject of court rulings and agency guidelines.

Non-Pay Issues

Two basic types of organizational practices have been considered discriminatory under Title VII, those that involve disparate treatment and those that result in disparate impact.[7] *Disparate treatment discrimination* occurs when sex (as well as race, color, religion, or national origin) is used as a basis for treating people unequally, such as rejecting women applicants of childbearing age for certain jobs. Under the disparate treatment standard, an organization is allowed to impose any job-related requirements as long as they are imposed on all employees alike.

In contrast, *disparate impact discrimination* refers to any organizational practice that affects women and men unequally, unless it can be justified as job-related and essential to the safe and efficient operation of the organization. For example, a company's use of a minimum height requirement for certain jobs was rejected as discriminatory when it was shown to rule out more women than men and was not essential to job performance. Under the disparate impact standard, whether or not an employer has discriminated intentionally in a personnel action is irrelevant. All that matters is whether the action has unequal results, unless it can be shown to serve a legitimate need (such as apprenticeship training for skilled craft positions and licensing requirements for nurses and teachers) and there is no alternative that would have less of a disparate impact.

In 1976, the Supreme Court ruled that General Electric did not violate Title VII by excluding pregnancy from coverage in its disability plan. It reasoned that the GE plan did not exclude anyone because of sex (even though only women get pregnant) but merely removed one physical condition, pregnancy, from the list of compensable disabilities. This led to the 1978 passage of the Pregnancy Discrimination Act amending Title VII, which banned unequal treatment of pregnant women for all employment-related purposes. It prohibits firing or refusing to hire or promote a woman solely because she is pregnant, prohibits mandatory leaves for pregnant women arbitrarily set at a certain time in their pregnancy rather than because of an individual inability to work, protects reinstatement rights of women on leave for pregnancy-related reasons, and requires employers to treat pregnancy and childbirth the same way they treat other causes of disability under fringe benefit plans.

Although the vast majority of cases involving Title VII have dealt with discrimination against women, discrimination against men is also covered. For example, a court ruled that a collective-bargaining contract that allowed women but not men to take unpaid leaves for childrearing violated Title VII. In addition, a court ruled against Pan American Airways in the early 1970s for limiting its flight attendants to women. Pan American cited survey results that passengers preferred female flight attendants, and a clinical psychologist testified that women are better at comforting and reassuring passengers simply because they are women. Nonetheless, they lost the case. Male flight attendants are commonplace today, and air travelers still manage to get their food and beverages with comfort and reassurance.[8]

The Title VII ban on sex discrimination makes an exception of discrimination that involves a "bona fide occupational qualification" (BFOQ). Use of a same-sex BFOQ has been upheld in situations involving personal hygiene (such as cleaning of washrooms during periods when they are in use), health care, and counseling of rape victims. A same-sex BFOQ may also be used for reasons of authenticity or genuineness; it is acceptable to prefer actresses to play female parts and actors to play male parts. However, the refusal to hire an individual due to customer preferences or stereotypical assumptions about the characteristics of women and men (such as in the Pan American case) is likely to be considered illegal. For example, an employer was not allowed to use sex as a BFOQ despite the fact that foreign customers would refuse to deal with a woman.

Another permissible exception to Title VII is discrimination based on a seniority system, as long as the system is not a guise for discrimination. For example, the Supreme Court ruled that an employer cannot be ordered to ignore a seniority system when making layoffs, even if the effect is to reduce the number of women or minorities hired under an affirmative action plan. The courts may award retroactive seniority to individuals who are the victims of past discrimination, but seniority systems themselves are not illegal.

Employee selection procedures such as testing that have a disparate impact on the employment opportunities of men and women are illegal under Title VII and Executive Order 11246 unless they are justified by business necessity. The Uniform Guidelines on Employee Selection Procedures, adopted by several government agencies, recommend an "80 percent" rule of thumb for determining adverse impact. According to this rule, a selection rate for one sex that is less than 80% of the selection rate of the other sex shall be regarded as evidence of disparate impact. This restriction may be applied to promotion and layoff decisions as well as selection decisions.

Employers are not required to meet hiring or promotion quotas for specific groups of workers (e.g., since 45% of the area's labor force or population is female, 45% of hires should be female). However, the language of Title VII has been interpreted to allow hiring quotas to remedy an imbalance caused by past discrimination. If prior hiring practices promoted sex discrimination, stronger affirmative action may be expected of employers to rectify past inequalities. EEOC guidelines state that employers may give temporary preference to qualified applicants from underrepresented groups to achieve a long-term balance in the representation of those groups among their employees.

Pay Issues

The terms used by the Equal Pay Act have been elaborated by various court decisions. The equal work standard requires only that jobs be substantially equal, not identical. Equal work is defined by four factors: skill, effort, responsibility, and working conditions. *Skill* refers to the experience, training, education, and ability needed to perform the job. The skill level of the job, not the job holders, determines whether two jobs are equal. For example, female nursing aides and male orderlies in hospitals perform equal work because similar skills are required. *Effort* refers to the amount or degree of effort, mental or physical, required for a job. *Responsibility* refers to the degree of accountability required in the performance of a job. For example, a wage differential may be justified for employees who are required to become acting supervisor in the absence of a regular supervisor. *Working conditions* refer to the physical surroundings and safety concerns of a job, such as inside versus outside work, adequate heating and ventilation, and so on. The fact that jobs are merely in different departments is not sufficient to demonstrate a difference in working conditions.

Pay differences are permitted between men and women engaged in equal work if they result from a seniority system, a merit system, a system that measures earnings by quality or quantity of production (e.g., a piecework incentive system), or some job-related factor other than sex such as a shift differential or a difference in experience. For example, a court upheld higher pay for salespeople in the men's department of a clothing store over those in the women's department because the company demonstrated that the men's department was the more profitable. However, in another case, women received 10% less pay than their male counterparts who did the same basic job. The men occasionally did heavier work, but this was infrequent and not all men did it. The court, ruling that the employer's lower wage rate for women was based on an artificially created job classification and that the extra duties of some men did not justify paying all of them more, awarded back wages to the women.

Pay disparities are often linked to job evaluation, a measurement procedure that helps organizations to set pay differentials. Job evaluations typically focus on *key jobs*, characterized by a standard and stable content across organizations, within *job clusters*, or groups of jobs that have emerged as a function of technological or administrative practices (e.g., lines of promotion), location, and common job content. The starting point for the setting of wages is what the marketplace currently pays for key jobs. Wages are assigned to the key jobs within a job cluster according to the wages typically paid in the labor market for that geographical location. Wages for non-key jobs are set according to how they compare in rated worth with the key jobs in the same job cluster. Thus, a computer programming job (typically a key job) that requires familiarity with advanced programming languages or has more senior responsibilities may be rated as worth more, and thereby deserving of more pay, than one that only requires familiarity with simple programming languages or has less responsibilities. Ideally, the result is a pay structure that is based on concern for both external equity—the relationship between the pay for key jobs inside and outside the organization—and internal equity—the relationship between pay and job content within the organization.[9]

The Equal Pay Act is based on the principle of "equal pay for equal work." An additional principle that has been proposed for determining whether wage discrimination exists is "equal pay for work of comparable worth or value." According to this principle, jobs that require comparable (not identical) skill, effort, and responsibility warrant equal pay.[10]

Claims of sex discrimination according to the comparable worth principle have been filed under the Title VII prohibition on sex discrimination in compensation. In considering such cases, the courts have typically examined a particular employer's conduct and not attempted to establish a general standard. The U.S. Supreme Court based a ruling against the County of Washington (in Oregon) on the fact that the county had already established an evaluation system that showed that the wage rates for women were too low. In a different case, a federal appeals court held that the State of Washington, because it did not create ? the inequity, could legally pay employees in predominantly male job classes more than employees in predominantly female job classes, even though a state-commissioned study had concluded that the two types of job classes were comparable in worth. In other cases, data showing that the differential value of jobs within an organization reflected their differential value in the external labor market, combined with affirmative actions by employers, have led courts to reject charges of wage discrimination.

Although comparable worth has not been accepted as a legal doctrine by the federal courts, it has not been rejected altogether. Its advocates have been more successful in getting laws mandating pay equity enacted at the state level, particularly for state workers, than in arguing wage discrimination under existing laws at the federal level. Perhaps local elected officials are more responsive to the concerns of their constituents than federal regulatory agencies or the court system.[11]

Employers need to make sure that sex discrimination does not enter into job evaluation or any other element of the compensation system. Wage discrimination does not legally exist if factors such as skill, effort, responsibility, working conditions, and differences between the wages paid for male-dominated and female-dominated jobs that are reflected in the marketplace account for pay disparities. However, if an organization has identified pay inequities that cannot be accounted for by job-related or market-related factors, then corrective action needs to be taken. This does not necessarily mean immediately rectifying all differences or lowering anyone's pay, but should foster a commitment over the long run to eliminate unjustifiable disparities.[12]

In summary, EEO laws ban sex discrimination by organizations in several forms. Organizations may not discriminate in the ways in which they treat women and men regarding hiring, firing, promotion, layoff, compensation, and other types of employment conditions. They may also be held responsible for the unequal impact of their policies on men and women, unless a legitimate need has been served by the policies in question. Most organizations are expected to take steps to eliminate sex discrimination in the distribution of individuals across jobs and in wage rates. In addition, they must demonstrate on a regular basis that they are taking such steps by filing reports and keeping their records open for monitoring to assure compliance.

The Influence of Organizational Culture

Despite the passage of EEO laws, sex discrimination remains in the workplace. In addition, many organizations adhere to managerial practices that are more appropriate for a homogeneous than a diverse work force. In this section of the chapter, we shall explore the influence of organizational culture on how employees from different groups are treated.

So far in this book, we have primarily attributed sex discrimination in organizations to individuals' tendencies to engage in gender stereotyping. Individuals who are more traditional in their attitudes, lower in self-esteem, less educated, and more authoritarian are more likely to rely on gender stereotypes than individuals with the opposite characteristics. Experience in working with members of the opposite sex and having more information about a person tend to reduce the tendency to apply gender stereotypes in work relationships. Token members of a group are more likely to be victims of gender stereotyping than minority members of a group with a more balanced sex ratio.

Thus sex discrimination may be viewed as an inevitable result of gender stereotyping, with individual characteristics and situational factors influencing the extent to which gender stereotypes operate at any moment. However, this explanation does not allow for the influence of the organization itself, other than through the cumulative effect of employment decisions about individuals on the sex ratio of groups and individuals' work experiences with members of the opposite sex. These decisions in turn are influenced by the organizational culture.

Attitudes Toward Equal Opportunity

Organizations may be divided into three categories according to their basic attitudes toward equal employment opportunity.[13] *Proactive organizations* would be equal opportunity employers even if EEO laws had never been passed. They have consistently and actively recruited female employees for male-dominated jobs and, as a result, have a stable population of female talent available for promotion. These organizations use a combination of career planning services, training and development programs, and other activities to develop managers of both sexes. *Reactive organizations* merely react to EEO laws. They typically at- tempt minimal compliance with those laws by adding token women as managers. Since their emphasis is on tokenism, these organizations are vulnerable to charges of sex discrimination and prolonged law suits. *Benign neglect organizations* do nothing to eliminate sex discrimination or to alleviate its effects. They see government activity in this area as a misguided and hopefully passing fad. These organizations are inclined to wait to see if laws really will be enforced before doing anything to promote equal opportunity. Sex discrimination is more likely to occur in reactive and benign neglect organizations than in proactive organizations.[14]

More organizations fall into the reactive category than the other two, principally because the federal government has sent mixed signals about the need to adhere to EEO laws. Laws against sex discrimination, beginning with Title VII of the 1964 Civil Rights Act, have had increasing public support as the proportion of women in the workplace has risen. However, presidential administrations have varied in the extent to which they have enforced these laws. Lack of enforcement makes it more likely that barriers to the progress of women into management and within the managerial ranks will go unnoticed. When enforcement is inconsistent and unpredictable, organizations are encouraged to adopt a reactive, play-it-safe strategy. They attempt to appear that they are in compliance with EEO laws just in case they are scrutinized, but they do not adhere fully to the laws' intent.

Another reason why so many organizations are reactive is that equal opportunity has received bad press. Assume for the moment that organizations may adopt two opposing philosophies of equal opportunity. According to one view, competence is the first screening criterion for hiring or promoting managers. Members of underrepresented groups such as women and minorities are given preference if they pass the screen. According to the opposite view, membership in an underrepresented group is the first screen, and competence is then used to choose among the candidates who remain. The first approach yields qualified and competent employees. The second approach yields the best of the available equal opportunity candidates, whether qualified or not.

Many people believe that the second view best captures how equal opportunity operates, even when the first view is more accurate. When they learn that a woman or minority group member has been hired into a managerial position, they jump to the conclusion that he or she is an "affirmative action hire" and, therefore, is likely to be incompetent. One study found that, when women managers believed that they were hired primarily because of their sex, they were less committed to their organizations and less satisfied with their jobs than those who believed that sex was not an important factor in their selection. As a result, both women and men tend to hold unfavorable attitudes toward affirmative action. With such widely held negative opinions, it is not surprising that many organizations have not been eager to initiate equal opportunity programs or to pursue them aggressively.[15]

Managers' attitudes toward equal opportunity are influenced by their concern about their own self-interest. Those with a low level of self- interest act with the best interests of the organization in mind. They seek only the individuals with the best skills for the organization and are willing to pay accordingly. Sex discrimination in pay or job opportunities then arises only if men and women are perceived as bringing different characteristics to the job.[16]

In contrast, managers' whose level of self-interest is high exhibit a "rational bias" by making decisions that are solely to their advantage rather than the organization's. These decisions may coincidentally result in hiring the best employees and helping them to succeed; however, they are made without regard for such concerns. Such managers are highly sensitive to what will help or hinder their own careers and seek information about what decisions are expected of them and may be personally advantageous. They may engage in sex discrimination even if they do not care for it personally, are aware of the laws against it, understand that the people being discriminated against are as capable as anyone else, or even belong themselves to the group being discriminated against.

How self-interested managers behave depends on the type of organization in which they work. Managers in proactive organizations are expected to refrain from sex discrimination and to actively promote equal employment opportunity through their decisions. In contrast, managers in benign neglect organizations are expected to ignore equal opportunity considerations. Self-interested managers have no trouble in deciding how to behave in either type of organization.

Reactive organizations call for more subtle behavior. Self-interested managers in these organizations are likely to sense that they will be rewarded for operating without regard for EEO laws, but that they will also be rewarded for a superficial change in behavior. They will be appreciated for paying lip service to equal opportunity considerations, but will modify their actual decision-making behavior little if at all.

Who is responsible for the discriminatory patterns of behavior exhibited by managers in reactive and benign neglect organizations? If managers are held blameless for acting with a high level of self-interest, then only their organizations are to blame for fostering a culture that encourages sex discrimination in managerial decisions.

Attitudes Toward Cultural Diversity

Organizations that promote equal opportunity do not necessarily value cultural diversity within their ranks. Equal employment opportunity was originally a legalistic response to the ban on discrimination according to sex, race, color, religion, and national origin mandated by the federal government. Affirmative action programs, which are an outgrowth of equal opportunity law and are regulated by executive orders and government agencies, have contributed to *quantitative* changes in the composition of the work force in many organizations. In contrast, organizations that value cultural diversity attempt to bring about *qualitative* changes through increased appreciation of the range of skills and values that dissimilar employees offer and increased opportunity to manage work groups that include members who are culturally distinct from the dominant group.[17]

Taylor Cox distinguished among three types of organizations according to their basic attitudes toward cultural diversity.[18] *Monolithic organizations* are characterized by a large majority of one group of employees, especially in the managerial ranks. Differences between majority and minority group members are resolved by the process of assimilation, whereby minority group employees are expected to adopt the norms and values of the majority group to survive in the organization. Such organizations are characterized by low levels of intergroup conflict, because there are few members of minority groups and such members have outwardly adopted, if not inwardly embraced, majority norms and values. Changes in work force demographics have led to a reduction in the number of monolithic organizations with white male majorities. However, many minority-owned businesses and foreign companies operating in the United States are monolithic organizations.

Plural organizations have a more heterogeneous work force than mono-lithic organizations, primarily because they take steps to be more inclusive of minority group members. These steps may include hiring and promotion policies that stress recruitment and advancement of members of minority groups and manager training on equal opportunity issues. Plural organizations, which may be either proactive or reactive, represent the typical large American business today. They emphasize an affirmative action approach to managing diversity by focusing on the numbers of majority versus minority group members in different jobs and levels, but not on the quality of work relationships between members of different groups. Although the primary organizational approach to resolving cultural differences is assimilation, intergroup conflict can be high if members of the majority group resent practices used to boost minority group membership. Even though overt discrimination may have been banished, prejudice is still likely to exist in plural organizations.

An organization that simply contains many diverse groups of employees is considered a plural organization. *Multicultural organizations* value this diversity. They respond to cultural differences by encouraging members of different groups to adopt some of the norms and values of other groups, in contrast to the assimilation practiced by monolithic and plural organizations. A multicultural approach "involves increasing the consciousness and appreciation of differences associated with the heritage, characteristics, and values of many different groups, as well as respecting the uniqueness of each individual."[19] Intergroup conflict in multicultural organizations is low due to a general absence of prejudice and discrimination.

Thus, to encourage both equality of opportunity and appreciation of diversity among their employees, organizations need to be more than merely proactive. They also need to be truly multicultural in their approach to managing their employees, rather than expect all employees to adhere to the values and norms associated with the traditional majority group.

Implications

So far, we have examined issues related to equal opportunity and valuing diversity from a legal and organizational culture perspective. Now, it's time to look at these issues from a practical perspective—what specifically should organizations try to accomplish, and how?[20]

Unfortunately, research offers little help. Only organizations that are proud of their efforts to promote equal opportunity and value cultural diversity have been willing to tell the outside world about their success. As a result, there are few comparative studies that identify the factors that most contribute to organizational success or failure in promoting equal opportunity and valuing diversity. We have to reach our own conclusions.

Setting the Proper Goals

Let's first consider the organization's goals regarding equal opportunity. Earlier, we placed organizations into three categories according to their basic commitment to equal opportunity—no commitment (benign neglect), commitment to meet legal obligations alone (reactive), or commitment as a guiding principle of conduct (proactive). We need to examine the consequences of equal opportunity commitment for each organizational category.

Benign neglect organizations are taking a foolish risk in hoping that EEO laws will fade away or that they will not be caught in violation of them. Enforcement may be sporadic, but, with the large number of women in the workplace, EEO laws will not be forgotten. Benign neglect organizations operate at considerable danger to their own livelihood as well as to their relations with employees.

Reactive organizations may achieve the minimal compliance with EEO laws that they desire. However, strategies of tokenism and double standards regarding equal opportunity foster negative employee reactions. These organizations are not really committed to ending sex discrimination. Instead, they may resort to reverse discrimination to achieve numerical balance if they think that will satisfy the law. They leave themselves vulnerable by following an intermediate, half-hearted strategy regarding equal opportunity, and they find themselves in frequent trouble over this issue.

Proactive organizations promote equal opportunity as a smart business practice. They recognize that the composition of the labor pool has changed, with larger proportions of women and members of minority groups in the labor market than ever before. If they were to deny opportunities to women and minorities, they would not be taking full advantage of the labor supply and would be limiting themselves to the relatively shrinking supply of white male workers. Whether considered as a moral, legal, or business issue, proactive commitment is the most appropriate for today's work environment.

A likely by-product of equal opportunity is a heterogeneous work force, but it's not the primary goal. If the goal were to balance men and women in all jobs and at all levels and managers were evaluated according to their contribution to achieving this balance, then they would make *all* employment-related decisions on the basis of sex, assigning women and men to positions according to formula. The result would be sex discrimination institutionalized as organizational policy, the opposite of equal opportunity intent.

The proper goal of an organization regarding equal opportunity, then, is to prevent sex discrimination from affecting its employment-related decisions in any way. This is attained by aggressively recruiting, hiring, and promoting the most qualified individuals without regard to their sex, and by not treating employees in any way differently on the basis of their sex. If the organization's goal is to end sex discrimination and managers are evaluated by how well they help achieve this, then *all* decisions must be made in a nondiscriminatory fashion, no matter what their outcome. This is what is really intended by EEO laws. And it is the attitude regarding equal opportunity that makes the most sense for an organization, because it emphasizes making the best use of all the human resources available.

Next, let's consider the organization's goals regarding cultural diversity. We have categorized organizations according to their basic attitudes toward cultural diversity as monolithic, plural, or multicultural. The attention to diversity exhibited by multicultural organizations may be justified for moral and legal reasons similar to those used to justify attention to equal opportunity. However, it may also be justified as a way for organizations to gain competitive advantage.[21]

Employee turmoil is costly. Women and people of color have higher turnover rates and often have lower job satisfaction levels than white males. This often reflects frustration over lack of career success (however defined) and discomfort with the dominant organizational culture.

Organizations with the best reputations for valuing diversity incorporate the needs and values of employees from all groups, including foreign employees, into the organizational culture. They are likely to have the lowest turnover rates and win the competition for the best personnel among women and minorities.

Because markets as well as organizations are becoming increasingly diverse, organizations that do not learn to function in a global economy in which diversity is a way of life are likely to suffer. Organizations with good reputations for valuing diversity have favorable public relations. They are also able to work effectively with foreign clients. Many people, especially women and ethnic minorities, prefer to buy from as well as work for such organizations.

Imagine, for example, that Company X has a sales force consisting entirely of white males and that Company Y has a sales force that is demographically diverse. Imagine also that both companies are competing for business from Company Z, whose purchasing department reflects the diversity of Company Y rather than the homogeneity of Company X. All other things being equal, including the quality of the products and services that Companies X and Y offer, which company is likely to win Company Z's business? Company Y, of course. The Company Y sales force will understand and relate to Company Z purchasers and be viewed positively by them. Thus, organizations will meet their operating goals better, both in keeping and gaining market share, by having a work force that reflects the heterogeneity of the labor force.

Diversity of viewpoints also enhances the creativity and problem-solving ability of work groups. It may be a way of avoiding the pitfalls of "groupthink," whereby groups forgo critical thinking because they are preoccupied with maintaining a sense of group cohesiveness. Excessive group cohesiveness, and the tendency toward groupthink that results, are more likely when the group is demographically similar than when it is made up of individuals from different cultures. Also, as work groups become more tolerant of different points of view, their organizations become more open to new ideas in general and generate more and better ideas. Such organizations are likely to be more responsive to changes in their operating environments than those that are more closed in their thinking and rigid in their approach to problem solving.[22]

Thus organizations benefit from setting a goal of being multicultural in their approach to diversity. This means movement away from the assimilation strategy of incorporating new employees into the existing organization, whereby they are expected to act in a manner identical to

Table 8.1 What Organizations Can Do

---

1. Inform top executives that they need to be fully committed to equal opportunity and appreciation of cultural diversity as organizational goals, and obtain their commitment by whatever means necessary.
2. Recognize equal opportunity and cultural diversity as business issues and present them that way to employees.
3. Assign responsibility for equal opportunity and cultural diversity programs and results to a top-line executive.
4. Set goals and objectives, measure performance to objectives, and reward or punish results regarding equal opportunity and cultural diversity just as any other kind of results.
5. Stress the importance of promoting equal opportunity and valuing cultural diversity in the mission statement.
6. Set up special committees to advise top executives on diversity issues.
7. Offer training programs in support of equal opportunity and cultural diversity goals.
8. Involve managers at all levels in the design and implementation of equal opportunity and cultural diversity programs.
9. Stress that competence is the first screen for filling open positions.

---

that of current employees to be fully accepted. Instead, it means encouraging employees at all levels, from top to bottom, (a) to be themselves and share the full range of their own skills, values, and ideas with other employees, and (b) to be open to and ready to take advantage of the full range of skills, values, and ideas of others. When organizations successfully cultivate this kind of sharing, they gain a competitive edge in today's economy.

Demonstrating Top Management Commitment

Assume that an organization has set the goals of being both proactive and multicultural in its employment practices. We shall now consider what it needs to do to achieve these goals. Table 8.1 outlines some of the steps that organizations can take. We shall discuss such steps in the remainder of the chapter.

Most writers conclude that top management commitment, demonstrated by assignment of responsibility and allocation of resources, is critical to achieving equal opportunity and cultural diversity. *In Search of Excellence* authors Tom Peters and Bob Waterman stressed the importance of the leader in setting an organization's primary values. Firms led by top executives who stress proactive values and devote resources to equal opportunity programs have higher proportions of female and minority managers than other firms. CEOs at companies like U.S. West, Payless Cashways, Pitney Bowes, and Fidelity Bank have had a major impact on the advancement of women within the managerial ranks. "Champions of diversity" are needed—people who take strong public and personal stands on the need for cultural change in the organization and act as role models for the new types of behaviors needed for change. What better role model than the top executive?[23]

Sometimes leaders can demonstrate their commitment ineffectually. For example, the CEO of Company A walks out of any meeting in his organization attended only by white males. How effective is this action? It certainly catches people's attention! However, it is likely to lead to token representation of lower-level women or minorities at meetings with the CEO. When the primary reason for having women at the meeting is to respond to the CEO's gesture, both the women and the rest of the group feel uncomfortable. Unless the CEO's action is accompanied by others that promote equal opportunity and valuing diversity, it is likely to be counterproductive.

The CEO of Company B follows a more typical approach of periodically sending a letter to employees stating that the company is an equal opportunity employer and that sex, race, color, religion, and national origin should not enter into any employment-related decisions by company employees. The letter is the same, word for word, each time it is sent, which is the same time each year. One can imagine a secretary annually observing in a tickler file that it is time to retrieve the standard letter from storage and prepare it for the CEO's signature. Signing this letter is the extent of the CEO's direct involvement with equal opportunity.

Like many organizations, Company B also has a policy of not revealing its goals and timetables for promoting equal opportunity for women employees to any internal or external source, other than to the government in its required affirmative action plan. Consider the effects of this policy on line managers. Denied knowledge of details about the company's equal opportunity program, they find it difficult to know how well they personally are doing in helping the company to reach its goals or whether they should do anything differently. They may then conclude that the real purpose of the letter is to meet government requirements to make the official policy known, rather than to promote any particular action on their part, and be inclined to ignore it.

How an organization "sells" equal opportunity and valuing cultural diversity to employees plays a large role in determining whether goals are achieved. Company C promoted equal opportunity and valuing diversity to its employees first as moral issues, then as legal issues, and finally as business issues. Its appeal to morality didn't work, because few people do the "right" thing unless it is personally advantageous. The legal argument didn't work either, because this angle suggested that compliance with the law was more important than ending sex discrimination and changing corporate culture and promoted the mentality of a reactive, plural organization. Company C has been more successful in promoting equal opportunity and valuing diversity as business issues because it has pointed to the effect on bottom-line profits, which most employees see as ultimately affecting their own livelihoods.

In conclusion, the person with primary responsibility for equal opportunity and cultural diversity programs should either report to or be a top-line executive. This person then has immediate access to and control over the managers who hold the key to program success or failure. For example, companies such as Corning and Allstate Insurance have a designated manager who oversees diversity programs companywide. If this responsibility is buried in the lower professional ranks of the personnel department, there is less impact on the organization as a whole, which gives managers the message that promoting equal opportunity and valuing cultural diversity are not really that important to the organization.[24]

Setting Up the Management System

A good sales pitch alone does not overcome resistance to organizational goals regarding equal opportunity and cultural diversity. An organization also needs a sound management system that analyzes its employment of women and minorities, identifies problem areas, establishes an action plan based on specific goals and timetables, and then monitors results against the plan. As one executive said in a Conference Board survey:

> How do you go about achieving EEO results in a company? The same way you achieve any other results. You analyze the problem carefully, determine what you need to do, and then set up an overall management planning and control system to make very sure that it happens—and on schedule.[25]

Such a system begins with an analysis of whether women and minorities are equitably represented throughout the organization. Required by Executive Order 11246 for government contractors, this analysis should compare the number of women and minorities in each job category with their availability in the relevant labor force who are qualified to fill jobs in that category. The relevant labor force could be defined as that located in the immediate city or town, the metropolitan area, or the nation, depending on the job category. Areas that underemploy women and minorities then become the appropriate targets of equal opportunity programs. Although not required by law, this analysis could also identify areas of underemployment of men, which the organization may wish to address.

Next comes the specification of objectives. Managers will put more effort into promoting equal opportunity and valuing diversity if they are expected to meet concrete objectives. For example, George Harvey, CEO of Pitney Bowes, mandated in the late 1980s that new professional hires and promotions include 35% women and 15% minorities. However, although this objective focused on results, it ignored the question of how they would be obtained. Since the goal is nondiscriminatory personnel decisions, objectives should focus more on how decisions are made than on their outcomes.[26]

The PQ Corporation, a specialty chemicals manufacturer in Valley Forge, Pennsylvania, has implemented a unique procedure to meet the objective of discrimination-free employment decisions. By fully documenting each hire or promotion, including job descriptions, a contrast of required skills to candidate skills, and a checklist of actions, it measures the nature and frequency of discrimination incidents and forces managers to confront and acknowledge discriminatory behavior in the hiring and promotion process.[27]

The key is the "selection checklist," a two-part document that the manager completes for each candidate interviewed for a position. The first part contains questions that address how free each step in the selection process was from possible discrimination, such as: Did you perform or do you have a current job analysis for this position? Was the position posted internally? Were reasons for rejection based on job-related deficiencies and not related to non-job-related factors such as a handicap or religious beliefs? Each question must be answered "yes," "no," or "not applicable." The questions answered "no" reflect possible incidents of discrimination. The second part documents the correlation between the job criteria (i.e., the skills and knowledge required to perform major job functions) and the attributes of the candidate.

Both parts of the document are intended to make managers aware of the process they use to make their decisions. Each manager's checklists are passed on to his or her superior, who is expected to investigate if the percentage of incident-free decisions is low. EEO objectives for managers are then stated in terms of percentages of discriminatory incidents. The focus of this procedure is clearly on discriminatory behavior rather than numbers of nontraditional hires and promotions. If a manager reports a potential incident of discrimination, upper management is able to take corrective action if necessary. If a manager does not complete the form accurately and attempts to cover up discrimination, then he or she is consciously exposing the company to the possibility of an EEO lawsuit.

The same principle may be used to promote acceptance of diverse skills and points of view. Irving Janis specified several actions that a group leader may take to counteract the groupthink tendency towards uncritical acceptance of majority points of view. The leader may (a) assign the role of critical evaluator to each group member, encouraging the group to share objections and doubts to ideas that seem to have majority acceptance; (b) refrain from stating preferences and expectations before the group has a chance to generate and evaluate alternative solutions to problems; (c) set up different groups to work on the same problems so that alternative solutions may be compared; (d) require each member to discuss the group's deliberations with colleagues outside the group and then report back their reactions; and (e) assign a member to play "devil's advocate" at each meeting, challenging the majority point of view. Effective leaders make sure that adequate consideration is given to the ideas of all group members.[28]

Leaders who manage their work groups in this fashion act as champions of diversity, even if the composition of the group is demographically similar, because they value diverse points of view and make sure that the group does too. When the group does have members from different cultures, they learn to expect that members from the majority culture will not impose their norms and values on the group simply because they are in the majority. Instead, group norms support open discussion and creative problem solving that draw on the ideas and talents of all group members.

How can the organization promote this kind of group process? A "group management checklist" could be instituted, on which both the leader and group members specified whether each of the above steps was followed as they addressed specific problems or projects. The group could be expected to review periodically the contents of its checklists and discuss how its problem solving process could be more effective. In addition, the supervisor of the group leader could review checklists to evaluate how well the leader seemed to be encouraging the expression and consideration of diverse points of view. The focus of this procedure is on the process by which the group makes decisions, rather than on the demographic composition of the group, because the presence of members from different cultures does not guarantee that diverse skills and points of view will be valued in the group.

Once an organization develops and assigns specific objectives, they should become part of the manager's overall performance appraisal. Managers should be made aware that that their supervisors will evaluate their success at promoting equal opportunity and valuing cultural diversity as they do any results. Then, good performance in this area should be reinforced with tangible rewards such as promotions, salary increases, and favorable task assignments. However, deliberate failure to comply with objectives (or benign neglect) should result in decreased salary or promotion opportunities.

These actions speak much louder than words of approval or disapproval. By giving managers explicit knowledge of the organization's goals to be proactive and multicultural and incentives to meet the objectives assigned to them, an effective management system helps to overcome any resistance they might feel to these goals.

Note that the emphasis is on the reinforcement of behaviors rather than attitudes. Unlike attitudes, behaviors can be readily observed, allowing progress or lack of progress to be directly monitored. Moreover, if people are motivated to promote equal opportunity and value cultural diversity despite holding other beliefs, they often come to believe in what they are doing.[29]

Becoming a Proactive and Multicultural Organization

Organizations may take many specific actions to promote a proactive and multicultural approach to management. For example, they may stress the importance of equal opportunity and cultural diversity in their mission statements, establish special groups to advise top executives on how current or proposed policies may affect employees from different groups, and include a component on equal opportunity and valuing diversity in their orientation programs for new employees.[30] Many of the initiatives that I recommended in previous chapters to counteract stereotyping and discrimination and to help employees achieve success in their careers and lives also promote acceptance of equal opportunity and cultural diversity.

Analysis of the organizational culture and how it influences the treatment of members of different groups should also be undertaken. The goals of a "cultural audit" should be (a) to uncover biases in decision making regarding recruitment, performance appraisals, promotions, compensation, and other management activities if present; and (b) to identify ways in which the organizational culture, especially if it is monolithic or plural, may put some employees at a disadvantage.[31]

Training programs are a popular way for organizations to promote equality of opportunity and appreciation of cultural diversity. *Awareness training* introduces the topics, provides information on changing work force demographics and the benefits to the organization of being proactive and multicultural, and offers exercises and role plays that raise participants' awareness of their own stereotypes, biases, skills, and values. *Skill-building training* helps employees to move beyond their stereotypes and biases and work well with members of diverse groups. For example, a skill-building program may focus on how to be an effective group member or leader by encouraging display of diverse skills and points of view. *Language training* is important to multinational organizations as well as those hiring Hispanic and Asian Americans, and foreign nationals; it may benefit Anglo-American employees as well.[32]

The participation of first-line supervisors, the people most responsible for getting work done in organizations, is critical to the success of equal opportunity and cultural diversity programs. The biggest problem most supervisors have with such programs is that they are perceived to result in the use of differential criteria for hiring and promotion and in differential treatment of employees with respect to discipline and discharge. If these programs are designed by staffing experts at the corporate level without consulting lower-level managers, then supervisors may feel that preferential hiring is taking place without regard to competence and may resent individuals whom they see as affirmative action hires in their units. Whether these beliefs are accurate, they may seriously affect morale in the supervisor's unit. Such perceptions can be prevented by including supervisors (and nonsupervisors if possible) in the development of programs and assuring them that qualifications and competence, not sex, race, or some other personal factor, will be the primary basis for employment decisions.[33]

Reverse discrimination hurts everyone. Conceivably, people who cannot gain a job otherwise may have a chance to show how well they can do. However, resentful coworkers are likely to make working conditions very difficult and success virtually impossible. The intended beneficiaries lose because others assume that they are incompetent and resent them. Other employees lose because they feel resentful about perceived reverse discrimination, even if it did not actually take place. Perceptions of reverse discrimination are in some ways more damaging than actual occurrences, because they trigger the negative attitudes that cause all parties to resist equal opportunity and cultural diversity programs. The best way to keep such perceptions from forming is to have women and men from all levels and from all cultural groups represented in the design and implementation of such programs.

In conclusion, all organizations benefit from promoting equal opportunity and valuing cultural diversity. Participation in goal setting and decision making leads to acceptance and commitment. Therefore, employees should be involved in the design and implementation of programs, setting goals to work towards, and identifying problems that hinder their achievement. Even organizations that have demonstrated such commitment throughout their existence need to make special efforts to have a pool of qualified applicants from all demographic groups and to offer them a satisfying job and culture in which to work. When organizations are proactive and multicultural in their management practices, they enhance their own bottom line and allow all of their employees to develop into "graceful swans."

Notes

1. P. Hellman, "Forget Your MBA, Read Cinderella," reprinted by permission of the publisher from *Management Review*, September 1990, © 1990, p. 63. American Management Association, New York. All rights reserved.

2. M. Eastwood, "Legal Protection Against Sex Discrimination," in *Women Working: Theories and Facts in Perspective*, ed. A. H. Stromberg and S. Harkess (Palo Alto, CA: Mayfield, 1978).

3. W. B. Johnston and A. E. Packer, *Workforce 2000: Work and Workers for the 21st Century* (Indianapolis: Hudson Institute, 1987); U.S. General Accounting Office, *The Changing Workforce: Demographic Issues Facing the Federal Government* (Washington, DC: U.S. General Accounting Office, 1992), pp. 23-35; H. N. Fullerton, Jr., "New Labor Force Projections, Spanning 1988 to 2000," *Monthly Labor Review, 112* (No. 11, November 1989): 3-12, calculations for the year 2000 based on table 4, p. 8.

4. L. L. Kessler, *Managing Diversity in an Equal Opportunity Workplace: A Primer for Today's Manager* (Washington, DC: National Foundation for the Study of Employment Policy, 1990), pp. 4-5.

5. This section of the chapter is primarily based on N. J. Sedmak and M. D. Levin-Epstein, *Primer of Equal Employment Opportunity*, 5th ed. (Washington, DC: Bureau of National Affairs, 1991).

6. J. Ledvinka and V. G. Scarpello, *Federal Regulation of Personnel and Human Resource Management*, 2nd ed. (Boston: PWS-Kent, 1991); pp. 63-65.

7. Ledvinka and Scarpello, *Federal Regulation of Personnel and Human Resource Management*, pp. 48-50.

8. Ledvinka and Scarpello, *Federal Regulation of Personnel and Human Resource Management*, p. 60.

9. D. P. Schwab, "Job Evaluation and Pay Setting: Concepts and Practices," in *Comparable Worth: Issues and Alternatives*, ed. E. R. Livernash (Washington, DC: Equal Employment Advisory Council, 1984).

10. P. England, *Comparable Worth: Theories and Evidence* (New York: Aldine de Gruyter, 1992); R. T. Michael, H. I. Hartmann, and B. O'Farrell, eds., *Pay Equity: Empirical Inquiries* (Washington, DC: National Academy Press, 1989); D. J. Treiman and H. I. Hartmann, eds., *Women, Work, and Wages: Equal Pay for Jobs of Equal Value* (Washington, DC: National Academy Press, 1981).

11. T. A. Mahoney, "Understanding Comparable Worth: A Societal and Political Perspective," in *Research in Organizational Behavior*, vol. 9, ed. L. L. Cummings and B. M. Staw (Greenwich, CT: JAI, 1987).

12. G. P. Sape, "Coping with Comparable Worth," *Harvard Business Review*, 63 (No. 3, May/June 1985): 145-152.

13. This section of the chapter is based on G. N. Powell, "Upgrading Management Opportunities for Women," *HR Magazine*, 35 (No. 11, November 1990): 67-70.

14. G. C. Pati, "Reverse Discrimination: What Can Managers Do?" *Personnel Journal*, 56 (1977): 334-338, 360-362. The labels of *proactive*, *reactive*, and *benign neglect* organizations are my own. Pati simply called them Category I, II, and III organizations, respectively.

15. G. B. Northcroft and J. Martin, "Double Jeopardy: Resistance to Affirmative Action from Potential Beneficiaries," in *Sex Role Stereotyping and Affirmative Action Policy*, ed. B. A. Gutek (Los Angeles: University of California, Institute of Industrial Relations, 1982); T. I. Chacko, "Women and Equal Employment Opportunity: Some Unintended Effects," *Journal of Applied Psychology*, 67 (1982): 119-123; M. E. Heilman, C. J. Block, and J. A. Lucas, "Presumed Incompetent? Stigmatization and Affirmative Action Efforts," *Journal of Applied Psychology*, 77 (1992): 536-544; M. E. Heilman, M. C. Simon, and D. P. Repper, "Intentionally Favored, Unintentionally Harmed? Impact of Sex-Based Preferential Selection on Self-Perceptions and Self-Evaluations," *Journal of Applied Psychology*, 72 (1987): 62-68; R. W. Nacoste, "Affirmative Action and Self-Evaluation," in *Affirmative Action in Perspective*, ed. F. A. Blanchard and F. J. Crosby (London: Springer Verlag, 1989); F. Tougas and F. Veilleux, "Who Likes Affirmative Action: Attitudinal Processes Among Men and Women," in *Affirmative Action in Perspective*, ed. Blanchard and Crosby.

16. L. Larwood, E. Szwajkowski, and S. Rose, "When Discrimination Makes 'Sense': The Rational Bias Theory," in *Women and Work: An Annual Review*, vol. 3, ed. B. A. Gutek, A. H. Stromberg, and L. Larwood (Newbury Park, CA: Sage, 1988); L.

Larwood, E. Szwajkowski, and S. Rose, "Sex and Race Discrimination Resulting from Manager-Client Relationships: Applying the Rational Bias Theory of Managerial Discrimination," *Sex Roles, 18* (1988): 9-29; L. Larwood, B. A. Gutek, and U. E. Gattiker, "Perspectives on Institutional Discrimination and Resistance to Change," *Group and Organization Studies, 9* (1984): 333-352.

17. M. Loden and J. B. Rosener, *Workforce America! Managing Employee Diversity as a Vital Resource* (Homewood, IL: Irwin, 1991), pp. 196-199.

18. T. Cox, Jr., "The Multicultural Organization," *Academy of Management Executive, 5* (No. 2, May 1991): 34-47.

19. A. M. Morrison, *The New Leaders: Guidelines on Leadership Diversity in America* (San Francisco: Jossey-Bass, 1992), p. 7.

20. Portions of this section of the chapter are based on Powell, "Upgrading Management Opportunities for Women."

21. T. Cox, Jr., and S. Blake, "Managing Cultural Diversity: Implications for Organizational Competitiveness," *Academy of Management Executive, 5* (No. 3, August 1991): 45-56; N. J. Adler, Chapter 4, "Cultural Synergy," in *International Dimensions of Organizational Behavior,* 2nd ed. (Boston: PWS-Kent, 1991); Morrison, Chapter 1, "Achieving Benefits from Leadership Diversity," in *The New Leaders.*

22. I. L. Janis, "Groupthink," *Psychology Today, 5* (No. 6, November 1971): 43-46, 74-76; Adler, Chapter 5, "Multicultural Teams," in *International Dimensions of Organizational Behavior.*

23. T. J. Peters and R. H. Waterman, Jr., *In Search of Excellence: Lessons from America's Best-Run Companies* (New York: Harper & Row, 1982); Morrison, Chapter 8, "Step Two: Strengthen Top-Management Commitment," in *The New Leaders;* A. M. Konrad and F. Linnehan, "The Implementation and Effectiveness of Equal Opportunity Employment," in *Proceedings: Annual Meeting of the Academy of Management,* ed. J. L. Wall and L. R. Jauch (Las Vegas, 1992); J. D. Leck and D. M. Saunders, "Employment Equity Programs: Effects on Hiring Visible Minorities," in *New Approaches to Employee Management,* vol. 2, ed. D. M. Saunders (Greenwich, CT: JAI, in press); B. Zeitz and L. Dusky, *The Best Companies for Women* (New York: Simon and Schuster, 1988); Cox and Blake, "Managing Cultural Diversity."

24. J. Cunningham, "Avoiding Common Pitfalls in Affirmative Action Programs," *Personnel Journal, 55* (1976): 125-127, 136; Cox and Blake, "Managing Cultural Diversity."

25. R. G. Schaeffer and E. F. Lynton, *Corporate Experiences in Improving Women's Job Opportunities* (New York: Conference Board, 1979), p. 21.

26. Zeitz and Dusky, "Pitney Bowes," in *The Best Companies for Women.*

27. J. C. Poole and E. T. Kautz, "An EEO/AA Program That Exceeds Quotas—It Targets Biases," *Personnel Journal, 66* (No. 1, January 1987): 103-105.

28. Janis, "Groupthink."

29. F. E. Gordon, "Bringing Women into Management: The Role of the Senior Executive," in *Bringing Women into Management,* ed. F. E. Gordon and M. H. Strober (New York: McGraw-Hill, 1975).

30. Cox, "The Multicultural Organization"; Loden and Rosener, Chapter 9, "Valuing Diversity in Leading-Edge Organizations," in *Workforce America!*; Zeitz and Dusky, *The Best Companies for Women.*

31. R. R. Thomas, Jr., "From Affirmative Action to Affirming Diversity," *Harvard Business Review, 68* (No. 2, March-April 1990): 107-117; Cox and Blake, "Managing Cultural Diversity."

32. Cox, "The Multicultural Organization;" Morrison, Chapter 5, "Creating Meaningful Development Opportunities," in *The New Leaders*.

33. T. H. Hammer, "Affirmative Action Programs: Have We Forgotten the First-Line Supervisor?" *Personnel Journal, 58* (1979): 384-389; F. S. Hall and M. Albrecht, Chapter 7, "Developing Systemwide Commitment," in *The Management of Affirmative Action* (Pacific Palisades, CA: Goodyear, 1979); D. A. Brookmire, "Designing and Implementing Your Company's Affirmative Action Program," *Personnel Journal, 58* (1979): 232-237.

9

Looking Ahead

The Times They Are A-Changin'?

There will be two large categories of changes between the working world of the present and that of the future. First, in the future there will be a greater accommodation of family life. In other words, there will be recognition by the working organization of the personal maintenance work of house and family care and a less rigid separation of these two aspects of their employees' lives. No one will be able to be treated as though he or she had no personal life or children. Second, the business and industrial organization will be less of a male-oriented, male-image culture. This will come about both through the greater participation of women in the actual processes of management and decision-making and through greater emphasis upon personal and emotional sides of men's personalities.

Jane W. Torrey[1]

In recent decades, we have witnessed a major transformation in the nature of male and female roles in the workplace. As more women have entered the work force, the working lives of women and men at work have been profoundly altered. Sex-related issues have not entirely disappeared from the workplace, however, and there is still room for change. The purpose of this chapter is to speculate about future changes in the working lives of women and men. Let's begin by assessing the current state of affairs.[2]

The Present: Stability and Change

There is evidence of both stability and change in the current state of male/female work roles. For example, we have seen that:

1. The majority of women have rejected the traditional role of the woman as "a homemaker." However, the vast majority of men still subscribe to the traditional image of the man as "a breadwinner." As a result, women and men are still experiencing considerable conflict and confusion over what roles they should play in their work and home lives.

2. New conceptions have developed about what it means to be male or female. Androgyny—a blend of masculine and feminine characteristics—has been touted as the new ideal for both sexes. However, much of society still endorses gender stereotypes depicting men as essentially masculine and women as essentially feminine. Further, the socialization experiences of young females and males continue to differ in ways that reinforce these stereotypes.

3. Barriers to the entry of women in the higher-paid, male-dominated occupations, including management, have been breaking down. A larger number of women have been preparing for and entering these occupations than ever before. However, men have not demonstrated a corresponding interest in the lower-paid, female-dominated occupations such as nursing, teaching, and secretarial/clerical work. Further, women's average full-time earnings, even in the same occupation or job, remain below those of men.

4. As the number of women in male-dominated occupations has increased, the sex ratios of work groups within those occupations have shifted from uniform (all male) to skewed (greater than 85% male) or tilted (65% to 85% male). Balanced sex ratios have seldom been achieved, however, and majority/minority dynamics remain between men and women in most work groups.

5. Many organizations have implemented and successfully enforced federal guidelines banning sexual harassment in the workplace. However, the incidence of sexual harassment in organizations continues to be alarming. In addition, men and women have

sharply differing views about what constitutes sexual harassment and what should be done about it, making it difficult for organizations to police themselves.

6. The myth that women are incapable of holding management positions has been successfully laid to rest. Except for women's greater tendency to be democratic leaders, female and male managers generally do not differ in aptitudes, abilities, and behaviors. Both sexes contain excellent, average, and poor performers. However, women remain in the minority in management, especially in its upper echelons. Although the proportion of women in management is above 40%, the proportion of women in *top* management positions is less than 5%.

7. There is evidence that better managers in today's work environment exhibit a high amount of behaviors traditionally regarded as feminine, using either a feminine or androgynous leadership style. Support for the belief that better managers are masculine remains strong, however, even though masculine managers seem to be only average performers.

8. Although the difference between women's and men's general career patterns is diminishing, important differences remain. Women with families are less likely to pursue careers in management than men with families. In addition, married male managers are more likely than married female managers to have a spouse who stays home and handles family responsibilities. Regardless of her occupation, the woman still performs most household activities in dual-career families. Thus, having a family typically imposes a greater constraint on women's careers than it does on men's.

9. A growing number of organizations offer their employees alternative work arrangements such as flextime and job sharing as well as assistance with child-care needs. However, women who take advantage of such arrangements often are relegated to the "mommy track" and are expected to accept reduced opportunities for career advancement. In addition, men are reluctant to participate in them because they do not want to be seen as less committed to their careers than a successful male should be.

10. Nearly all employers now provide more equal opportunity to their employees and job applicants than they have at any previous time. However, these actions are often token attempts to achieve minimal compliance with EEO laws rather than true commitment

to ending sex discrimination. When perceived as reverse discrimination, they encourage resistance to equal opportunity among
all employees, including the intended beneficiaries.

11. Change in the demographic mix of job applicants and the increased internationalization of business have led the labor force
to be more diverse in sex, race, ethnicity, and nationality than
ever before. However, many employers see increased cultural diversity among their employees as a disruptive influence to be mini-
mized, rather than as a welcome influence that gives the organization a competitive advantage.

How much stability versus how much change has there been in male
and female work roles? This question is as difficult to answer objectively as "Is a glass that contains 50% liquid half-full or half-empty?"
In Chapter 2, we distinguished between the tendency to exaggerate sex
differences in basic abilities and behavioral inclinations (alpha bias) and
the tendency to minimize them (beta bias). The amount of change people
see could be affected by their personal biases or dispositions. Perhaps,
when people consider the relationship between the sexes, similar biases
lead some to emphasize change in social relations and others to emphasize stability.

This would explain why, although most people agree there has been
some change, some observers see mostly progress in male-female relations in our society while others see mostly preservation of the status
quo. For example, one member of the latter group complained that a
Business Week cover story titled "Corporate Women: They're About to
Break Through to the Top" (emphasizing change) should have been
titled "Corporate Women: The Barriers to the Top Still Persist" (emphasizing stability). Another observer emphasized both stability and change
in applying an old saying to apparent changes in the workplace regarding male/female roles: "The more things change, the more they stay the
same."[3]

Alternative Scenarios for the Future

Two diametrically opposed scenarios may be envisioned for the roles
that women and men will play in the workplace of the future. They are
extreme scenarios, presented to illustrate the dramatic but very conceiv-
able results of current trends.

Scenario #1

Virtually all organizations have been striving for some time to be proactive and multicultural in their management practices, and they have gone about as far as they can toward reaching these goals. Sex discrimination as well as discrimination on the basis of race, ethnicity, and other job-irrelevant characteristics has become taboo behavior in the workplace. Managers who are guilty of such discrimination are subject to immediate dismissal or other strongly punitive action. In contrast, managers who find creative ways to take advantage of cultural diversity among their subordinates are strongly rewarded. At the same time, EEO laws are being rigorously enforced, and organizations that do not adhere to the dictates of these laws are putting themselves at considerable risk.

Organizations have made great strides in helping their employees to meet both their work and their family needs. Couples have also been making their own internal adjustments to enable both members to pursue their careers with equal satisfaction. As a result, family concerns are now having similar influences on the careers of both partners.

These changes have in turn affected the socialization experiences of children. Because their parents are leading more similar work lives, girls and boys are developing the same career aspirations and perceptions of the workplace. They see few barriers to their working in any career they would like to pursue.

With the resulting reduction in the sex segregation of occupations, most work groups now have balanced sex ratios. Male and female coworkers treat each other essentially as individuals, without regard to sex. Gender stereotyping in the workplace is a subject that has been relegated to books or articles about working conditions in the United States up until the latter part of the 20th century.

The proportion of women managers has become equivalent to the proportion of women in the labor force as a whole, a condition that primarily reflects individual goals rather than family or organizational constraints. The proportion of men and women at different levels of management is relatively balanced, with neither sex having a monopoly on the most powerful positions. Androgynous and feminine individuals are generally preferred as managers over masculine individuals, because they have the best capability of eliciting their subordinates' ideas and commitment.

Organizations are operating at peak performance levels because they are finally making the best possible use of all their available talent. They distribute monetary and other rewards equitably, and their employees are achieving maximum job satisfaction because they hold the positions that are best suited to their particular skills and interests.

Scenario #2

Organizations pay lip service to EEO laws, which are seen as more relevant to a distant past (if they were ever relevant then) than to the present and are generally not enforced. Affirmative action plans that are submitted to the government have no connection with the reality of the workplace and are not intended to be the basis for any real action. Organizations allow managers to take sex, race, ethnicity, and other personal characteristics into account in decision making if they believe that it is important. Top executives occasionally make speeches about the importance of equal opportunity and valuing diversity and send out form letters on the subject to employees, but everyone knows that these are simply empty gestures.

Most organizations let their employees fend for themselves in satisfying their family needs. Work is assumed to be a good employee's primary concern, with family issues relegated to the home. Working couples slant decisions on the handling of household responsibilities in favor of the male, because his career is implicitly seen as more important than his partner's. This message is reinforced in the socialization experiences of children. Young girls and boys learn that, if a couple is forced to compromise on careers, the woman's interests will be subservient to those of her male partner.

The sex ratios of groups are heavily skewed in favor of either males or females depending on the occupation. Anyone who pursues an occupation that is atypical of his or her sex will probably achieve the unenviable position of being the only man or woman in the work group. Gender stereotypes are the primary basis for predicting and evaluating people's behavior.

Within the ranks of management, the proportion of women managers has stabilized at a level below the proportion of women in the labor force. The more powerful the position, the less chance a woman has of holding it. There are very few women in the ranks of top management. A masculine management style, emphasizing attention to task rather than the needs of people, remains the norm.

Organizations have not increased their productivity levels because they have not made any real changes in their utilization of their employees. Men continue to receive a higher share of monetary and other rewards than women. Not surprisingly, men also report generally higher levels of satisfaction with their jobs and careers, while women report either frustration with or reluctant acceptance of the constraints placed by their families and organizations on their careers.

Critical Forces

Five types of forces are most likely to reflect and influence the future roles of women and men at work. The prevailing trends in these forces will determine which scenario, if either, will win out. The forces are:

1. *Management issues*—what the proportion of female and male managers is overall and at different managerial levels, and what management style prevails if any.
2. *Societal norms and gender stereotyping*—what norms remain concerning the proper roles of men and women, and how gender stereotypes influence interactions between men and women at work.
3. *Equal opportunity and cultural diversity issues*—what the EEO laws are, how extensively they are enforced, and how much the culture of organizations stresses proactive and multicultural practices.
4. *Socialization experiences*—how girls and boys are socialized, and how their experiences affect their choice of occupation.
5. *Work and family issues*—how couples learn to balance their work and family responsibilities, and how organizations help employees meet their family needs.

Management Issues

How large will the proportion of women managers become? Table 1.2 shows that this proportion has more than doubled since 1970, increasing from 16% to 42%. Will the proportion of managers who are women rise further? If so, to what level? 50%? 60%? 70%? Higher?

Currently, fewer female than male managers are married or have children. If the impact of family considerations on women's careers does not change, the proportion of women managers may remain below the proportion of women in the labor force. However, if family life becomes less constraining on women's careers or if more women forego family lives to pursue managerial careers, this proportion could rise above 50%. Changes in the managerial aspirations of women relative to men, the amount of organizational support for employees' pursuit of their family lives, and the presence or absence of sex discrimination in hiring decisions for management positions could also influence the future proportion of women managers.

How will the proportions of women at various managerial levels differ? The proportion of women managers is greatest at the lower management levels, smaller at the middle, and smallest at the top. This imbalance is not surprising, since new managers typically start at the bottom of the management ranks, which most women managers have entered in recent years. If there were no barriers to upward mobility for women managers, the proportions of women at middle and top managerial levels should increase simply as a function of time.

An alternative view is that the present imbalance may continue for any of the following reasons: (a) sex discrimination in hiring and promotion for middle and top management positions, (b) sex discrimination in the development of lower-level women managers that leaves them unprepared to rise within management ranks, or (c) less interest among women to attain higher-level management positions. There is some evidence to support the first two reasons, but little evidence to support the last reason.

Organizational efforts to promote equal opportunity and end sex discrimination within the ranks of management will play a big part in answering this question. Individual commitment and decisions about management careers will also be factors. It seems likely that the proportions of women in middle and top management levels will rise as some of the women presently in the lower management levels are promoted. Since few women are presently at the very top levels of organizations and since most organizations do not fully commit to equal opportunity, it also seems likely that imbalanced distribution of women across managerial levels will remain.

What will the predominant management style be? The increase in women managers in recent years has not affected beliefs about what makes a manager more effective. Support for a stereotype of the "good manager" as masculine has remained steady among American women and men, who as managers continue to see themselves as masculine on the whole. As long as women managers remain similar to men in this regard, we have little reason to expect a change in the predominant management style.

However, women managers may have adopted a masculine style simply because men have been the majority group in management. In the opening passage, Torrey predicts an androgynous organizational culture. She expects that there will be less of a masculine, male-oriented culture as women are more involved in essential management activities and men are freer to express their feminine qualities. If women ever became the majority sex in power, perhaps a feminine, female-oriented culture would emerge and men would feel compelled to conform to a new standard of behavior set by women.

A feminine or androgynous management style may lead to greater success as a manager in today's global economy. If this is indeed the case (and more research is needed to determine whether it is), astute managers may eventually realize it and shift their behavior accordingly. However, predominant management styles are very difficult to change, even for the right reasons.

Societal Norms and Gender Stereotyping

Will traditional norms about women's and men's roles disappear? The proportion of individuals who believe that the proper place for women is at home and for men at work has decreased considerably in the latter half of this century. If these prescriptions for behavior become even more out of touch with the reality of how women and men live their lives, we can expect the size of this group to shrink even further.

Will gender stereotyping diminish in the workplace? Gender stereotyping most often occurs when people know little about individuals except their sex. Thus, the degree of gender stereotyping in the workplace depends on the extent to which women and men actually work with each other in their jobs. After working with or for women, men have more positive attitudes toward them as coworkers and managers and are less apt to see them in stereotypical terms. A similar shift in attitudes and perceptions about men occurs for women who have men as coworkers for the first time. If the experiences that women and men have at work become more similar and the sex ratios of work groups become more balanced, gender stereotyping will be less frequent. However, if work groups remain imbalanced or if any increase in minority group members is seen as due to preferential treatment rather than competence, gender stereotypes will remain in force.

Equal Opportunity and Cultural Diversity Issues

Will EEO laws become modified in practice? Although concern for the employment situation for women played a small role in the initial passage of EEO legislation, support for the laws has increased as the proportion of women in the workplace has risen. Unless there is a sharp reversal in this trend, the laws will probably not be curtailed. If anything, they are more likely to be strengthened, especially at the state and local levels where organized groups of voters have greater influence than they would at the federal level.

However, interpretation and enforcement of EEO laws at all levels have varied between strictness and leniency according to the political and social philosophy of elected officials and ruling judges. It seems more likely that this kind of variation will continue than that the laws themselves will change.

Will more organizations be proactive in their approach to equal opportunity? Organizational behavior on this score is affected by EEO laws, top management attitudes, and the composition of the labor market. If the enforcement and interpretation of EEO laws are lenient, top managers feel less compelled to promote equal opportunity in employment-related decisions and policies. Also, if the organization does not reward the achievement of affirmative action goals, managers could be influenced by rational bias.

However, enlightened top executives may still decide that promoting equal opportunity is a good organizational practice. If more women than men are seeking to enter the workplace, employers that emphasize equal opportunity have an advantage in attracting new talent. Such a situation would encourage even top managers who do not see equal opportunity as a moral imperative to promote it for their own good. It is unclear whether more top executives will make strategic decisions for their organizations that would also promote equal opportunity.

Sex discrimination is most difficult to eliminate when there is little information about the individuals being judged, typically when hiring decisions are made. It is less likely to occur when more is known about the individuals under consideration, such as when promotions and salary increases are decided on. However, discrimination in the form of prejudice and resentment occur when the equal opportunity program promotes—or is perceived to promote—preferential treatment rather than decisions based on individuals' qualifications and competence. Thus, the ways in which equal opportunity programs are conceived and communicated play a major role in determining whether they ever achieve their intended purpose.

Will more organizations be multicultural? Given changes in the applicant pool, it will be very difficult for monolithic organizations to avoid becoming plural organizations without engaging in rampant discrimination. Whether plural organizations become multicultural organizations is determined more by top management attitudes. Thus the process by which individuals are selected to be top executives is critical. There should not be a "glass ceiling" that restricts the advancement of women or minorities into the upper management levels. In addition, the individuals chosen to be top executives should possess values that embrace the contributions of all employees, not just members of groups with which they have more in common or feel more comfortable. Unless top executives are willing to be champions of diversity and reward lower-level managers accordingly, cultural diversity will be more tolerated than appreciated.

Socialization Experiences

Will the sex difference in children's socialization experiences disappear? These experiences are primarily influenced by parents, school systems, and the mass media. The latter two influences reflect societal changes in women's and men's roles, although on a delayed basis, but children learn most from their parents' way of life. Young boys and girls now receive more similar messages about who can and should work. However, when the mother's work contributes less to the family's total income than the father's work (as is now the case in most families), the unspoken message is that women's work is less essential than men's.

In addition, children are influenced by the nature of their parents' occupations. For example, compared to male managers, relatively few female managers have children. The influence of parents on children's socialization experiences will not change very much if the couples who are most likely to have children remain those who have more traditional occupations.

Will the sex difference in occupational choices disappear? Individuals' choices about if, where, and when they will work are influenced by the parental "messages" they have received about work while growing up, as well as by the existing distribution of men and women across occupations. Sex segregation is reduced, however, only if the occupational choices of males and females become more alike and men and women are admitted to occupations in more similar proportions. Given this vicious cycle, it is amazing that any change has taken place in the nature of women's and men's occupational choices.

Once the sex ratio of an occupation changes, however, it spurs further change by affecting the occupational choices of those who are just entering the labor market. The difference between aspirations and expectations, which influence occupational choices, is greater for females than for males. However, when the opportunities for women in a given male-dominated occupation seem to be greater, girls become more likely to make it their occupational choice and to prepare themselves by gaining the necessary education or training. Adolescent boys, however, see fewer constraints on the achievement of their occupational aspirations and show little interest in female-dominated occupations.

The sex imbalance in occupational choices will be reduced if women continue to seek more entry-level positions in male-dominated occupations and if the success of female "pioneers" lets other women believe that they can achieve their aspirations. However, unless men feel a corresponding desire to enter female-dominated occupations, some sex imbalance in occupational choices will remain.

Work and Family Issues

Will women and men share family responsibilities more equally? Working people always have to decide how much time and energy to put into their careers versus their home life or other interests. Potential demands placed on individuals by their family situations range from the minimal demands on the single person with no children to the slightly higher demands on "dinks" (double income, no kids) to the heavier demands on dual-career parents to the heaviest demands on the single parent. Parents or elderly relatives must also be considered.

In dual-career families, women generally perform more of the household activities than men, leaving them less time and energy to devote to their careers. Thus, it is invariably the woman who takes time off from the workplace or leaves it altogether to attend to family needs. If couples chose to allocate their household responsibilities equally, they would more evenly distribute the impact of their families on their careers. However, this would require even more extensive change in societal norms about women's and men's roles than has taken place already.

Will organizations make it easier for employees to satisfy family needs? The opening passage predicts that this will happen, and there is a trend in

this direction. Some employers are revising their policies and procedures in an attempt to allow for the impact of employees' families on
their working lives. Work and family programs now include alternative
work patterns, parental leaves, child care and elder care, and counseling
services that help employees to better satisfy their family needs. Such
programs alleviate the burden of family on women and enable them to
have careers that are more like men's, that is, uninterrupted and free of
concerns about family arrangements during working hours. Men also
welcome these programs because they require less renegotiation of
household roles.

Most organizations still have a long way to go in helping their
employees deal with work/family conflicts. If dual-career couples allocate their household responsibilities more equally, organizations will
not need to change their policies as much. For the proportion of women
in the labor force to increase further while women still handle most
household responsibilities, organizations will have to either make it
easier for their employees to satisfy family needs or offer higher wages
to attract and retain female employees. However, if the allocation of
household responsibilities is not changed and organizations do not
offer their employees more options, the proportion of women in the
labor force and seeking to enter it may level off or decrease. The result
could be a reduction in the overall skill level of the work force.

Which Scenario Will Prevail?

The trends that I have described will help to shape the future roles of
women and men at work, whether in managerial or nonmanagerial
positions. I have generally stated trends in "either-or" terms. If all or
most of them go one way, it will make the experiences of women and
men at work more similar than they already are and Scenario #1 will be
achieved at some point in the future. If they go the other way, it will
reinforce or increase the current distinctions between the sexes in their
work experiences, resulting in Scenario #2. These trends and scenarios
suggest some final questions for us to consider:

Which scenario would be better to achieve? It should be no surprise that
I vote for Scenario #1. Since you picked up this book and have read this
far, I suspect that you do too.

Toward which scenario have we been heading in recent years? I believe
Scenario #1, primarily because women have made substantial progress

in entering male-dominated professions and because the difference between women's and men's earnings and typical career patterns has been reduced. However, the continued gender gap in earnings and the male domination of the upper ranks of most professions suggest that Scenario #2 cannot be completely rejected as a possibility.

Which scenario best reflects today's realities? That's an "Is the glass half-full or half-empty?" type of question that is difficult to answer. I believe that (a) reality lies somewhere between the two scenarios, (b) we are not as close to Scenario #2 as we once were, and (c) we still have a long way to go to achieve Scenario #1. However, I find it difficult to select one that better represents the current state of affairs. What do *you* believe?

Toward which scenario are we more likely to proceed as a society? It's hard to tell. All of us, women and men, girls and boys, have a large stake in how this question is answered. Further research is needed to give us more guidance on how to eliminate sex discrimination and minimize the relevance of sex as an individual characteristic in the workplace. In the meantime, if we promote proactive and multicultural practices in our organizations, encourage each other in the pursuit of satisfying lives in and out of work, share the family responsibilities that are there to be shared, and personally strive to do in life what we are best at and most enjoy, we can contribute to making Scenario #1 happen in our lifetimes.

Notes

1. J. W. Torrey, "The Consequences of Equal Opportunity for Women," in *Women in Management*, ed. B. A. Stead, 1st ed. (Englewood Cliffs, NJ: Prentice Hall, 1978), pp. 304-305.

2. An earlier version of this chapter appeared in G. N. Powell, "Male/Female Work Roles: What Kind of Future?" *Personnel, 66* (No. 7, July 1989): 47-50.

3. "Corporate Women: They're About to Break Through to the Top," *Business Week*, No. 3004 (22 June 1987): 72-78; "Readers Report," *Business Week*, No. 3007 (13 July 1987): 10-13; V. R. Fuchs, *Women's Quest for Economic Equality* (Cambridge, MA: Harvard University Press, 1988), p. 32.

Appendix

Additional Resources

If you are teaching a course on women and men in management or women in management, or offering a training program on either of these topics, there are additional resources that may be of assistance. I expect to publish an accompanying volume to this book, tentatively titled *Women and Men at Work: A Resourcebook,* that will consist of structured experiences to be used by teachers and trainers.

In addition, *Women and Men in Organizations: Teaching Strategies,* edited by Dorothy M. Hai and published by the Organizational Behavior Teaching Society (OBTS) in 1984, is an invaluable reference. It contains articles on teaching issues (including one by me on "Issues for the Male Teacher"), classroom exercises, sample course syllabi, and a bibliography on the topic of women and men in management. It may be ordered from the OBTS, Center for Economic and Management Research, University of Oklahoma, Norman, OK 73019. Another excellent book for teachers and trainers that contains articles, exercises, and a bibliography of books, films, and videotapes is *Preparing Professional Women for the Future: Resources for Teachers and Trainers,* edited by V. Jean Ramsey and published in 1985 by the Division of Research, Graduate School of Business Administration, University of Michigan, Ann Arbor, MI 48109.

If you are *not* a teacher or trainer but are interested in further reading on the topics in this book, I recommend any of the following books:

1. Anne F. Scott, ed., *The American Woman: Who Was She?* (Englewood Cliffs, NJ: Prentice Hall, 1971).

2. Paula Reis and Anne J. Stone, eds., *The American Woman: 1992-93* (New York: Norton, 1992); also other volumes in this series.

3. Joe L. Dubbert, *A Man's Place: Masculinity in Transition* (Englewood Cliffs, NJ: Prentice Hall, 1979).

4. Michael S. Kimmel, ed., *Changing Men: New Directions in Research on Men and Masculinity* (Newbury Park, CA: Sage, 1987).

5. Steve Craig, ed., *Men, Masculinity, and the Media* (Newbury Park, CA: Sage, 1992).

6. Joseph H. Pleck, *The Myth of Masculinity* (Cambridge, MA: MIT Press, 1981).

7. Carol Gilligan, *In a Different Voice: Psychological Theory and Women's Development* (Cambridge, MA: Harvard University Press, 1982).

8. Robert D. and Candida G. Brush, *The Woman Entrepreneur: Starting, Financing, and Managing a Successful New Business* (Lexington, MA: Lexington/Heath, 1986).

9. Laurie Larwood, Ann H. Stromberg, and Barbara A. Gutek, eds., *Women and Work: An Annual Review*, vols. 1, 2, and 3 (Newbury Park, CA: Sage, 1985, 1987, 1988).

10. Barbara F. Reskin and Heidi I. Hartmann, eds., *Women's Work, Men's Work: Sex Segregation on the Job* (Washington, DC: National Academy Press, 1986).

11. Barbara F. Reskin, ed., *Sex Segregation in the Workplace: Trends, Explanations, Remedies* (Washington, DC: National Academy Press, 1984).

12. Claudia Goldin, *Understanding the Gender Gap: An Economic History of Women* (New York: Oxford University Press, 1990).

13. Francine D. Blau and Marianne A. Ferber, *The Economics of Women, Men, and Work*, 2nd. ed. (Englewood Cliffs, NJ: Prentice Hall, 1992).

14. Christine L. Williams, *Gender Differences at Work: Women and Men in Nontraditional Occupations* (Berkeley: University of California Press, 1989).

15. Jerry Jacobs, *Revolving Doors: Sex Segregation and Women's Careers* (Stanford: Stanford University Press, 1989).

16. Rosabeth M. Kanter, *Men and Women of the Corporation* (New York: Basic, 1977).

17. Constance Backhouse and Leah Cohen, *Sexual Harassment on the Job: How to Avoid the Working Woman's Nightmare* (Englewood Cliffs, NJ: Prentice Hall, 1981).

18. Dail A. Neugarten and Jay M. Shafritz, *Sexuality in Organizations: Romantic and Coercive Behaviors at Work* (Oak Park, IL: Moore, 1980).

19. Lisa A. Mainiero, *Office Romance: Love, Power, and Sex in the Workplace* (New York: Rawson, 1989).

20. Jeff Hearn and Wendy Parkin, *"Sex" at "Work": The Power and Paradox of Organizational Sexuality* (New York: St. Martin's Press, 1987).

21. Natasha Josefowitz, *Is This Where I Was Going?* (New York: Warner, 1983).

22. Ann Howard and Douglas W. Bray, *Managerial Lives in Transition: Advancing Age and Changing Times* (New York: Guilford Press, 1988).

23. Alice G. Sargent, *The Androgynous Manager* (New York: AMACOM, 1981).

24. Ann M. Morrison, Randall P. White, Ellen Van Velsor, and the Center for Creative Leadership, *Breaking the Glass Ceiling: Can Women Reach the Top of America's Largest Corporations?*, updated ed. (Reading, MA: Addison- Wesley, 1992).

25. Marilyn J. Davidson and Cary L. Cooper, *Shattering the Glass Ceiling: The Woman Manager* (London: Chapman, 1992).

26. Baila Zeitz and Lorraine Dusky, *The Best Companies for Women* (New York: Simon and Schuster, 1988).

27. Barbara A. Gutek and Laurie Larwood, eds., *Women's Career Development* (Newbury Park, CA: Sage, 1987).

28. Uma Sekaran, *Dual-Career Families* (San Francisco: Jossey-Bass, 1986).

29. Lucia A. Gilbert, *Men in Dual-Career Families* (Hillsdale, NJ: Lawrence Erlbaum, 1985).

30. Francine S. and Douglas T. Hall, *The Two-Career Couple* (Reading, MA: Addison-Wesley, 1979).

31. Faye J. Crosby, *Juggling: The Unexpected Advantages of Balancing Career and Home for Women and Their Families* (New York: Free Press, 1991).

32. Marianne A. Ferber and Brigid O'Farrell with La Rue Allen, *Work and Family: Policies for a Changing Work Force* (Washington, DC: National Academy Press, 1991).

33. Sheldon Zedeck, ed., *Work, Family, and Organizations* (San Francisco: Jossey-Bass, 1992).

34. Robert S. Weiss, *Staying the Course: The Emotional and Social Lives of Men Who Do Well at Work* (New York: Free Press, 1990).

35. A. Hochschild, *The Second Shift* (New York: Viking Penguin, 1989).

36. Nancy J. Sedmak and Michael D. Levin-Epstein, *Primer of Equal Employment Opportunity*, 5th ed. (Washington, DC: Bureau of National Affairs, 1991).

37. James Ledvinka and Vida G. Scarpello, *Federal Regulation of Personnel and Human Resource Management*, 2nd ed. (Boston: PWS-Kent, 1991).

38. Barbara S. Gamble, ed., *Sex Discrimination Handbook* (Washington, DC: Bureau of National Affairs, 1992).

39. *Promoting Minorities and Women: A Practical Guide to Affirmative Action for the 1990s* (Washington, DC: Bureau of National Affairs, 1989).

40. Robert T. Michael, Heidi I. Hartmann, and Brigid O'Farrell, eds., *Pay Equity: Empirical Inquiries* (Washington, DC: National Academy Press, 1989).

41. Ann M. Morrison, *The New Leaders: Guidelines on Leadership Diversity in America* (San Francisco: Jossey-Bass, 1992).

42. Lorence L. Kessler, *Managing Diversity in an Equal Opportunity Workplace: A Primer for Today's Manager* (Washington, DC: National Foundation for the Study of Employment Policy, 1990).

43. Marilyn Loden and Judy B. Rosener, *Workforce America! Managing Employee Diversity as a Vital Resource* (Homewood, IL: Irwin, 1991).

44. Nancy J. Adler and Dafna N. Izraeli, eds., *Women in Management Worldwide* (Armonk, NY: Sharpe, 1988).

Index

About the Authors

Gary N. Powell, Ph.D., is Professor of Management in the School of Business Administration at the University of Connecticut. He is a nationally recognized scholar and educator on women and men in management. His graduate course on women and men in management won an award for innovation in education from the Committee on Equal Opportunity for Women of the American Assembly of Collegiate Schools of Business (AACSB). He has also won the University of Connecticut School of Business Administration's Outstanding Undergraduate Teaching Award. He has served as chairperson, program chair, newsletter editor, and on the Executive Committee of the Women in Management Division of the Academy of Management. He has published over 50 articles and presented over 50 papers at professional conferences. He has served on the Board of Governors and as Co-Chair of the Status of Minorities Task Force of the Academy of Management. He is a past president of the Eastern Academy of Management. He has served on the Editorial Board of *Academy of Management Review and Academy of Management Executive.*

He is a former project engineer and systems analyst with General Electric, having graduated from its Manufacturing Management Program. At GE, he designed and implemented automated project scheduling systems as well as systems for inventory control, production control, materials procurement, facilities management, and so on. He has provided management training and development for several companies, including GE-Capital, General Signal, Apple Computer, Monroe Auto

Equipment, AllState, and CIGNA, and has conducted numerous other workshops.

He received his Ph.D. and a master's degree in business administration from the University of Massachusetts and a bachelor's degree from MIT. He is a member of Beta Gamma Sigma, a business honorary association.

Lisa A. Mainiero (co-author of chapter 7) is Associate Professor of Management in the School of Business at Fairfield University. She has published several papers on women and power, office romance, and career strategies for technical professionals in journals such as *Administrative Science Quarterly, Academy of Management Review, Journal of Management, Personnel, Personnel Journal,* and *Training and Development Journal.* She is the author of *Office Romance: Love, Power, and Sex in the Workplace* and co-author of *Developing Managerial Skills: Exercises, Cases, and Readings in Organizational Behavior.* She received her doctorate in Organizational Behavior from Yale University in 1983.